/11

D0938053

SIMMS LIBRARY

*This book was given
in memory of*

Van Dorn Hooker III '72

a gift of his family

·ALBUQUERQUE ACADEMY·

PLACE MAKERS

With an Essay on Planning and Policy

Ronald Lee Fleming

Renata von Tscharner

with GEORGE MELROD and BEVERLEE SERONICK BARNES

PLACE MAKERS

CREATING PUBLIC ART THAT TELLS YOU WHERE YOU ARE

Harcourt Brace Jovanovich, Publishers

Boston   San Diego   New York

HBJ

Front cover photo credits, top to bottom, left to right:

Brick reliefs on Anatole Hotel, Dallas, Texas, by Mara Smith. Photo by The Townscape Institute. See page 41.

Mississippi River pavement relief, Mud Island, Memphis, Tennessee, by Roy Harrover-Ass. Photo courtesy of Mississippi River Museum, Mud Island, Memphis, Tennessee. See page 143.

"Prospect V–III Miners' Monument." Sculpture and interpretation, Frostburg, State College, Maryland, by Andrew Leicester. Photo by Bruce Peterson. See page 29.

Gate to electrical substation, Viewlands/Hoffman, Seattle, Washington, by Keating, Markovitz, Simpson. Photo by Seattle Arts Commission. See page 167.

"Solar Borealis." Road portal at International Airport in Fairbanks, Alaska, commissioned by the State of Alaska, by Robert Behrens. Photo by Scott Harper, Denver, Colorado. The sculpture of welded steel covered with special diffraction grating reflects and scatters light with the daily and seasonal changes in the natural light conditions of the region.

Ceramic flower container in electrical substation, Creston-Nelson, Seattle, Washington, by Merilyn Tompkins. Photo by Joyce Moty. See page 167.

"Krewe of Poydras." Kynetic sculpture in New Orleans, Louisiana, by Ida Kohlmeyer. Photo by Charles Wolff, III. See page 89.

"Bricklayer and Ballplayer." Brick sculpture with drinking fountain in Cambridge, Massachusetts, by David Judelson. Shown with the Hon. Thomas P. (Tip) O'Neill, who grew up in this neighborhood. Photo by Renata von Tscharner. See page 128.

"Clinton Square Map." Bronze and granite pavement relief, Highland Park, Illinois, by Gregg Lefevre. Photo courtesy of the artist. See page 35.

Copyright © 1987 by Harcourt Brace Jovanovich, Inc.
Copyright © 1981 by The Townscape Institute, Inc. and Ronald Lee Fleming and Renata von Tscharner

All rights reserved. No part of this publication may be reproduced or transmitted in any form or by any means, electronic or mechanical, including photocopy, recording, or any information storage and retrieval system, without permission in writing from the publisher.

Request for permission to make copies of any part of the work should be mailed to: Permissions, Harcourt Brace Jovanovich, Publishers, Orlando, Florida 32887.

Library of Congress Cataloging-in-Publication Data
Fleming, Ronald Lee.
  Place makers.

  Bibliography: p.
  Includes index.
  1. Public art—United States—Case studies.
2. Urban beautification—United States—Case studies.
I. Von Tscharner, Renata. II. Townscape Institute
(Cambridge, Mass.) III. Title.
N8844.F53 1987   709'.73   86-14807

ISBN 0-15-172000-2
ISBN 0-15-172013-2 (pbk.)

Designed by G.B.D. Smith

Printed in the United States of America

A B C D E

709.73
FLE
1987

Contents

* The placemaker stories that are marked by the asterisk are new in the second edition of this book.

The Townscape Institute

Cambridge,
Massachusetts

The term *townscape design* has been defined as the art of giving visual coherence and organization to the collage of buildings, streets, and spaces that make up the urban environment. The Townscape Institute, a not-for-profit, public interest planning organization in Cambridge, Massachusetts, utilizes this concept of design to improve both the legibility and the livability of cities, towns, and neighborhoods. Its range of endeavors supports the townscape concept that the whole can become more than the sum of its parts.

Through advocacy for the visual enhancement of the built environment and projects combining public art and urban design, the Townscape Institute affirms, enhances, and reveals a sense of place. The Townscape Institute continues the decade of design work by its principals, Ronald Lee Fleming and Renata von Tscharner, in both the public and private sectors. Projects revealing 'place meaning' seek to encourage a sense of proprietorship that can nourish the notion of an ethic for the built environment. To achieve this goal, The Townscape Institute develops strategies to strengthen people's

capacity to lay claim to their environs through such projects as Main Street revitalization, cultural identity programs, computer software, and the commissioning of public art.

To stimulate a broader interest in this approach, The Townscape Institute produces educational publications—both books and posters—that illustrate how buildings, spaces, and objects can reinforce identification with place. These publications form an integral part of The Townscape Institute's advocacy role. The first three books in the series are *Place Makers, On Common Ground,* and *Facade Stories.*

Facade Stories: Changing Faces of Main Street Storefronts and How to Care for Them, by Ronald Lee Fleming, depicts the building fronts that line the business districts of American towns and records what happened to them over time. Before and after photographs show facades that have been preserved, restored, adapted, left as freestanding sculptures, reduced to fragments, or recalled as wall murals. The appendix, written with Noré V. Winter, illustrates how facades should be analyzed and maintained.

On Common Ground: Caring for Shared Land from Town Common to Urban Park, by Ronald Lee Fleming and Lauri A. Halderman, is a practical book that examines the history of New England's common grazing lands as a basis for defining guidelines for their protection and enhancement. On Common Ground explores the original notion of a shared "proprietorship"—the guiding principle of the early village greens—in order to demonstrate how corporations, foundations, and community groups from New York to California can utilize this traditional concept for the design and management of new shared spaces.

The Massachusetts Historical Society nominated this trilogy, entitled The Power of Place: Towards an Ethic for the Built Environment, for a Pulitzer Prize in 1982. The most recent addition to this publication program is New Providence: A Changing Cityscape, a full-color picture book which documents the physical evolution of a typical small American city between 1910 and 1987.

Acknowledgments

Since many of the works of art profiled here had not been substantially documented before, we are very grateful for the collaboration of artists, craftsmen, arts administrators, historians, and reporters of the urban scene. They helped us to research the trajectory of the projects from initial concept to implementation, providing us with factual information and helping us to assess the impact of many placemakers. We must, of course, take complete responsibility for our own evaluations, but we want to express our profound thanks to these many people who took the time to correspond or talk with us. They often provided material that was not available in any archives. We appreciate their cooperation in the sometimes tedious task of information gathering, as well as the efforts of many who reviewed our profile drafts. The role of contributors is so extensive that it can serve as a resource inventory for those who seek to advance their own place responsive art and amenity projects. We have listed these names in a separate section at the end of the book.

Special tribute should be paid here at the beginning, though, to those who have given us particular counsel and support. Some of the ideas about the potential of placemaking were developed in a dialogue with our friend, Grant R. Jones, FASLA, the landscape architect and poet. We gave a joint presentation of these ideas to the annual meeting of the American Society of Landscape Architects in November, 1980. Grant Jones' comradeship and strength of character as well as the support from his office, Jones and Jones of Seattle, are deeply appreciated.

A number of our friends who are writers also served as critics and allowed us to test some of our ideas against their experience. In this regard we pay tribute to Roberto Brambilla and Brent Brolin, New York, Mary Hemingway, Kittery Point, Maine, and Carole Rifkind, New York. Carole Rifkind's work for the Partners for Livable Places, Washington, D.C., focused on cultural tourism in gritty cities. She and the president of the Partners, Robert McNulty, encouraged our interest in showing how designers can learn from literary techniques to better reveal place meaning, and they supported our paper on this subject at a conference sponsored by the Partners in Paterson, New

Jersey, in the spring of 1980. Our friend, Professor Nathan Glazer, encouraged us to write more about the policy implications of place-making art in the second edition by inviting us to contribute to his issue of *Public Interest* on public art.

We are grateful for an intrepid band of supporters whose particular allegiance and guidance have helped us to carry forward the integrity of our purpose. Some among them serve on our board of directors and others are on our advisory board. They include Philip H. Behr, Philadelphia, David Bird, Cambridge, E. Pope Coleman, Cincinnati, Lester Glen Fant III, Washington, D.C., Mrs. Ree Overton Fleming, Laguna Hills, California, Dr. Richard H. Howland, Washington, D.C., Frank Keefe, Boston, Edmund H. Kellogg, Esq., Pomfret, Vermont, Mr. and Mrs. Roger Kennedy, Washington, D.C., Roger S. Webb, Boston, William Sutherland Strong, Esq., Boston, and William H. Whyte, Jr., New York. Dr. Charles G.K. Warner of Cambridge, Massachusetts, has, in addition, painstakingly read through parts of the 1981 manuscript and helped shape its style, as did Townscape staff member Lauri A. Halderman. George Melrod, who assisted us in researching and did much of the writing of the first edition, played a substantial role in shaping our evaluations of the objects we ultimately included from the many that we reviewed. Beverlee Seronick Barnes, a planner on our staff, researched and drafted some twenty new stories for the second edition. For the second edition we relied on editors Didi Stevens and Fern Reiss as well as copy editor Roberta Reeder.

This book and the related activities of The Townscape Institute, Inc., a non-profit, public interest organization, have depended upon the financial assistance of individuals and foundations. David Bird, Cambridge, Henry J. Heinz II, Pittsburgh, William I. Koch, Dover, Mass., Charles Muller, New York, Ann Roberts, New York, and Robert A. Sincerbeaux, Esq., Woodstock, Vermont, are friends who were helpful either in securing funds from foundations with which they are affiliated or in providing direct support. In the first edition, the Charles Sumner Bird Foundation, and the H.J. Heinz Charitable and Family Trust gave financial assistance, which helped to bring this project to fruition. In the second edition, we are grateful for funding support from Mrs. Ree Overton Fleming and the William I. Koch Foundation.

In achieving this work which, we hope, charts some new terrain as well as makes connections between territories that have already been tentatively mapped, we were often reminded of a short quotation that hangs on our office wall. It expresses the larger aim of The Townscape Institute as well as our particular conviction in writing this book.

> If society were different, we might
> be content just to do something well.
> But we are not pleased simply to do
> what we do. What is important for us
> always is what doesn't yet exist.

We hope this book can encourage others not only to create what does not often exist—new environments which resonate with place meanings—but also to do as well as or better than the designers of the projects we briefly describe here.

Ronald Lee Fleming
Renata von Tscharner-Fleming
CAMBRIDGE, MASSACHUSETTS

First edition 1981
Second edition 1987

Preface

This is the second edition of *Place Makers* following six years after this collection first appeared in 1981. It creates a physically larger and in some ways more expansive book. There are twenty-three new "placemakers" here that add increased geographical reach to this review. The introduction and final chapters have been revised, and the discussion about public art planning has been considerably expanded. The interest in the Environmental Profiling technique encouraged the authors to more fully annotate this process based on experiences with it during the past five years.

Despite the variety of locales, materials, objects, and sponsors, most of the elements profiled here are organized in the same textual format. A background section explains how and why a particular art element, amenity or fragment that we designate as a placemaker happened to be created or how it survived over time. Following is a technical description of what the placemaker looks like and how it is made. And finally there is an analysis of the impact of the project, capped by a summary containing essential data: cost, size, time of commission, and so forth.

For some placemakers such as carved tree trunks, a brief description is given under the caption "Summary." Although the aesthetic quality of an object or design element may be questioned and examination may reveal only a marginal impact on context, inclusion in this book indicates that the analysis is in general positive, since this second edition has offered the authors a chance to refine some earlier choices. Where possible the impact section for each case study includes evaluations of the work culled from interviews, reviews or other written sources. Some of these comments have an ingenuous quality that the editors have taken pains to preserve in order to let those involved with the works speak for them.

Introduction

CONDITIONS THAT
REQUIRE PLACEMAKERS

There is a spectre haunting America, but it is not the spectre that Karl Marx wished upon us in the opening line of his *Manifesto*. It is not the spectre of a different form of government—a dictatorship of the masses—that is haunting us, but the spectre that grows out of our own society with its mass consumerism, throwaway economy, and technological fixation. It is the spectre of placelessness. We have in the generations since World War II created a banal sameness everywhere in America—a sameness that haunts not only the older commercial strip along the road to the airport but also the new development that is massively changing the profile of many a city center. It is a pervasive dullness of building surface, highway abutment, corporate sign, and franchise design which obscures with the security of sameness our connections to particular places, and which, in the aggregate, obliterates our very image of ourselves. The impact of this phenomenon has vastly increased in the past decade. And yet it is not the design community or local government or preservationists who have generally rallied effectively against it, but rather some writers who have seen it with an unmerciful eye. Vladimir Nabokov satirized this phenomenon of placelessness in the motel rooms where *Lolita* briefly closeted with her elderly lover. James Dickey drove his weekend recreationists through it on their way to the wild river of *Deliverance*, and Alistair Cooke damned it as the saddest sight in the concluding essay of his book *America*. In truth there are now two generations of Americans at city edge who live, move and have their being in spaces—whole environments of speculative, transient buildings—shopping centers, suburbia, franchise strips—spaces that never become places. This is the spectre now haunting America, whether it is Co-op City or Tyson's Corner, and it is of our own making.

When confronting this condition of placelessness and trying to combat it, the community must seek ways to connect people to such environments. We need, as Roger

Kennedy, director of the National Museum of American History, says, "small directional signals deliberately inserted in the monotony of most places to help us know we have arrived somewhere." Of course, it is difficult to find an anchor for our sensi-

Sidney Goodman's 'Figures in a Landscape' evokes a sense of the personal isolation in a country where land-use policies spread people in thin socio-economic layers across an increasingly standardized landscape.

The larger failure of American urban design and the isolation of different land uses is poignantly revealed in Nancy Wolf's drawing of a cityscape with a juxtaposed "historic district," Corbusian superblocks, and commercial strip, and the resultant alienation which graffiti commemorates.

bility in the twirling franchise signs that mark the widening gyre of commercial detritus at the city's edge. There is not much to remember in the new phalanx of concrete slabs and mirrored glass that envelops such disparate cities as Hartford, Connecticut and Austin, Texas with an anonymity that their nineteenth-century builders would have abhorred.

The resonance with the sources of our identity is rapidly vanishing in most of our cities. Indeed, like the swimmer in John Cheever's story, traversing the endless pools of suburbia, we can interminably tread the barren public plazas in downtown developments or meander through the sterile shopping centers of suburbia without finding clues that could help us endow them with meaning—with any connection to our roots or our aspirations. They remain dead spaces that tell no tales and offer no support, only a general feeling of the angst and anomie that social commentators ascribe to our age.

In such a world, indeed, placemakers and placemaking actions should be welcome. This book profiles some examples of the kinds of objects—works of public art, urban design, and artifacts—that can help us to

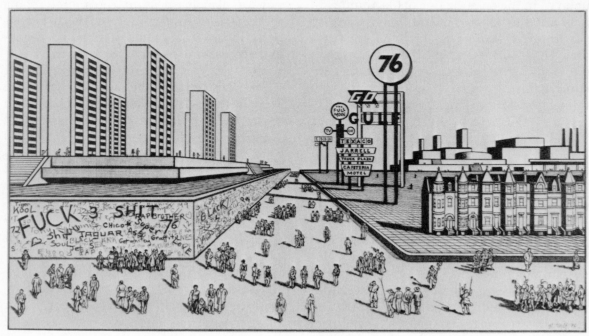

define, reveal, enrich, expand or otherwise make accessible the meanings of a particular environment. Its purpose is to help the concerned layman, planning commissioner, arts council executive, downtown improvement activist, architect, artist or urban designer to put into practice Roger Kennedy's dictum that they should indeed arrive somewhere.

It is a book about sculptures and castings, carved reliefs and embedded pavement inserts, fountains and fragments, benches and bollards, murals and markers. It even includes a forest reasserting itself in a Richmond shopping mall, the painted tracery of an abandoned shoreline in New York's financial district and a Victorian cast-iron flower stand perched on a massive plaza in downtown Cincinnati, Ohio. Each element tells a special tale about the evolving character of its location. These objects are meant to intrigue. They lay claim to our memories and sometimes even to our affections. They can stimulate anecdotes to humanize the face of new developments, and their presence can build a sense of future value for a neglected older neighborhood.

That value is based on associations and images conveyed so strongly that they imprint themselves on what we call "the landscape of the mind." This creation of a mental context can transform our view of environments that were previously anonymous or forlorn by populating the mind with images of the community—its history, characters, geography—often with a decorative richness, whimsy, even humor. These mental associations help us to regain a feeling of belonging, and perhaps with it to secure a sort of inner harmony. For we seek to make durable reference to the often nebulous connection between people and their locale and thus vouchsafe a certain grace, intangible and yet profound, that has gone out of the lives of two generations of Americans whose feeling for place has been eclipsed by the automobile, and whose sense of community has often no more palpable impression than spending Saturday morn-

Two views of Hartford poignantly reveal a planned nineteenth-century cityscape, where two subsequent capital building silhouettes provided an ascendant dignity, which early twentieth century corporate towers respected. These early insurance buildings are now obscured by chunky, contemporary sky scrapers which were not required to respect comprehensive urban design guidelines—at this ultimate scale for placemaking action.

ing at the shopping mall. By recovering or reinventing this mental landscape of associations, we can create a resonance with place like the timbre that figurative illusions evoke in a lively conversation.

David Harding, long-time artist-in-residence in the Public Works Department of Glenrothes, Scotland, created this casting on the sides of a concrete underpass in 1971. This is one of several which he transformed by simply carving styrofoam to mold concrete images. This underpass symbolizes the changing industrial base of the town from mining and paper milling to electronics, as the community expanded under the British New Towns Program.[1]

Harvard University's underpass connecting the Old Yard to the Science Center and Law School would have been an ideal site to communicate the history of the university on the concrete walls, but Harvard has not yet made a policy commitment to utilize public art as a way of enriching campus and community life, though individual buildings have sometimes included artists' work.

A PERSPECTIVE ON PRESERVATION: CREATING A PAST FOR THE FUTURE

One objective of this book is to emancipate ourselves from limiting notions of what is traditionally important or architecturally significant in the built environment, and to invest more meaning in the ordinary streets and spaces where we live and work. Of course, this is not to suggest that the commissioning of a few works of public art or urban design will create a sense of value powerful enough to overcome some of the larger determinants of our urban condition. We are a mobile and uprooted people, living amidst a technology of standardized parts in an economy based on rapid depreciation of the built fabric, and with a contemporary architecture that is bereft of a decorative tradition that could carry pictorial content. Nevertheless, recent movements in architecture, art, and literature seek to restore more discernible meaning. Post-Modern architecture is rediscovering decorative idioms; music takes tentative steps away from atonal abstrusiveness and toward lyricism and melody; and painting celebrates the return of the figure in a new realism.

These trends come at a time when the existing content of the built environment—the evidence of the past—is perceived as increasing in economic value—as creating a supportive context for today's investments. In effect, as a consequence of changes in public attitudes and via the tax laws, the battle to save significant buildings and spaces has launched a thousand surveys, guides, and "lost architecture" books. Conflicts still arise in the form of struggles over specific pieces of property, but the preservation forces have gradually fulfilled a "territorial imperative" like the early American land acquisition. Beginning in the affluent residential precincts, many of which have spectacular architectural assets, the preservation idea has found new support for historic district designation and commensurate design controls growing in blue-collar neighborhoods and on Main Street.

This broader recognition of value in the building environment is an important stimulant to new thinking about placemaking, with its focus on the associative elements and pockets of memory that can give environments an increased meaning in the lives of their users. For although placemaking is a separate activity from architectural preservation or conservation, it is symbiotically connected to both preservation and conservation. Placemaking seeks to expand the sense of meaning in the built environment. It does not aim to freeze a moment in time; rather it leads us to understand the compression of many moments, and by preparing us for the *evolution* of places, it promises an environment secure for continued use into the future. This is because placemaking actions can record that evolution, making it more recognizable and significant to the generations of its users.

The cases illustrated in this book seek to advance beyond current battle lines over what we should be saving now. Instead, they attempt to discover how, by saving old objects or introducing new ones into the environment, *value* can accrue to the future. *Though the authors of this book consider themselves to be preservationists, they are equally concerned about how new environments can be created to have enough place meaning to warrant future care and perhaps eventual preservation.* In our judgment, the view of many preservationists, popularized by the motto of Colonial Williamsburg— "The future may learn from the past"— should be allied with an equal concern about creating a past for the environment that will be built in the immediate future. Such a concern can produce a larger future constituency for these places than the numbers now interested in the preservation of old buildings. It should be a constituency of people who feel connected to the meanings that are created or reinforced in these new environments, whether they are city corners, neighborhood malls, or public schools. Indeed, one of the best tests of our architecture is to evaluate what it is that we are building *now* that people will in the future fight to preserve. We can best achieve this by creating architecture that will give people the capacity to imagine the past—even if it is only the geology of the terrain or the significance of a place name.

This plywood model of a Catholic Church in Milwaukee, once the heart of a blue collar Italian neighborhood, is used annually when the neighborhood returns to the site, now a tangle of interstate ramps, to commemorate the emotive power of a (lost) place. The evergreens are the landscape's more permanent and less tangible tribute. Ironically, but not atypically, the landscape designer has the modest residual role of providing a little token planting around the marker commemorating the church location.

The brutal functionalism of Gund Hall, the Graduate School of Design at Harvard University, stolidly illustrates the environmental obstacles to recreating a decorative tradition. Constructed in 1970, already in its short life the interior had to be redesigned to more satisfactorily serve the needs of several disparate faculties and their students. Perhaps an enlightened administrator will one day encourage a student design competition for enriching the exterior and the dead space adjacent to it, lest another generation of students be deprived of exposure to the particular pleasure of decorative richness in their immediate educational environment.

THE FUNCTION OF PLACEMAKING ELEMENTS IN URBAN DESIGN STRATEGY

In an urban design sense, placemakers have few limitations. They can be located anywhere, no matter how modest or how grand; the same creation can affect several populations differently; they can be sponsored and created by disparate groups and individuals, and they can be made of a wide range of materials, sometimes at modest cost. Carved bricks, inlaid pavements, painted walls, mosaic covered benches, salvaged architectural fragments, cast aluminum reliefs, or sculpted tree trunks can help to express the distinctive features or the popular aspirations of everyman's environment. They represent a level of detail and of craft, a sort of thoughtfulness about locale that is missing from most design and construction projects, where the builders are divorced from the lore of place information.

Though a few placemakers entirely transform the locations they celebrate, and more provide merely decorative richness, historic insight, commemorative relief, or just a whimsical bump in the mind, many others remain isolated objects in space. Their effect could be more pronounced if architects and urban designers sought to relate them to each other—in effect, to create a choreography of meanings. The Chelsea streetscape project, which incorporates a number of placemakers—a "memory wall," bronze sculptures of living Chelsea residents, inserts in sidewalks and street pavement—has been a pioneering effort in this direction. Even there, however, the orchestration could be more densely realized if the memory wall's porcelain enamel panels celebrating Chelsea's past were used as a sounding board on which chords of place meaning might merge with the surrounding cityscape. The harmony thus created could then reinforce the resonance of the panels by linking the people and incidents depicted to art objects nearby. For example, the panel of Laura Lee, the Chelsea feminist, shown wearing the earliest American bloomers, could be related to a pair of her celebrated pantaloons, cast in bronze, on the rim of the newly renovated fountain in Chelsea Square. This would enable people to reinvent her in their own minds and to imagine what she might be doing today. Had she lived in these less constraining times, she would probably have remained true to her then Bohemian char-

"Chelsea Conversation" figures prominently populate a renovated square, as the sculptor, Penelope Jencks, sought to encourage future use of the space by claiming it with the animation, albeit frozen, of community residents—a well-known high school athlete and a science teacher who has motivated many Chelsea youngsters to go to college.

Chelsea Memory Wall, part of a cityscape revitalization program, is an outdoor "photo album" featuring Laura Lee, an eccentric feminist who reputedly modeled the first bloomers in America. Miss Lee and other local figures juxtaposed on porcelain enamel panels help the visitor reinvent the complexity over time of even such modest places as Chelsea, Massachusetts.

acter and perhaps have slipped off the pantaloons for an early morning dip *au naturel*. Such a fluid view of the history of just one local character can strengthen our grip on the multiple realities of place meaning over time.

Placemaking should be the handmaiden of urban design. The elements of placemaking serve broad objectives that go beyond their intrinsic value as works of art or artisanry or their function as amenities. Below are four objectives that can give a placemaker an intrinsic role in urban design. Probably more often than not, it is difficult to realize all four in one placemaking strategy:

An entry sign on the main street of a small Louisiana town illustrates how an event animating the street inspired the sign design now marking it. The carved sign includes a building on a cake which recalls the Bake Festival when "cake buildings" were confected to raise money for the historic survey that led subsequently to historic designation.[2] This connection between a community action and commemoration of that action in a design element creating a resonance of meaning echoing over time is not used often enough by contemporary designers. Even if they use behavioral analysis, they rarely make the time to elicit the potential emotive power of community events as a basis for design ideas.

- Placemakers can provide *direction*: they can help us navigate through space. The eye can be moved artfully from object to connecting object, forging a trail of little encounters through space.

- Placemakers can create a sense of *connection*: they can bind a space together in a matrix of meanings. The eye often encounters a series of relationships that are visually tied together in contrast to the incremental discovery and direction of the trail system approach.

- More usually, placemakers merely strengthen identity with a particular site, serving as an *orientation* to space.

- Placemakers can be called upon to *animate* space, for example, by staking out an area for specific activities, like the embedded dance steps at a Seattle bus top, or by cueing activities through installation of a symbol—like the Judge's Bench in a Boston square that encourages the programming of a space. The presence of the Bench has inspired the TV news teams to cover the daily court reports from this rostrum. (See photos on pp. 77, 78, and 215.)

The Spectrum of Placemaking and its Effect

How do we measure the effect of the assemblage of design elements and art objects that are evaluated here? Certainly, few of them alter our experience of a place as dramatically as do the sinuous multicolored benches that now embrace the cold marble formalism of Grant's tomb like a Gaudi necklace. Those benches also provoked a strong reaction from the Civil War buffs who felt a proprietary interest in the status quo ante. For when the invested meaning of a place transcends the neighborhood claims on it—which the necklace of bright tile represented—then there may be considerable conflict over place definition and the competing resonances that certain alterations obtain. Obviously, the notion that placemaking requires a sort of community compact is facilitated by a design process that secures consent. Some art elements—such as the community portraits at the Louden-Nelson Community Center in Santa Cruz or the Oakland murals—are special because they represent such a high level of consent. One can almost feel the community waiting to have its portrait painted in the Louden-Nelson mural. The impact is bolstered by the intimacy of the compact.

Many placemakers have a more modest objective. They add a layer of decorative richness that does not transform an environment, but rather embellishes and sometimes commemorates it. The carved brick friezes along the ground floor exterior walls of the new Anatole Hotel in Dallas, the ceramic tile hopscotch pavement by Lilli Ann Killen Rosenberg in Boston, and the bronze Dancer's Steps embedded in the Seattle pavement all perform this function. Some of the older placemakers, though smaller, have a grander effect than decorative embellishment. As fragments of an earlier era, the Burke Building arch in Seattle, the Cincinnati flower stand, and the steaming kettle in Boston achieve a special sanctity, a sort of transfiguration through endurance over time. We celebrate their tenacity as a part of their value! Yet few people know their stories, for some American cities appear to have made a habit out of failing to interpret what they have saved. There is an unrealized potential for employing such artifacts more frequently in contemporary urban de-

Mara Smith's carved brick reliefs on the exterior of Lowe's Anatole Hotel in Dallas, constructed with union labor in 1978, illustrate the potential narrative powers of this simple medium which was used by the Chaldeans so impressively to decorate the walls of Babylonia thousands of years ago.

The classical formalism of Grant's Tomb now entwined with this Gaudi necklace of a bench represents the collision of two different constituencies—Civil War buffs and neighborhood activists—with different attitudes about the meaning of this site and how it should be used.

sign, but with a deliberate concentration and within the embrace of some community ritual. The public yearns for symbolic objects, a wish that often finds banal fulfillment in the sporadic outbreaks of vernacular adornment—whitewashed wagon wheels or bathtub madonnas on suburban lawns.

A guerrilla action restores place meaning: working clandestinely, preservationists reinstated this fragment of the original ornamental design into the contemporary utilitarian handrail of the Kirchenfeldbruecke, Bern, Switzerland.

This leads us to speculate on some of the ways in which placemaking objectives can be categorized, for certainly their range and levels of impact are varied. If we think of them on a continuum, one end might be titled simply the *placemarker*. This would be a work of art or a piece of urban design that makes no specific reference to a physical or social context, but merely enables one to remember a particular node because it is there. After a period of time, people sometimes cherish such an object because of its familiar association to location; it may also take on particular meanings because it comes to represent a certain state of technology, or be valued as representing a particular design period or sensibility. The large CITGO sign above Kenmore Square in Boston, which was restored after a great hue

and cry, is an example of such a place marker.[3] It is simply there; it does not mark the site of a filling station or an oil company headquarters. This type of placemarker—which is arbitrary and perhaps even capricious—usually achieves its prominence through scale and design quality. It should be used sparingly—like the Eiffel Tower!

Placemarkers can achieve considerable prominence in a highway-oriented culture. It is possible to think about orchestrating them as part of the design of a new highway commercial corridor. They may achieve prominence because of their dramatic visibility, rather than because of what they express implicitly or explicitly. Placemarkers may be self-conscious—created to make an effect—and sometimes they gain notice only because their context has shifted. For example, the ruin of a church in Boston's Back Bay, which has now been incorporated into new condominiums, becomes more of a placemarker now as a fragment of the past

When the CITGO sign was scheduled to be demolished in Boston, architectural critics came to its defense, hailing it as an example of the neon craft and as a traditional marker since 1965. It was subsequently restored in 1983. Both location and cost raise a serious question about how many such "place markers" a city requires, and whether this widely publicized action was worth the resources that went into it. The residential neighborhood near it sees blinking lights rather than a landmark's aura.

Isamu Noguchi's "California Scenario" has obvious sculptural presence as a place marker between corporate glass walls and a concrete parking garage in Costa Mesa, but even during a sunny February noontime the space is too glaring to serve a primary function as a rest area for employees in the adjacent towers. It poignantly demonstrates the failure of even large and integrated public art commissions to respond to the behavioral information that would affirm them as places for people rather than merely spaces for the arrangement of objects.

than it did when it was intact and had a congregation to fill it.

In the second category an object is called a *Generic Placemaker* when it responds directly to the content of what it celebrates, but without reference to a particular site or event. Such objects may commemorate a certain function, like the Creston/Nelson substation in Seattle that pays tribute to the generation of electric power, or Andrew Leicester's sculpture that honors the mining industry in Frostburg, Maryland. Generic themes may take the form of the dancing steps embedded in the bus stops of Seattle's Broadway, or the street people painted on the walls in downtown Palo Alto. They can reinforce a general impression of the character of a region—its geographical identity—the light, the terrain, whether it is desert or mountainside, and of course the vegetation—as does Isamu Noguchi's "California Scenario," a sculpture garden of symbolic elements in a corporate plaza demarked by mirrored glass towers and concrete garages that could be anywhere in the golden state.[4]

Such elements as the Noguchi sculpture can add a considerable power to a space through an abstraction that enables them to be interpreted in many ways. Conversely, their generalized symbolism may be felt less acutely than the *Specific Placemakers*, a category of design elements that responds to particular locations or commemorates particular people or events. Many specific placemakers evolve out of the special circumstances of a designated group or environmental condition. The specific placemakers form the most eccentric category. They can bear the appellation of 'lovable object' with great equanimity, considerable frequency, and a special grace. Our preference in this book is to describe these elements because they concentrate human interest and because they plead special circumstance. Many of them were generated by particular constituencies who bore the responsibility of their proprietorship with the fiercest intent. Of the three categories just described, they are the most *closely attached* to place, and their value which depends more on the vesting of association than on their intrinsic worth as art objects might significantly decline if they were moved.

There is a final category, the *Place Enhancer*, which is clearly the most comprehensive and probably the most frequently utilized. This category is composed of decorative elements created by artisans that reinforce the identity of a place. As discrete elements, they usually lack the power to be place-transforming, but, in the aggregate, such elements—cast concrete panels, wrought iron detailing, stained glass scenes, crafted street furniture, specially designed manhole covers, benches, or bollards—can impart great richness and indeed define the character of a place, particularly if the decorative elements come together to complete a generic composition or related set of themes. Kenneth Treister, developer and architect, realized this integration of place enhancement and architectural design in the Mayfair at Coconut Grove, Florida. As owner and designer, Treister had the freedom to create an environment in which decorative chased copper trash receptacles combine with walls of cast concrete impressed with decorative motifs that thematically reinforce the tropical garden in the atrium of his shopping center.

Cast bronze frieze of early fire fighting relieves a bland modern firehouse and modestly reasserts a decorative motif (left). It is the result of Philadelphia's One Percent for Public Art ordinance, among the first in the country.

The Civil War frieze, white terra cotta against red brick, bands the Pension Building of 1882–1886 with the movement of marching troops, galloping horses, and careening caissons (right and bottom). Only 180 feet of the frieze is the original design—but the artists made it stretch 1000 feet around the building by adding or subtracting minor elements to give it the variety which belies the small amount of original work required; a technique that could be more widely employed today to encourage more comprehensive integration of craft in new architecture.

reveal an expanding capacity to locate craftsmen to execute rich decorative elements in an age that has been popularly called high tech—high touch. This increased awareness of craft and demand for craftsmen is probably a happy result of the burgeoning rehabilitation of old structures where more intricately worked surfaces create a market for the renewal of the craftsman's skills. This trend connects building enrichment to the preservation movement which increasingly recognizes that the evidence of craft is a principal reason why many people want to save old buildings. Some developers of new building projects understand the market value of this new enrichment better than the architects they hire. Usually architectural training has not included a mastery of the historic styles which make it easier to design a mantelpiece or a reflective ceiling—a ceiling that relates to a design motif on the floor.

An architect-developer, Kenneth Treister, enhanced his shopping center at Coconut Grove, Florida, with cast concrete forms fashioned from carved styrofoam by Cuban work crews. Such decorative elements were an unusual departure from the severity and simplicity of shopping mall design in the 1970s and require a level of intervention in the construction process that most architects are not trained, or required by the client to understand or philosophically motivated to undertake.

The recent spate of books on decoration, particularly the *Sourcebook on Architectural Ornament* by Brent Brolin and Jean Richards evidence an increased popular concern for the insertion of these enhancing elements into architectural design. They also

Dimitri Gerakaris designed and forged this twenty-seven-foot iron tree as part of a gateway he was commissioned to make for Eagle Square, a public plaza that replaced a fire-damaged building set within a row of mid-nineteenth-century façades on Main Street, Concord, New Hampshire. Completed in 1983, the gateway's 40-foot wide horizontal entablature relates to the cornices of the surrounding historic architecture, while upon close inspection providing a degree of intricacy and human interest.

These new stained-glass windows of the Beverly Restaurant in historic downtown Staunton, Virginia, are part of the 1981 rehabilitation. The façade was restored to its original appearance as a hardware store in 1886, but these clerestory edibles, the work of a new generation of craftsmen now living in Staunton, replace simple ornamental panels.

Façade after renovation in 1981.

An 1890 photo of the original façade, when the building served as a hardware store.

PLACEMEANING AS ENERGY SOURCE

The fact that the Chelsea placemakers escaped vandalism in the first three years after their installation in this blue-collar community, with its melange of ethnic identities and bevy of late night bars, encouraged us to believe that they release a particular kind of energy[5] an energy that translates into feelings of care and proprietorship for place. The fact that children in Chelsea now ask visitors if they have seen the bronze purse, the crabs, or the lunch on the bollard demonstrates in a small but perhaps significant way how feelings of pride and respect can be built into places.

We believe that architects and designers can apply this experience elsewhere. Certainly this special pride is true of a number of projects profiled here. The miners and their families who donated their memorabilia and ideas to the Miners' Monument in Frostburg, Maryland, showed pride as did the children and adults who molded the baker's dough for Ruth Asawa's bronze scenes of San Francisco on the Hyatt Fountain.

At a time when fossil fuel is in short supply, we are rethinking our attitudes toward both energy and our level of mobility, attitudes that formerly sanctioned a disposable built environment—one that we could move away from at will. Placemakers can now have an added significance by helping, even in a small way, to prevent the waste incurred by disinvestment in older neighborhoods. By encouraging pride of place, they release community energy for maintenance and conservation, just as they help save the energy that might otherwise be expended to demolish older neighborhoods and construct new ones. The placemakers help to kindle a connection between objects in the environment and the layers of association with that environment that can impress itself on the minds of the city's dwellers, and

nourish a feeling of belonging, even proprietorship.

In 1982 Andrew Leicester created this monument to miners, entitled "Prospect V–III." Located in Frostburg, Maryland, this tribute to miners everywhere is of special significance here in a coal mining community dating from the 1860s. The artist enlisted the help of miners and their families in the creation of his artwork.

Artist Ruth Asawa involved 300 people in the clay moulding of these scenes of San Francisco, that were then cast into this bronze fountain at the stepped entry to the Hyatt Hotel in Union Square.

THE LANDSCAPE OF THE MIND

The connection between placemakers and the memories and associations they release we call "crystallization." It is a word that Stendhal used in his treatise *On Love* more than a century and a half ago to describe the way objects in the environment recalled associations between a lover and his beloved and consequently enriched the lover's view of the beloved. He derived the analogy from the observation of how a bare tree branch left in a salt mine is covered in time with dazzling salt crystals. We use the term crystallization to describe how objects in the environment create or reinforce a mental landscape of associations in the minds of people who experience a particular locale.

The embroidered granite bollards for the new subway station in Cambridge's Porter Square illustrate the crystallization process. Unlike many bollards used in contemporary landscape design that are as rough and clumsy as tank traps, these are delicately carved by the sculptor Will Reimann in patterns based on the textiles and other artifacts of the diverse ethnic groups that have inhabited the Porter Square area over three centuries. The patterns used in weaving, embroidery, floor tiles, and jewelry span a time from Penobscot Indians to recent French-Canadian immigrants. Because the carvings are subtly worked into the stone, they will probably receive only an occasional glance from some of the hurried subway users, who may appreciate their decorative relief as a discrete counterpoint to the high-tech industrialized surfaces of the station. For others they will be an act of discovery, the discovery of a layer of meaning that may have been carried in the subconscious for most of a lifetime. An embroidery pattern carved in granite can crystallize an earlier association with a pattern reminiscent of the one on the antimacassar of grandmother's half-forgotten parlor sofa, bringing back the memory of

This Spanish fourteenth-century tile pattern and the relief which sculptor William Reimann created by sandblasting it in this granite bollard at the Porter Square subway station plaza, Cambridge, illustrates a subtle technique that 'softens' a hard surface by "crystallizing" images for passersby who may have a Spanish heritage or a love of craft.

childhood visits, the smells of cooking in the old house, and the special aura of family feasts.

Writers have used this crystallizing technique to create a literature of remembrance. It is a technique that could be widely employed by designers to sustain a system of mental recollection. In *Swann's Way*, the first novel of Marcel Proust's epochal *Remembrance of Things Past*, he wrote of sipping tea as a grown man in Paris. The first bite of the tea cake recalled to him the country house where a favorite aunt had served him tea in his youth. To Proust the smell and taste of things contained the "tiny and almost impalpable drop of their essence," as he believed senses were "poised like souls" to recover the "vast structure of recollection."[6] What the delicate almond scent of the *madeleine* awoke in the private domain of Proust's consciousness, placemaking public art could, we believe, evoke in the public domain in our cities.

PLACEMAKERS AS AN ANTIDOTE TO THE DEAD SPACE OF MODERN MOVEMENT URBAN DESIGN

It is this Proustian capability of both recalling past time and allowing users to reinvent its meaning in the present that is missing from most contemporary urban design. Today's leading architects have usually been trained to think about making their own bold statement; the context of such a statement was not a major concern in most architectural schools during the 1950s and 60s. The effort has been toward new creation—a bold new effect—and the architectural magazines have rewarded innovation, not the subtle fitting in or retrofitting of an existing environment. The architectural view has been for the most part antihistorical, first because of a rather naive confidence that the present was better than the past, and then because that view encouraged the design of buildings that were not easily accommodated to future change. Buildings were constructed for a specific current use, and the spaces designed usually resisted change. Indeed, there was little behavioral analysis either in the schools or in the professional journals that would demonstrate how, in fact, people used space or were abused by it. Often spaces looked best in a bird's eye view, or in the proverbial sketch of couples sauntering through flower-lined paths with a baby carriage and a balloon vendor in the foreground.

This period produced many banal environments that lacked a capacity for mental resonance in which past and future meanings could reverberate and populate spaces with their imagery. In effect, the emergence of new placemaking objects during the past ten years, when many of the pieces in this book were created, appears to be one reaction to the then-prevailing aesthetic impact of the Modern Movement in urban design. The tenets of that movement emphasized the integrity of function that expressed the new technology in abstract design of glass and steel and concrete. For a half century the disciples of the Modern Movement looked on ornament as part of the decadent embrace of the nineteenth-century historicism and thus eschewed the ornamental narrative that such decoration creates. Placemakers of a representational character, with intricately worked surfaces and a wide range of materials, now serve as a counterpoint to these abstractions.

The new Edwardian Bar at the Loeb Theatre, Harvard University, "retrofits" the stark interior of this bland modern structure built in 1960. The American Repertory Theatre's prop shop fashioned this ornate wooden structure in 1984. The decorative carving seeks to humanize an austere space while recalling memories of intermission time in London theatres.

While the Modern Movement is now undergoing a period of reassessment, a new generation of architects—the Post-Modernists—are playfully, if often shallowly, addressing its authoritarian pretensions with whimsical juxtapositions of earlier historical styles. These practitioners display a re-

Bird's eye view of Pemberton Square, Boston, reveals the architects' preoccupation with the aerial view of their composition. On foot, dull concrete bollards and aggregate planters punctuate space often in shadows, where the patterning of the brick is barely noticeable. Perhaps the return of a richly decorative tradition is the next step in the evolution of Post-Modernism, but it will require closer collaboration with artisans at the schematic design stage than is currently done by most of the leading Post-Modern architects.

newed interest in decorative elements but, for the most part, the quality of urban *spaces* still echo the rigidity of design and absence of intimate detail that characterized the modern order. It is on the ground too—where this sustained bleakness provokes the strongest popular reaction—that most placemakers are located. Some, like the old building arch and terra cotta fragments on the new Federal Building Plaza in Seattle, or the forest on display in the Best Products parking lot near Richmond, Virginia, appear to redress the grievance of these hard abstractions—the concrete and brick plaza and asphalt parking lot.

However, few placemakers achieve an environmental scale, like the forest building by SITE, and many are afterthoughts that fill assigned or even leftover spaces. The creators of the placemaker have rarely been involved in the preliminary design of new spaces, but were called in to redress a problem area, the way the Judge's Bench becomes part of an amenity strategy for animating the barren Pemberton Square Plaza

Aerial view of model of BEST Products store outside Richmond, Virginia, reveals how the meaning of forest and its partial preservation becomes the guiding design principle.

in Boston. This isolated quality appears to be another legacy of the Modern Movement, in which technology divorced the artisan and artist from the design process, in contrast to the integrated work that had distinguished the earlier Beaux Arts tradition. The problem remains to rebuild a *modus operandi* that can enable artists and artisans to collaborate successfully. Despite some highly lauded and publicized projects, there is precious little to point to so far.

SOME PERILS FOR PLACEMAKERS

We have noted that placemakers have often been isolated from the design process, conceived or sited on such a limited scale as to

be swallowed up in a vast space, like Fountain Square's handsome little Flower Stand in Cincinnati. But placemakers must contend with another problem that often afflicts them in the shopping malls and public plazas: a surfeit of undistinguished, usually standard but often implacaby situated street furniture. Vast rows of barren benches, bollards, berms, baskets, and kiosks march in phalanxes through these spaces, invariably blocking significant vistas and sometimes incapacitating the space as well. Some benches are so massive that they appear able to resist nuclear attack—as well as the backsides of their prospective patrons. Well-intentioned but stolid, such street furniture ultimately denies the dignity of places because it inhibits their use and diminishes the focus of authentically special elements—without a considerable amount of heavy lifting!

Set amidst the cluttered anonymity of standard street furniture, placemakers may also have to compete with specially designed objects that are often forced and af-

SIMMS LIBRARY ALBUQUERQUE ACADEMY

City Hall bench, Boston, Massachusetts, part of an award-winning building and plaza design, but built for nuclear assault, not for the backsides of the users or the caress of the eye.

The cast-iron bench from Mexico City is a recent reproduction reflecting the design idioms of an Aztec and Spanish colonial heritage.

fected. Witness the didacticism or false sentimentality evoked by some publicly commissioned art objects. Mags Harries' bronze purse and gloves on the Chelsea bus stop bench are poised between these conditions—the ponderous street furniture and

the affected object. The bronze has a sculptural quality, and it also generates anecdotes about old ladies who try to lift the purse before boarding the bus. It can be appreciated both as a sculptural arrangement of shapes and as a source of community entertainment that elicits a certain affection. As a placemaker, it qualifies for an additional sobriquet as a lovable object, though without becoming cute or precious.

This distinction between objects that convey affectation and those that have a capacity to inspire lasting affection or lovability is an important element in the evaluation of works of art and design meant for wide popular acceptance. For by their definition, placemakers, whether described as art, like Seattle's "Waiting for the Interurban," or as design, like the manhole cover maps, or as artifact, like the Boston steaming kettle, must appeal to more than a few cognoscenti.

Mags Harries' bronze purse in Chelsea has the formal properties of sculpture but also acts as an armature for anecdotes. It is the sort of non-heroic, small encounter which can be encouraged by public art planning that does not put the entire arts budget into monumental works.

We have attempted to exclude objects that in our view try too hard to be charming, and that thus in a glance must be taken for caricature, like some Norman Rockwell portraits. Placemakers, when deliberately created as art work, should retain a certain privacy, even if we find them lovable—a privacy that allows the viewer to explore them, not just once, but over time. We also sought to avoid the many objects that appeared to be overly self-conscious like this fountain sculpture in Santa Fe, New Mexico, of a boy dressed for the sand-lot in cut-off jeans, T-shirt and baseball cap, squirting a water pistol. Yet we certainly count as a placemaker the popular Brussels sculpture of another boy whose constant act of relieving himself in the Rue d'Etruve has generated a stream of legends since the early fifteenth century. Perhaps "Manekin Pis" is saved from being considered merely cute because everyone in Brussels knows the legend of the sculpture—that it was given by a father who vowed he would commission a statue of his missing son in whatever position he found him. This mental context combines with the age of the sculpture to give it a special presence. Sometimes the distinction between the cute and the lovable is narrow, and a few pieces profiled in this book may, in the judgment of some, cross the fine line into the realm of the coy.

Besides cuteness, there is another sort of self-consciousness that can impair effective placemaking. These are the growing numbers of exaggerated objects on the floors of our cities that, like pedants on a college campus, are conspicuous because they convey an undue sense of self-importance. Something as inherently simple as a drinking fountain is transformed by the over-zealous designer into a monument; a telephone booth is transformed into a toadstool! Although the Modern Movement postulated that form should follow function, these overdramatized objects exaggerate their function in the context of the city. Their recent predominance, particularly in the new pedestrian environments—the downtown

Bronze baseball player in Santa Fe, New Mexico. He plays a coy game in his sandlot outfit and is too contrived and predictable for place making.

"Mannekin Pis," Brussels, Belgium. Though naked, this figure has more dignity born out of a historical setting that clothes him in myth rather than sandlot gear.

malls—seems to be an unintended consequence of Modern Movement ideology. The emancipation of form from the constraints of context, well documented in recent books on architectural design, has created devastating acts of self-assertion in the streetscapes that have passed almost unnoticed by architectural critics.

A provoking example of misplaced monumentality commands a small traffic island in downtown Portland, Maine. From a distance the shape suggests a giant black toadstool. Is this a creative expression of the city's seafaring tradition? Is it a comment on the capstans that mark the wharves? No one in Portland seems to know, and the landscape architects have never explained. Closer inspection reveals that the mushroom merely houses two public telephones.

vealed where waters were meant to flow. The dynamic of street definition and eye contact between shoppers and storefronts across the street was obliterated, and with it any sense of urbanity. Similarly, Eugene, Oregon, has disfigured its central pedestrian mall intersection with a more complicated pyramidal series of brutal concrete slabs that are intended to be covered by running water during part of the year. Perhaps the citizens will one day consider removing this impediment to the use of their space in fewer years than it took St. Louis to rid itself of the Pruitt-Igoe housing project, which came to symbolize the failure of Modern Movement architecture. There are now hundreds of these ugly mall monuments waiting for another generation of merchants to remove them in disgust.

Mushroom behemoth, Portland, Maine, is an awkward example of streetscape overkill, where form outweighs content. The kiosk only houses telephones, so what is the point? The traditional lobsterman sculpture turns his back from the folly of it all.

Structural Tank Trap (a sometime fountain) in Eugene, Oregon's pedestrian plaza represents the kind of mall "amenity" where the architect's need for a design statement gets in the way of urbanity. It is probably more important for most people to be able to see across the plaza.

Such efforts litter new public places across the country, and in many of them the cost far outweighs even the intended utility. Sacramento's downtown mall was studded with large geometric concrete shapes 1970–1986; a green patina of mold on their surface re-

PLACEMAKING AS PART OF A DESIGN PROCESS

Perhaps the continuing presence of toadstools and geometric concrete slabs in our public areas make a more eloquent plea for placemaking than the objects profiled in the following pages. Those irrelevant artifacts bear mute but all too visible witness to the need for a process that integrates different design talents with community information. And yet that process is only rarely attempted. Though some innovative theorists and designers give lip service to context as a way of justifying their preoccupation with form and style, little heed is actually paid to authentic integration in their work.

Patan Square, Nepal, illustrates how the integration of craftwork, sculpture, architecture, and urban design can mutually reinforce the meaning of a place. Compare it to the banality of most recent American urban spaces.

Examine, for example, Philadelphia's Guild House project by Venturi & Rauch, a firm nationally recognized for its effective critique of the Modern Movement both as theory and in their own architectural design. This housing project for senior citizens in a run-down and unfashionable nineteenth-century neighborhood should have created opportunities for placemaking in an area sorely in need of them. Instead, there is a shallow design play of changing window scale and brown and white brick detailing on a very ordinary building that tries to register its significance through the exaggerated symbolism of billboard-like graphics and an oversized entryway.

Guild House was originally crowned by a large golden television aerial, an emblem that may have represented the architect's

The facade of the Guild House Senior Citizens residence in Philadelphia was widely publicized in architectural journals, but in retrospect, it is fair to ask whether the spaces adjacent to it encourage pedestrian use and enjoyment.

assumption of the residents' main activity. The building is surrounded by barren space with a few conventional concrete and wood slab park benches enclosed by a high chain link fence. A few years ago the golden aerial was removed, though the chain link remains. Hailed by its designers as a break with the formal iconography of International Style design, and for its adoption of pop idioms that relate to the "ugly and ordinary" character of average people's environment—a favorite Venturi phrase—Guild House does not become a place for people. A style has been imposed, architectural ideas have been advanced in the professional journals, and in the process some old people have probably been patronized. The whole environment is harsh and sterile, a mockery, we believe, of what architecture should achieve.

The contrast between Guild House and Seattle's Viewlands/Hoffman electrical power substation is illuminating, because the substation that houses machines appears to offer a friendlier environment for people than the Guild House, which was intended for them. Hobbs/Fukui Associates, the architects for this power substation, which is located in a modest blue-collar neighborhood, transformed the very "ugly and ordinary" necessity of a power substation into a neighborhood park and meeting place. Aided by the city's one-percent-for-public-art requirement, which in this project was interpreted for the first time as calling for coordination with an arts team at the earliest stage of design, the team, made up of a printmaker, a painter, and a conceptual artist, worked with the architects and landscape architects to transform the entire environment of the station into something attractive, humane, and even witty.

Unlike the harsh chain-link fence that encloses Guild House, the cyclone fence at Viewlands/Hoffman is rounded into a trellis form, inviting the visitor to inspect a stand of whirligigs on one side of the enclosed power area. The whirligigs are made of tin and scrap materials by two elderly folk artists and serve as whimsical windmills playing off color-coded power turbines and a background mural. The rounded fence opens to allow visitors to pass through the site and see the whirligigs. In front, a piece of fence has been shaped into a table and chair, spoofing the very material of this standard power station accoutrement.

It is our conviction that the process that led to the Viewlands/Hoffman station could serve as a useful model for other projects across the country. Indeed, with some refinements in the form of the collaboration, it has already influenced another Seattle substation design, Creston/Nelson, also illustrated in this book. Of course, these collaborative approaches are not without pit-

Viewlands/Hoffman substation, Seattle, Washington, demonstrates where a collaborative team of architects and artists transformed very harsh design elements—power transmitters, chain mesh fencing—into a place of whimsical delight.

Viewlands/Hoffman power substation's whirligig forest by folk artists Emil and Verd Gehrke.

falls. Rarely does the architectural team allot sufficient time for research on place associations, apparently assuming that the perfunctory and usually rudimentary meeting with neighborhood groups will suffice. Seldom, too, do the designers who value their own creativity welcome other creative voices in the preliminary design process. And the artists themselves usually lack experience in working effectively on a grander scale, when they first undertake public work. In addition, they often need to learn how to modify a proposal without having to go back to scratch with a new concept. This is the kind of experience that architects seem to have acquired more readily in their own practice.

In the Appendix at the end of this book, we make bold to suggest one procedure that we believe can both strengthen the collaborative process and provide increased place content. It calls for the engagement of a multidisciplinary team—to include artists, neighborhood historians, and perhaps a geographer or sociologist—who together can create an "Environmental Profile," a *written* analysis that acknowledges the design context and opportunities, the site history, demography, and traditions, and a behavioral analysis of how the space is used. This brief then is used as the gist for fashioning metaphors and themes. The resulting environmental profile statement combining the site brief and the metaphors can then guide the commissioning process.

Only a few of the placemakers we describe in this book had the benefit of such a formal process that integrated local information and then inspired metaphors at the beginning of the design process. But a number benefitted from collaborations over time, as spaces were retrofitted and art works connected to community experience so that there was some resonance between objects and space that builds a context of place meaning. We are optimistic about the future application of this method because of the significant increase in city and county ordinances requiring that a percentage of public construction funds be used for public art. This process also should lead to art decisions based on a wider consensus than is usually appealed to by corporate or federally funded art projects. As the Seattle experience demonstrates, accountability to the community need not reduce the quality of the art that comes out of it. We believe that there is a diversity of urban groups that will seek a broader collaboration and that this movement is growing stronger every year. Certainly the dramatic growth of the local arts council movement from a single council in Winston-Salem in 1947 to more than 2200 organizations in 1986 and the concomitant broadening of this movement to embrace environmental arts as a mechanism for supporting community identity, augurs well for more effective collaboration.[7]

TOWARD AN ETHIC FOR THE BUILT ENVIRONMENT

The larger goal of these collaborative procedures is to increase the likelihood of achieving and sustaining an imagery of place that affirms an increased sense of identity in both old and new American environments. We need to find images in our built environment that activate our curiosity about where we are, inspire some reverie about our future there, and perhaps elicit a whimsical smile about where we have been. We need art and urban design that make the stored humanity of places accessible to the community as a whole, not just to architects or planners. This is because we live in our consciousness as well as in our architecture. As Professor Juan Carlo Bonta put it rather severely in his book *Architecture and Its Interpretation:*

Architects are deluding themselves if they believe that they are addressing submissive audiences . . . that their public wants by all means to understand the meaning of architecture as seen by the designer. Nothing could be further from the truth. What people want is to see their own meanings in the environment, their own systems of values, from their own frames of reference, and this is exactly what they do whether designers like it or not.[8]

It is only by making these meanings more accessible that we can restore a vision of place as a declaration of public value. It is this mental linkage to a sense of value, to a connection with community, that becomes the basis for an ethic. It should be the unifying reason for treating the built environment more responsibly. The forester and teacher Aldo Leopold, working as he did in the natural environment earlier in this century, recognized this connection between ethic and image when he wrote:

> An ethic presupposes the existence of some mental image of land as a biotic mechanism. We can be ethical only in relation to something we can see, feel, understand, love, or otherwise have faith in.[9]

Now our concern is how to extend this ethic beyond the natural environment—which Leopold describes so movingly in *Sand County Almanac*—to the cities and suburbs where most of us live. A newly recognized need to conserve that environment and a keener sense of the meaning of what we have already destroyed can reinforce the extension of this ethic. Placemakers are a kind of armature that supports this extension. They can, as Leopold puts it, "enable us to feel, understand, love, or otherwise have faith in" a particular environment.

Indeed, we must use this ethical sense to guarantee a future environment worth caring for. We must ensure that what we build in the next twenty or thirty years—which may be as much again as we have built in the past century—will be worth remembering. Placemakers are, of course, only one means of connecting people to the emotive power of the built environment; however, they have the formidable virtue of broadening the constituency for care, because, as the profiles in this book suggest, such a di-

A sculpted podium by Will Reimann between the rock of the courthouse façade and the hard place of Pemberton Square, Boston, illustrates a modest animating solution to the dilemma of being "between a rock and a hard place" (left and above).

versity of people and organizations are interested in their creation and maintenance. It is only with the consolidated energy of this *broader* constituency that we can successfully confront the haunting spectre of placelessness that we evoked at the beginning of this chapter. It is only with a much *deeper* awareness of how to create this emotive value in the built environment that we can assert alternatives to the banality that surrounds us.

We can challenge that banality, as the profiles reveal, by preserving forests in asphalt parking lots, transforming power stations with sculptures, or even engraving bollards to evoke a community fabric. These asphalt parking lots, steel power transformers, and stone bollards have hard surfaces that resist change, but the problem, as we see it, is not the old dilemma of being caught between a rock and a hard place. Rather, the problem this book seeks to address is how changing the surface of the rock can make it less hard to affirm a sense of place wherever we live.

Miners' Monument

Background

The Miners' Monument, perched on the open hillside above Frostburg State College suggests, at first glance, a defunct mining site. The wood frame structures resemble a montage of archetypical mining components—furnace, tipple, and company rowhouses.

Closer observation reveals the structure's true identity—a series of interlocking sculptures that people can walk into, or view casually from the outside—a monument to miners and the mining industry.

George Washington noticed the coal seams of Allegheny County in Western Maryland,

NAME: *Monument For Miners (Prospect V–III)*

PROJECT: Sculpture on hill site at Frostburg College—memorial to mining industry and miners of the region

ARTIST: Andrew Leicester

AGENCY: Commissioned by Maryland State Arts Council for state-owned institutions. Owned and maintained by Frostburg State College.

SIZE: 127 feet long, 26 feet high, up to 15 feet wide

DATE: 1982

COST: $35,000 with additional $15,000 worth of labor, donated services

MATERIAL: Wood with some steel and brick, and various mining tools and artifacts

PHOTOGRAPHY: Miners' monument photos— Bruce Peterson; Miners' monument drawings—Andrew Leicester; Horton's Tree Plaza—Roy Ascott; Cobumora—Andrew Leicester

in 1782, while overseeing the first geological survey of the area. In the 1860s, Frostburg became the site of the first bituminous coal mining operations in the U.S. Since then, mining has been an ever present fact, the region's economic backbone. The industry peaked in the late nineteenth century and slumped around 1927, when the mines shut down. After World War II, the industry came back to life with the development of strip mining. Though it is still the predominant industry in the area, the new practices employ fewer miners than were necessary using traditional mining techniques.

Besides its economic impact, mining has dramatically altered the visual landscape in Frostburg. For long years before the introduction of strip mining, miners using various techniques for extracting coal, iron ore, and clay burrowed through the hills and valleys, leaving behind man-made remnants— mine shafts, furnaces, tracks and buildings. Strip mining, however, has erased many of these physical reminders of the late nineteenth and early twentieth centuries, when thousands of miners and their families withstood the hardships of working conditions before mechanization. The Miners' Monument is a tangible tribute to this increasingly obscure period of mining history.

In 1981, the Maryland State Arts Council commissioned Andrew Leicester, a British-born artist now living in Minneapolis, to create a sculpture for the campus of Frostburg State College. This was to be the first of five projects for the Fine Art in Public Places Program, funded in part by a state grant. Sites and artists had to be chosen for all five projects. The Arts Council supervised an initial survey of forty-five state-owned sites and chose a jury of five curators and artists from across the nation to select the five final sites, based on their particular spatial and behavioral attributes and interviews with site sponsors. After site selection the panel handpicked five artists from 800 applicants, a decision based on the quality of the applicants' previous artwork and on the committee's perception of how well the artists could meet the particular needs of both the site and the site sponsor. The Arts Council advertised for applicants in national periodicals, including *Artforum*, *Art in America*, and *American Artists*. Project announcements were also sent to all State Arts Commissions.

When the Arts Council and the jurors visited Frostburg State College, the college representatives asked for a sculpture for the balcony of the new library. According to Cindy Kelley, State Arts Council administrator, the jurors convinced the college committee to choose instead a site in the open landscape because of the natural beauty of the area, and because no outdoor art or public monuments existed in the three adjoining counties, excepting a single pile of cannonballs. The college committee agreed, and Andrew Leicester, whose previous work included outdoor environmental art, was chosen for the project. The panel then flew Leicester to Frostburg, where he spent a week studying the area and spoke with a state archaeologist documenting the chapter of early mining history which had been wiped out by strip mining. This encouraged Leicester to think about commemorating the region's mining industry. He decided to create a sculptural ensemble giving the public a more intimate view of miners' lives in the past, and recognizing the labor force behind the industry.

Leicester chose a hillside location overlooking the George's Creek Coal Basin, the historic center of the region and site of a reclaimed strip mine. The site also captures a connection between late nineteenth-century miners and the present academic setting. Local miners collected donations at the entrances of the mines to purchase this land in 1898 for the first secondary school in Frostburg. Later the site was given to the state to build the college.

Although a committee of administrators and faculty from Frostburg State College advised Leicester, he wanted accounts of the mining community from first hand sources, and therefore he sought out local miners and their families who gave him information about their daily lives. This helped him create an incisive and inclusive view of the social and physical aspects of life in the mines which influenced his schematic design and caused changes and refinements even during the construction phase. After completing a site analysis, Leicester chose indigenous materials—timber and steel. Leicester built the series of sculptures in seventy consecutive days, with the help of an eight member team composed of students from Frostburg State College, three sculptors from Minnesota, and local builders.

Leicester intended his piece to be completed in 1982—the bicentenniel of Washington's 1782 geologic survey when the coal seams were first discovered. This also marked the centennial of the miners' strike in 1882. Lasting six grueling months, this strike was a dramatic episode in mining history. Frostburg miners received sixty cents per ton from 1880 to 1882, when the companies cut their wage to fifty cents per ton. Because of this cut, the workers formed the first coal mining union, called the Knights of Labor, and demanded $2.50 per day *minimum* and ten-hour workdays. These miners, mainly from the British Isles and Germany, were highly skilled and familiar with the Pillar and Room method of extracting coal. They carved out rooms around a pillar of coal that was left standing, forming a honeycomb pattern. When all the coal was extracted, they collapsed the columns in a sequential order and retreated back to the entrance. Instead of meeting the strikers' demands, management stuck to their decision to pay reduced wages of fifty cents per ton without any assurance of a minimum daily wage and hired "scab" labor who were not skilled in the Pillar and Room method. Subsequently, columns collapsed before the coal was recovered, and much of it was lost forever. It was this "trapped coal" that lured the strip miners into the region.

The Miners' Monument was dedicated on October 3, 1982. The artist was paid $35,000 by the State for the completed work. Leicester estimates that he and his associates donated an additional $15,000 for labor and services.

Description

Leicester's artwork is a series of wooden structures 128 feet in length. Although each piece is an independent entity, the series is linked physically and thematically. Using an architectural language—tower, bridge, house, rotunda, tunnel—the artist creates a vertical and linear sequence. Vertically the path leads from open air to underground, while horizontally it begins at a fixed point, the tower, and moves in one direction until it terminates in the mine shaft. The axis of the work points to the origin of the first coal survey at Savage Mountain seen on the horizon. In a similar linear framework, the chronological path of a miner's life is traced from birth to death along the sequence of sculptures. Thus, a linear passage of time overlays a linear path through space.

The visitor reaches the sculpture by climbing a staircase under the miners' houses. In one direction a ramped footbridge, which is elevated on a wooden frame skeleton of stilts, leads to a twenty-three foot high observation tower resembling a furnace. The view is spectacular, encompassing the college campus, the city of Frostburg below, the mountains, and the George's Creek coal basin. Returning back down the footbridge and past the entrance staircase, the visitor reaches a series of three consecutive wooden shacks attached like miners' rowhouses. Visitors can continue along the ramp or enter the rooms—each corresponding to a stage in life. The first, infancy, is portrayed by a low-ceilinged house; a coal cart symbolizing a cradle is poised on the tracks leading towards the mine shaft, representing the inevitable career choice for many men in the region. On the walls, images of red, yellow and blue-colored butterflies are transformed surrealistically into pairs of black lungs—a reference to the respiratory disease miners can contract from exposure to coal dust. The viewer then enters the next room, which pays homage to a miner's prime of life. Aptly, it is a typical miners' work-setting depicting the Pillar and Room method for extracting coal.

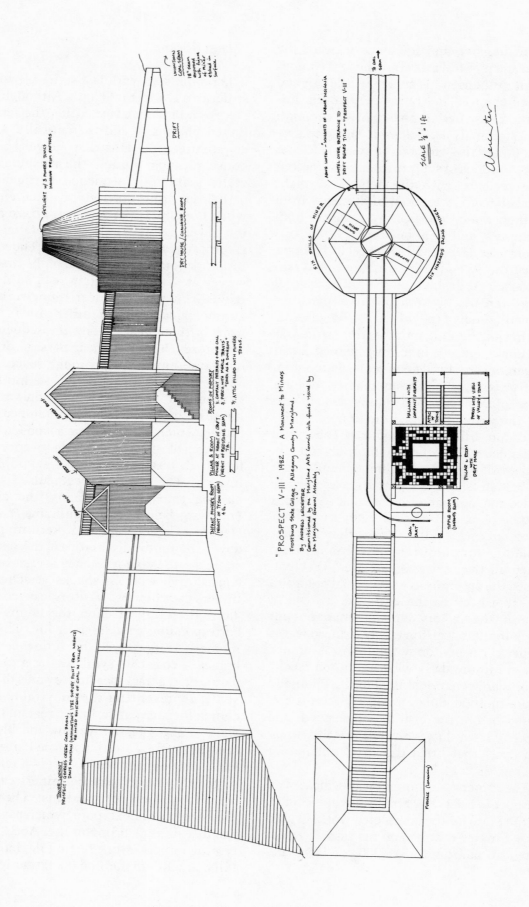

"PROSPECT V-III" 1982. A Monument to Miners

Frostburg State College, Allegany County, Maryland.

By ANDREW LEICESTER
Commissioned by the Maryland Arts Council with funds issued by
the Maryland General Assembly.

Andrew Leicester's drawing of the Miners' Monument, Frostburg, Maryland

The shiny black-tiled interior alludes to the grim walls of coal and the proximity to death when using this dangerous method. The last adjoining shack, a tribute to retirement, contains miner memorabilia—picks, shovels, lunch pails, metal tokens signifying a day's work, and family photographs donated by the townspeople.

The octagonally-shaped Rotunda is the final structure before the visitor descends into the shaft which represents the miner's tomb. It resembles a miner's changing room. Stenciled on the walls are images of the six skills a miner was expected to possess, and the six dangers the miner encountered underground. On the floor a track leads into the shaft. Its midsection shifts away from the direction of the shaft, so the track is no longer a continuous path leading into the mine. From a skylight above hang three miners' uniforms, which appear to float between earth and sky.

The last stop on the tour is the mine shaft. The visitor travels a connecting hallway framed in a series of wooden posts and lintels, into what has been described as "death beyond culture, deepest blackness."[1] Here is an exposed coal seam fashioned into a bed. Leicester explains, "Cut into the bed is the effigy of a figure—reminding us of the life cycle of the miner at his eventual resting place." The image comes from a line of a mining ballad, "Dark as a Dungeon," written by Merle Travis in the 1920s. "And I'll watch from the doors of my heavenly home and laugh at the miner a-digging my bones." The view inside reveals tracks that disappear into the blackness beyond. The view in the opposite direction passes through the sequence of spaces which the visitor has just traversed and opens into a vista of the bright outdoors. It is ironic that the crew working on the artwork inadvertently struck coal.

Design Impact

The Miners' Monument attracts a diversified audience. Travelers driving along the nearby highway catch a fleeting vision of the architectural character of past mining

villages. Students and visitors on campus enjoy Prospect V-III as a place for viewing the surrounding countryside. The piece holds special meaning for community residents like septuagenarian Tony Urbas, one of the miners who donated his advice and artifacts to Leicester's work. Mr. Urbas remarked, "This is something the area has been in need of, something in memory of the miners who worked this area."[2] Dr. Nelson P. Guild, President of Frostburg State College says, "This is about the first thing that has ever been done in the area in recognition of the life of the coal miner."[3]

The relationship between Leicester's design and the contemporary mining community can be described as symbiotic. Both nurtured each other. Leicester calls this project "the most exciting thing he has ever done" and likened the results to "spontaneous theatre because the design, especially the interiors, was an additive process, ever-changing even while being built." Local newspapers reported the sculpture's progress and each day more and more miners and their relatives stopped by the site to offer suggestions and contribute miners' artifacts. Community response *became* part of the art work; it was not merely used as background information. In turn, building a tribute to miners roused sentiment and caused the community to translate their sense of pride into action. When representatives from the College Art Department attempted to discourage Leicester from including images like black lungs in the artwork because they thought this would be offensive, Leicester and members of the mining community met with the College and simply persuaded them that these unpleasantries were part of the true story and should be told. The College conceded on this point. However, they successfully discouraged Leicester from decorating the exterior of the mining shacks with plastic flowers because they lacked dignity; though they were a decorative item often seen around miners' housing. At meetings between the college and the mining community, conces-sions made on both sides improved relations and probably engendered some mutual understanding between these two very different groups of people.

As a result of the Miners' Monument, an ad hoc committee was formed and is currently lobbying to have the state build an underground mining museum adjacent to the monument. They propose that the museum house large machinery and other memorabilia originally offered for inclusion in the sculpture. In an ironic twist, a work of public art could, in time, inspire a building project—rather than the more common event of a building project becoming the occasion for commissioning art.

Though Leicester's work was directly inspired by the Allegheny County mining experience, he intended his piece to be a tribute to mining and miners everywhere. "I choose to emphasize themes of human conditions which are common to mining worldwide."[4] Prospect V–III's imaginative iconography mixes mining imagery with symbols from other sources to express the dialectic forces—heaven and earth, confinement and freedom—which Leicester feels operate in a specially heightened way for miners and their families. A miner's daily life, says Leicester, "subjects him more intensely than most other people to these extremes."

Frostburg State College maintains the sculpture, which is open to the public three afternoons a week in the spring and fall. Those wishing to visit the sculpture at other times can sign out a key from the Frostburg State College Library, near the site. A pamphlet explaining the piece is also available at the library. While the physical condition of the monument has been well maintained, unfortunately, some mining artifacts inside have disappeared.

Of the five public artworks commissioned by the Maryland State Arts Council, three others have been installed on state college campuses, and one is located at a state mental hospital. Cindy Kelley, a State Arts Council administrator, considers Leicester's work "the most historically-based," and believes it has succeeded in reaching new constituencies, one of the Arts Council's goals.

Leicester has created several subsequent outdoor works including "Toth," a memorial to the gold smelting industry in Rapid City, South Dakota, which is a timber replica of the support system built underground to extract gold; and Horton's Tree Plaza, outside St. Joseph's Hospital, in Brainerd, Minnesota, is a mosaic patterned design inspired by a mathematical formula derived from research on the human pulmonary and circulatory systems. This latter design also symbolizes similar patterns found in nature: rivers, tributaries, and tree roots. The artist has also completed "Cobumora" (COw, BUll, MOuse, RAt), an outdoor plaza on Washington State University campus in Pullman. Shaped like a bull's skull, it is adjacent to the College of Veterinary Medicine and is a sculptural tribute to the ancient legacy of veterinary medicine. Snakes and cows—ancient medical symbols, and mice and cats—animals used in modern laboratory practice, are integrated in the mosaic wall, tiled floor and entrances to the plaza.

Andrew Leicester's model for "Cobumora" on the Washington State campus in Pullman is a sculptural tribute to veterinary medicine.

Horton's Tree Plaza adjacent to St. Joseph's Hospital in Brainerd, Minnesota, contains mosaic patterns inspired by the root and branch systems of trees and the pulmonary system of the human body.

Clinton Square Map

Background

Highland Park residents may feel a little like Alice in Wonderland as they roam around a miniature bronze map of their city that is embedded into the pavement of the plaza of new Port Clinton Square, a mixed-use redevelopment project in the downtown area. Like Alice after drinking a magic potion, visitors to the map appear many times larger-than-life size, as they walk within a diminutive landscape relief that is both familiar and fanciful.

The City of Highland Park, an affluent suburb north of Chicago, developed a revitalization plan for the downtown area in 1980 which included building new office and retail space, making façade and streetscape renovations, and adding landscaping, new benches and lighting to the downtown area.

The Highland Park Streetscape Office, the city agency that sponsored the revitalization plan, hired Sasaki Associates to do the landscape plan. The firm included funds for public art, and chose artist Gregg LeFevre

Description

People freely explore the 15 ft. by 15 ft. map of embedded bronze and granite, which depicts the entire twelve square miles of Highland Park in low relief. Gregg LeFevre's piece plays on the notion that all maps are abstracted versions of reality. Using traditional mapping elements like earth textures and geological features, LeFevre's map piece evokes the delight which results when the familiar is contrasted with the unexpected. Well-known symbols for city blocks and streets are juxtaposed with abstract topographic lines and trees. This mix of familiar and unexpected is augmented by the more than 300 three-dimensional "surprise" elements sited in the base map. These include frogs, turtles, crabs, starfish, autos, golf tees, divots, footsteps that suddenly stop, and a woman walking her poodle. LeFevre also includes local landmarks such as the high school, the water tower, and a ship that sank offshore years ago. These visible buildings and landmarks suggest the neighboring buildings and landmarks which have not been included in the map.

The process was a long one, involving many steps before casting. LeFevre and his associate Kate Burke crafted patterns of wood and foam core, with paper, cardboard, and plastic pieces used to form the details of the relief. Next, resin-bonded sand molds were made from these patterns, and then bronze was poured into the molds. The burnishing process included chasing, polishing and finally patination. The twenty-five finished bronze panels and another seventeen cut-granite pieces were installed in jigsaw puzzle fashion by local masons. To affix and align the map pieces, adjustable anchors were attached to the back of each section, and then a rubberized wooden mallet was used to line the pieces into place. The map took eight months to construct and was installed in July, 1984.

This piece is just one facet of LeFevre's work as a landscape artist. Like landscape and cityscape painters of the past, he is in-

NAME: *Clinton Square Map*, Highland Park, Illinois
PROJECT: A bronze and granite low-relief map embedded in the plaza of Port Clinton Square in downtown Highland Park.
ARTIST: Gregg LeFevre
AGENCY: Highland Park Streetscape Office (city agency), Sasaki Associates (landscape architects)
SIZE: 15 feet x 15 feet
DATE: Unveiling—October 1984
COST: $50,000—includes artist's fee, materials, installation and delivery
MATERIAL: Bronze, granite
PHOTOGRAPHY: Gregg LeFevre

of Waltham, Massachusetts to create a pavement piece for the 17,000 square foot public plaza. The Highland Park Streetscape Office was pleased with the inclusion of public art as the city had little of it. However, Robert Ballou, the director, wanted this to be "a safe piece—less controversial" than a previous public sculpture designed for Highland Park by Peter Voulkos, an artist known for his large-scale non-representational bronze pieces. Voulkos' piece—a large, bronze tubular work, according to Ballou, provoked a highly critical response from the public. The city officials wanted to avoid a similar controversy in this next project. Gregg LeFevre, a sculptor who is interested in land forms and textures, had worked with pavement inserts before and suggested a concept of a map of Highland Park.

terested in the celebration of both nature's beauties and manmade constructions. Unlike his predecessors, though, he works three-dimensionally, often in cast bronze and with cast paper, and his perspective is an aerial one. Much of his work appears abstract until one compares it with birdseye views, and then it seems realistic.

Design Impact

The Clinton Square Map, located on a new plaza in the retail shopping area, has become a focal point because of its prominent location and its capacity to encourage public participation. Local people walk on the map, stopping to point out where they live or work. It has become a landmark for shoppers and other visitors, says Ballou. People now say, "Meet me at the map in Port Clinton Square."

Community members, designers and construction workers on the site told LeFevre that it was the one piece in the entire revitalization plan which was unequivocably accepted and enjoyed by all. The artist believes that it is successful because of the number of details which encourage closer examination. LeFevre blends landscape and cityscape into one sculpture that simultaneously expresses a recognizable rendition

Detail of Highland Park Map depicting the City Hall and the public library.

A grouping of the brick-sized bronze casts embedded in Winthrop Lane, a pedestrian alley, that evoke the character of Boston, Massachusetts.

of the actual city and LeFevre's own personal view of it.

There will be an added dimension to this sculpture as time goes by. Says LeFevre, "The nature of the burnishing will change, as people walk on the map. None of the recesses are greater than a quarter of an inch, and these may turn green like weathered copper."

LeFevre has executed numerous public and corporate commissions. One project, installed in Boston in May 1985, is entitled "Boston Bricks." Over one hundred bronze reliefs crafted by LeFevre and Burke are embedded in Winthrop Lane, a pedestrian alley near Downtown Crossing and the heart of Boston's department store district. Each makes reference either to historic events, symbols of Boston, or local architecture.

Haas Murals

Background

For the past eleven years, Richard Haas has been painting facades onto empty urban walls. To the uninitiated, the illusions, suddenly noticed, are startling. Locals quickly adopt the murals as landmarks. Simultaneously eluding, confounding and teasing perception, Haas' urban *trompe l'oeils* are always site-inspired.

Raised in the shadow of Frank Lloyd Wright's Taliesin studio in Spring Green, Wisconsin, Haas once seriously considered architecture as a career. He chose art school, but his earlier interest sustained itself during study at two Midwestern universities, travels to Europe, and an eventual relocation to SoHo in 1968. For a while, Haas constructed sculptural boxes depicting urban scenes. It was then that he realized that the focus of his concern was in "the dialogue between architecture and city space, how things coexist by accident and fail to coexist by design." Subsequently, his mural work has imaginatively redressed the haphazard weave of the city fabric.

SoHo Mural

New York City, Haas' home, houses several of his most inventive works. His first mural in the city, painted in 1974, stands on the corner of Green and Prince Streets. It was commissioned by a mural group called City Walls, who until then had selected mainly abstract designs. The SoHo mural was a distinct change. One of Haas' most representational works, it continues the Victorian cast-iron façade of a building over to its exposed side wall. The detailing is intricate: each column and façade relief is meticulously shadowed, and identical. But as uniformity does not make reality, the painting is punctuated with traces of human intervention—sporadic air conditioners, occasional opened or boarded windows, a single cat gazing from a sill. Two real windows are woven into the fabric of the mural. Now fading with age, the work was described by critic Paul Goldberger as "witty and reverential . . . one of the few pieces of public art anywhere in the city that's fun to look at."

Peck Slip Mural

The Peck Slip Mural was painted in 1978. Located within the eleven blocks of crumbling Federal-style brick buildings and wooden piers that comprise Manhattan's historic South Street Seaport, it is a striking image: a Greek arcade framed with four Ionic columns, opening towards the Brooklyn Bridge. The mural is adjacent to a print shop, also painted. Commissioned by Con Edison

NAME: *SoHo Mural*, New York City
PROJECT: Mural depicting cast-iron Victorian façade, located at the corner of Green and Prince Streets in Soho.
ARTIST: Richard Haas
AGENCY: City Walls, Inc.
SIZE: Approximately 60 feet by 55 feet
DATE: 1974
COST: Unknown
MATERIAL: External mural paint
PHOTOGRAPHY: Renata von Tscharner

the type of Classical Revivalist structure that actually could have been added to the New York streetscape during the second half of the nineteenth century.

NAME: *Peck Slip Mural*, New York City
PROJECT: Mural at historic South Street Seaport depicting classical Greek Arcade opening to Brooklyn Bridge, and facade of Federal-style building and adjacent print shop
ARTIST: Richard Haas
AGENCY: City Walls, Inc.; Consolidated Edison of New York
SIZE: Approximately 100 feet by 50 feet
DATE: 1978
COST: Approximately $15,000
MATERIAL: Exterior mural paint
PHOTOGRAPHY: Renata von Tscharner

for the side of their electrical facility, the mural captures the essence of the neighborhood with a gentle wit. The view of the bridge through the arcade presents the perspective that would be visible if the plant were not there, and the Manhattan and Williamsburg Bridges, spanning the horizon of the painting, emphasize the theme of Manhattan as an island and a port. Tucked between two Federal-style buildings, the arcade is simultaneously absurd yet plausible—

Times Building Mural

Haas' largest New York City piece, completed in spring 1980, attempts to commemorate a specific lost facade—the New York Times Building which was built in 1905 and demolished in 1965. The inspiration for the mural was the site: the ten-story Crossroads Building located on 42nd Street and Broadway in the hub of Times Square across from the site of the old Times Building. The Crossroads Building's elevator shaft was never finished and had not been decorated; however, it was highly visible.

NAME: *Times Building Mural*, New York City
PROJECT: Mural on ten-story tower in central Times Square, depicting demolished 1905 New York Times Building
ARTIST: Richard Haas
AGENCY: 42nd Street Redevelopment Corporation; New York City Office of Planning and Development; New York City Office of Economic Development
SIZE: Four walls, each approximately 35 feet by 100 feet, plus a lower portion 15 feet by 200 feet
DATE: Started 1979, completed 1980
COST: Approximately $60,000
MATERIAL: Exterior mural paint
PHOTOGRAPHY: Robert Livingston Pell

The mural covers all four sides of the elevator shaft and was created according to Haas' standard procedure. The initial drafting was made in his studio, enlarged with the aid of an assistant, and finally applied to the wall surface by professional sign painters under Haas' supervision.

The project took three months to complete. Although the newspaper had no part in funding the work, the word "Times" in old English text lettering still appears under the arch on the front of the building, as it had on the original building which no longer stands.

Of his feelings for the old Times building, and his motivations for doing the mural, Haas said: "For me [the building] never left. . . . It declared the identity of Times Square. Some buildings don't go away." The *New York Times*, in an editorial on the mural, took the opportunity to decry the loss of the building and the chronic destruction of meaningful historic sites: "They wanted a sense of place back badly, but this is the only way they are going to get even a little bit of it. It's ingenious, probably worthwhile, but I'm not sure it's enough." Viewed as a wall painting rather than as an attempt at historic restoration, the work represents an element of reclamation amidst the deterioration of this world-famous site.

Design Impact

Haas' paintings have more than once accompanied urban redevelopment, at times preceding large-scale rehabilitation projects. The Times Building, in fact, was just one component of a $350,000 program of public improvements on the street, which set the stage for the proposed revitalization of the entire 42nd Street area. Originally planned in 1980 to include new gardens, restaurants and theaters, the new plan includes four office towers, the restoration of nine historic theatres, a hotel complex and a merchandise mart, at an estimated total cost of $2 billion. This program includes two other, small-scale Haas murals depicting ceremonial gateways to decorate two walls of the intersection of Dyer Avenue and Forty-second Street, opposite the Lincoln tunnel.

Similarly Haas' Peck Slip mural in 1979 became a preface for the comprehensive revitalization of the historic maritime district. The first phase was completed in 1983 and included renovation of federal-style buildings and the addition of a marketplace, developed by the Rouse Company, which renovated Quincy Market in Boston. Today, South Street Seaport is a thriving retail center, attracting large crowds of visitors daily.

In July, 1985, a new complex opened on nearby Pier 17.

Haas' portfolio, meanwhile, has been expanding by tens of thousands of square feet per year, transforming urban spaces across this country and more recently in Europe as well. There are four Haas murals in Chicago, two in Boston, and one each in Des Moines, Iowa; Galveston, Texas; Seattle, Washington; Philadelphia, Pennsylvania; Cincinnatti, Ohio; and Munich, Germany.

One prominent mural, which appears on the back wall of the Boston Architectural Center, shows a cross-section of a domed Renaissance structure, an allusion to one of the great historic styles that is part of every architecture student's vocabulary. In addition, the painting points out the sharp juxtaposition between this historic style and the building's own Brutalist form: a concrete Modern Movement structure looming above two- and three-story nineteenth-century brick townhouses.

A small mural covers three sides of a snack bar in New York's Central Park. Renovated in 1980, the flat surface is painted to depict fieldstone and lattice-work. The materials in Haas' mural recover the spa-like character of an original nineteenth-century

structure—the Mineral Spring House designed by Calvert Vaux. The mural alludes indirectly to the mineral springs that used to flow through the park, evoking both natural and built environmental imagery.

One of the two Richard Haas murals in Boston, alas, disguises only one side of the brutalist concrete Boston Architectural Center.

Anatole Hotel Reliefs

Background

Rising fourteen stories from the flat Texas plain, Loew's Anatole Hotel is a cube-like red brick structure with twin pyramidal skylights, which looks so stark and symmetrical it conjures images of ancient Middle-Eastern civilizations. Mara Smith's five large brick bas-reliefs, located along the ground floor exterior of the hotel in separate

arched panels as well as the subsequent three panels and frieze she created for the addition to the hotel, reinforce that atmosphere. The merging hieroglyphics, mythical forms, and contemporary themes of the panels add an element of warmth usually not found in structures of such large scale.

The first phase of the artwork evolved out of competitive bidding between contractors

NAME: *Anatole Hotel Reliefs*, Dallas, Texas
PROJECT: Series of five bas relief brick murals, displaying mythological and modern imagery, along ground floor of modern luxury hotel, with a later addition of three similar murals and a frieze in the annex
ARTIST: Mara Smith
AGENCY: Beran and Shelmire, Architects; Crow Development Co.
SIZE: Phase 1, 2 panels 15 feet × 18 feet; 3 panels 15 feet × 23 feet
Phase 2, 3 panels 18 feet × 22 feet and a frieze 1 foot × 200 feet
DATE: Phase 1, 1977–1978
Phase 2, 1983
COST: Phase 1, $32,000 (construction $12,000; artist $20,000)
MATERIAL: Clay brick from Fairbury, Nebraska
PHOTOGRAPHY: Ronald Lee Fleming

when the hotel was in its planning stages. The Acme Brick Company, in an effort to enhance their bid as subcontractors, included a proposal for brick carvings with their submission. They approached the Texas Women's University for artistic talent, because the school had included brick carving in their curriculum for over 15 years. When it was agreed that the reliefs would be incorporated into the hotel design, Mara Smith, a sculptor and teacher working towards her Master's degree, was selected from five candidates to prepare the artwork. After the designs were chosen, Smith worked closely with the architect and the brick manufacturer to integrate the murals and the architecture as fully as possible.

Description

In the reliefs and throughout the hotel, fourteen-pound bricks were used. Regular bricks weigh four pounds. This larger than standard size brick helps to visually reduce the volume of the building. Because they were made from a clay bearing traces of iron ore, the bricks change color with the light, their hue ranging from burnt sienna to purple. Smith carved the bricks while they were still wet, using a curved knife, broken saw

blade, and drill, among other tools. Owing to the murals' massive size—two panels are 15 feet by 18 feet, three are 15 feet by 23 feet—this process required that the artist spend seven weeks on her knees. Once the so-called green bricks were carved and individually numbered and the firing completed, the walls were assembled by union crews.

The reliefs combine mythological signs, hieroglyphics, symbols used by Native American tribes of the Southwest and modern cityscapes into what the artist describes as a blending of "the contemporary with the primitive," and "an ebullient mythology of my presence on earth." Many of the characters and forms derive from the mythical themes of the Egyptians, Mesopotamians, and Mayans—those cultures most widely known for sculpted brick carvings. Scenes depict galloping unicorns, highcheeked Indians, flowers, and, frequently, desert vegetation and animals. The stylization is rich and graphic, with flowing lines and curvaceous figures. Each relief is set in an arched, recessed panel along the exterior of the hotel's ground floor; two flank the entranceway, and three more face the parking lot on the side.

In 1983, Smith added three more reliefs—each 18 feet × 22 feet, entitled "Garuda,"

"Wolf" and "Expedition" on the annex of Loew's Anatole Hotel, which also depict figures from mythology and history. In addition, a 1 × 200 foot frieze runs along the top of the exterior wall of the auditorium, where the artist experimented with a deeper cut technique for this abstract design.

Design Impact

Smith's narrative artworks are especially useful in countering the sterile atmosphere so frequently associated with modern hotels. The reliefs help compensate for the enormous size of the structure, the vast spaces formed by the towers and atria, and the rigid, impersonal ordering of rooms, windows and floors. The murals, placed next to the main entrance of the hotel, are visible to everyone, and provide a human-scaled welcome. Despite their size, however, the eight panels remain dwarfed next to the overwhelming scale and geometry of the building.

The reliefs complement the "ancient" vocabulary of the architecture, which is further reinforced by sunken gardens. Against the flat, desert background, the ancient theme seems appropriate. The hotel design incorporates a potpourri of architectural motifs which have no connection to their locale—including Continental, Mexican, and Chinese-style restaurants, a modern discotheque, Egyptian obelisks, and turn-of-the-century London-style streetlights for the indoors atrium plaza. Conversely, Smith's reliefs are the only design elements that reflect the local culture, with folklore themes indigenous to the region.

Members of the brick industry have been enthusiastic about the Anatole reliefs, and the potential for future large-scale brick carving. Similarly intrigued with the medium, Smith has completed over fifty large-scale murals since her first Anatole murals in 1978. Her richly carved figurative reliefs adorn an array of public places across the country—hotels, banks, utility buildings and cemeteries.

Smith created six murals—two 6 × 18 feet, and four 8 × 20 feet, commissioned for the Pacific Northwest Bell Building, in Seattle Washington. Based on historic themes of Seattle's past, they were installed in 1985. Reading, Pennsylvania hosts another of Smith's murals based on a similarly regional theme. This 15 × 60 mural for the American Bank and Trust company illustrates Reading rowhouses, trains, coal mines, and Amish farmers.

A recent creation is a horizontal series of four 8 × 10 foot abstract murals of faces and creatures for a staircase at One Bethesda Plaza near Washington, D.C., one of several commercial structures where public art was encouraged through the zoning process (see p. 198).

Smith classifies her work into three categories—historic regional themes for public buildings, experimental deep cut abstract work for commercial buildings, and site-specific "lyrical" murals for smaller projects. Since creating her first murals in 1978, when few others were working in this medium, Ms. Smith has learned of twelve other brick sculptors working in the United States today. She gives credit to the brick industry for this growth. Smith believes the industry is reviving an interest in using long-lasting building materials which reflect "the return to the past intimate relationship between artists and the industrial world."

BOSTON, MASSACHUSETTS

City Carpet and Mural

Background

Children play hopscotch once again on the sidewalk of School Street in downtown Boston, on a red-hued grid executed by Newton artist Lilli Ann Killen Rosenberg. There is no longer a school in sight of this cluster of government and commercial offices, although the Boston School Committee maintains its chambers just down the street. The pavement insert recalls a time, however, when small shops and houses lined the street where America's first public school stood. Established in 1635 only a few years after the settlement of Boston, the Latin School is the oldest institution of its kind in America today. Still thriving, it has long since moved out of the downtown. It was first replaced by the Suffolk County Courthouse designed by Charles Bullfinch, built between 1810 and 1812. In 1860 this courthouse was considered too small and the site was designated for yet another Boston landmark—the City Hall, a robust Second Empire granite structure, home of city government from 1865–1968. When city government moved a few blocks away and the future of this structure was in doubt, the Architectural Heritage Foundation under the leadership of Roger Webb stepped in to rehabilitate the building into office space and one of Boston's tonier French restaurants. In an effort to better interpret the significance of the building and site, The Townscape Institute developed a comprehensive Arts and Amenities Plan for Old City Hall. The Freedom Trail, a continuous red line weaving through the city, linking together its historic highlights, passes directly by and provided further incentives for siting interpretative art at this location. The first element to be implemented from this art catalogue was the City Carpet, a pavement insert on School Street.

Description

Rosenberg crafted her hopscotch field from brass, stained concrete, and ceramic pieces, packing a wealth of detail into the 25 square foot area of her work. Human figures, symbols and inscriptions are woven together like a patchwork. The ten hopscotch squares show children playing traditional games like marbles, hoops, jacks and jump rope. The earth-toned ceramic tiles are studded with small red, purple, green, and blue stones. These brilliant accents, together with the aggregate-textured concrete in which the tiles sit, add further liveliness to the scenes of children at play. Edged around the perimeter is an alphabet made of old block type, interspersed with an A to Z of objects, some associated with Boston history. For example, a grasshopper, like the one on the top of the weather vane on Faneuil Hall, depicts the letter "G". The layer of brick surrounding the entire piece visually links the "Carpet" to the nearby red brick Freedom Trail. At the upper part of the hopscotch court, beneath a bronze image of the early school, is inscribed the school name and Latin motto "Labor Omnia Vincit," "Omnibus Opportunitas" ("work conquers all"—"opportunity for all"). Also inscribed here is a quotation from a famous graduate, Benjamin Franklin. His maxim, "Experience keeps a dear school, but fools learn in no other," wittily connects the memory of Boston Latin with experience gained through life.

Design Impact

The carpet commemorates the once novel concept of free education, an egalitarian policy that allowed boys of little means (like Ben Franklin) to improve their lot in life. It also informs passersby that such notable

NAME: *City Carpet*, Boston, Massachusetts
PROJECT: Pavement insert in the shape of a hopscotch game to commemorate America's first public school
ARTIST: Lilli Ann Killen Rosenberg
　Design development: Ronald T. Reed
AGENCY: Architectural Heritage Foundation; The Townscape Institute
SIZE: 25 square feet
DATE: October 1983
COST: $7500
MATERIAL: Ceramic pieces, stained concrete, brass, brick
PHOTOGRAPHY: Lilian Kemp, Renata von Tscharner

"Sons of Liberty" as Samuel Adams and John Hancock studied their primers at the Latin School. Not simply an historical marker, the hopscotch game is a vibrant part of the street life, causing some people to stop suddenly and stare at their feet. Occasionally people even use it for what it was designed for—hopscotch! Since its installation, gas lighting has been added along School Street, and bollards have been placed near the piece to protect it from cars which sometimes park on the sidewalk across from the Parker House Hotel. Its colors and whimsical nature contrast with the utility gray of the sidewalk, so that a few people gingerly step around it. One observer, a professional calligrapher who has worked in the district for over forty years, likened City Carpet to "a whole history book embedded in the ground." He said, "People should bring their children to City Carpet, and let them learn from an artwork that is such a wealth of knowledge and beauty." The City Carpet inspired the expansion of the Freedom Trail itself.

Six months after the completion of the City Carpet, the building owners implemented the second project in the Arts and Amenities Plan. A trompe l'oeil mural now covers the bare entry portal at the end of the entrance hall leading into the building. As a result of 1960s fire codes, which preceded the wave of historic rehabilitations that Old City Hall pioneered, the developer gutted the interior of the structure, and re-

placed the elaborate architectural elements, including a handsome central stairway, with unadorned wallboard. The granite-hued mural, designed in collaboration with The Townscape Insititute and executed by Joshua Winer and Campari Knoepffler, restores some of the architectural richness that had been lost, while adding a new narrative element.

Second Empire pilasters, which seem to be an extension of the exterior style, carry the names and dates of all the mayors who

NAME: *Old City Hall Entrance Mural*, Boston, Massachusetts
PROJECT: Trompe l'oeil mural in vestibule of Old City Hall
ARTIST: Joshua Winer, Campari Knoepffler
AGENCY: Architectural Heritage Foundation, The Townscape Institute
SIZE: 16' × 16'
DATE: November, 1984
COST: $3500
MATERIAL: Canvas mounted on the wall, acrylic paint, sealer
PHOTOGRAPHY: Renata von Tscharner

were in office at this School Street building. To reflect the time which has elapsed, the mayors' names are done in four graphic styles, each set in a typeface used during their term of office. Two allegorical figures with architectural tools of the trade—a T-Square and a triangle—hover over the arch; each carries a scroll depicting both the old and new city halls, which were the products of design competitions. A painted sparrow perched on the cornice adds a whimsical touch, and the artists depicted the building owner's red umbrella leaning against the wall. It is supposed to remind the viewer that the painting was executed in the mid-1980s. This wall painting surrounding the main entrance has been followed by a trompe l'oeil mural in the interior which Lisa Carter painted.

In another Massachusetts city, other pavement inserts help animate a downtown district. The Bridgewater Improvement Association, with state funding, included imprinted bricks, and a five-foot granite city seal embedded in the pavement in front of the town hall, as part of a streetscape improvement program around Central Square at the heart of the small town of Bridgewater. Throughout the newly paved area, the viewer can find bricks with a small im-

Some 100 bricks with town logo are embedded in the sidewalk around Central Square, Bridgewater, Massachusetts.

print depicting the key buildings of the Square, including the granite fountain that gives the town green its particular character. A local brick manufacturer, Stiles and Hart, offered their help. The imprinted bricks installed in the fall of 1984 were designed by Klaus Roesch of The Townscape Institute and executed by Marvin and Lilli Ann Rosenberg. They were fired at a high temperature to produce a harder consistency.

Grant's Tomb Mosaics

Background

The tomb of General and President Ulysses S. Grant, in New York's Riverside Park on the Upper West Side, is a severe, dignified adaptation of a Greek mausoleum. Also reminiscent of Roman tombs and President Garfield's memorial, the tomb was built in 1897 with funds provided by popular sub-

scription. Pedro Silva's undulating, Gaudiesque ceramic benches, embracing the tomb like a spectacular snake, were created at the behest of the National Park Service in 1974, through a populist organization called Cityarts. From the day of their installment, the benches were controversial. At the time, artists and community groups praised the

work for attracting and involving local residents, while architectural and historical organizations deemed them utterly incompatible with their environment, and demanded their removal.

In the patriotic years following WWII, the tomb was a popular attraction, drawing over half a million visitors annually. By the early 1970's, however, the number of tourists had steadily dwindled, and the site, which was far from most city attractions, became the object of increasing vandalism. The National Park Service, which owns and maintains the site, became concerned. David Dame, then Parks Service Superintendent for Manhattan Sites, commented tersely on the situation:

> Gang fights. Rival gangs using the tomb to settle their differences, often with knives. There was heavy graffiti on the tomb itself, beer cans, trash, people using nooks and crannies for bathrooms. The thing to do at Grant's Tomb was not to build a high fence and hire extra guards, but rather to give the community up there pride of ownership of the site. It's the difference between the island-mindset that shuts people out and welcoming them into what is, after all, theirs.

In 1972, the Park Service engaged Chilean sculptor, Pedro Silva, assisted by architect Phillip Danzig and others, to create a bench design that might involve members of the community and act as a diversion from vandalism. Charged with supervising the project was the Cityarts Workshop, an organization with a background of involving local communities in public art. Silva received approval from the Department, then over the course of two years constructed the benches: first the framework of iron rods, wire mesh and poured concrete, afterwards the tilework. Volunteers from the neighborhood—children, high school and college students, adults—assisted in designing and laying the many mosaics.

Description

The colorful, free-form benches stretch more than 350 feet in length, surrounding all sides of the mausoleum but the front, and are set back 25 feet from the building. The mosaics include a portrait of General Grant as well as depictions of his travels and achievements, including a geyser that commemorates his designation of the Yellowstone National Park. The images form an energetic medley: wild dragons, owls, racing cars, sunflowers, damsels, castles, firefighting scenes, portraits of local residents, and a notorious Matisse-like trio of dancing naked women. The contours of the bench often change with different scenes, at times forming fullsize gateways and arches.

Design Impact

Paul Goldberger, *New York Times* critic, described the benches as "surely Manhattan's finest piece of folk art of our time." Other praise has come from the American Institute of Architects' *Cityguide*, which deems them "sinuous, colorful, amusing . . . wonderful" and the *New York Amsterdam News*, which credits the benches with creating "a vital and exciting urban plaza for the entire neighborhood."

The juxtaposition of the joyous free-form artwork and the austere Presidential burial site has, simultaneously, enraged several national organizations. Various preservation societies, such as Classical America and the Victorian Society, see the benches as a disgraceful eyesore. They are "a note of inconceivable grotesqueness," said one Classical America bulletin, "Utterly at loggerheads with the mausoleum's overwhelming

Doric flavor, the benches are repellently ugly in themselves. We would avert our eyes from them in any setting." Descendants of General Grant, supported by the Civil War Roundtable, an organization composed of Civil War buffs, have similarly expressed outrage. "It's like having a roller-coaster ride running up and down the Lincoln Memorial," a Roundtable spokesman noted, "It may be fun but it's not history."

Groups arguing for the removal of the benches contended that there was little community involvement, but Cityarts and other supporters of the artwork produced memos indicating many hundreds of local helpers. Residents of the Morningside Heights neighborhood still largely favor the work, as witnessed by the increased number of local events at the plaza, and greater use of the site as a park. The local approval of the benches was formalized when Community Planning Board #9 voted fifty to one in favor of keeping them in place. However, the controversy continued for approximately ten years, with City Councilmen and State Senators joining the battle lines on both sides of the issue; it has died down since 1984, according to Diane Dayson, Site Supervisor of Grants Tomb, National Park Service. Despite periodic cleanings, the mausoleum walls continue to be marred with graffitti. "Today, Grant's Tomb is an eyesore, sorry, and neglected." confirms *New York Times* editor Peter McCabe. In contrast, the benches have remained in good condition.

Central to the concern of the National Park Service was the desire to upgrade the site in the preparation for the centennial of Grant's death, in 1985. In May 1981, the Park Service issued a statement weighing various courses of action and assessing public opinion, as gleaned from people who had written in with comments. It was concluded that the building and site should be restored to their appearance in the period 1929–1959, the benches to be moved at a future time, when suitable location and funding could be arrived at, though it is ques-

NAME: *Grant's Tomb Mosaics*, New York City
PROJECT: Undulating mosaic benches surrounding Grant's Tomb
ARTIST: Pedro Silva and assistants
AGENCY: National Park Service; Cityarts Workshop
SIZE: 350 feet long, varies from 3 feet to 10 feet wide
DATE: Started 1972, finished 1974
COST: Approximately $50,000
MATERIAL: Iron supports covered with wire mesh, poured concrete and small pieces of tile and broken ceramic
PHOTOGRAPHY: Renata von Tscharner

tionable whether the benches with their hollow, rib-supported frame would survive a relocation. Other additions for the tomb cited were the construction of a new visitors' center and the placement of a 24-hour guard.

However, as of January 1985, the National Park Service had no plans to remove the benches from the site. For the 1985 centennial they concentrated on, "restoring the natural beauty of the site," i.e. removing graffitti from the mausoleum walls, establishing twenty-four hour patrol service, and improving the Visitors' Center located inside the monument. They have sponsored two celebrations on the site with guest speakers from West Point and the National Park Service commemorating Grant's birth (April 27) and his death (July 23).

Horse Race Clock

Background

The Kentucky Derby causes quite a stir once a year in Louisville. However, for those who prefer horse-racing on a daily basis, the Race Clock in the downtown Louisville pedestrian mall offers an alternative to traditional equine entertainment. The clock tower consists of a mechanized horse race which circles around a gazebo structure, topped by the clock itself. Louisville Central Area (LCA), a private downtown group composed of businesses and corporations dedicated to revitalizing the city center, was instrumental in activating construction of this mechanical toy. The idea had been part of the original plan for the River Street Mall, now called the Fourth Avenue Mall, a five block-long pedestrian mall that LCA helped establish in August, 1973. A platform for the proposed clock had been built in the center of the long pedestrian space, but a clock was never crafted. After the mall was completed in the fall of 1973, the Chamber of Commerce hired a consultant to evaluate the downtown area, including the mall, and to generate ideas for enhancing the area with public art. The consultant suggested that a clock be located on the platform already in place, and even drew a sketch of a miniature City Hall with a clock on top.

The consultant's suggestion coincided with a meeting convened by Wilson Wyatt, Jr., executive director of LCA, and 200 prospective private donors who were interested in underwriting art for the downtown mall, the Belvedere, and the Federal Plaza. Wyatt included the clock idea on his agenda at the last minute, assuming it would have low priority. He estimated the project's cost at $60,000—5 percent of the mall's budget for construction. But Henry Heuser, president and director of the Henry Vogt Machine Company of Louisville and president of the Vogt Foundation, one of the largest private foundations in the city, immediately took an interest in the clock idea. When a second

NAME: *Horse Race Clock*, Louisville, Kentucky
PROJECT: A mechanized horse race crowned by a clock, set on a gazebo in Fourth Avenue Mall, a downtown pedestrian mall
ARTIST: Barney Bright
AGENCY: Public/private partnership—Jefferson County Government and Henry Vogt Foundation, with Louisville Central Area Inc.
SIZE: 40 feet high, 26 feet in diameter race track
DATE: Completed 1976
COST: $210,000, additional $20,000 of labor donated by artist, $20,000 by mechanical engineer and $10,000 by electrical engineer. $20,000 annual maintenance cost
MATERIAL: Painted cast aluminum
PHOTOGRAPHY: Overall view—Sam Moseley, Moseley Photography. Detail—courtesy of Louisville Central Area Inc.

donor also made a commitment, LCA formed a committee of nine representatives, with civic, financial and artistic expertise, to define the project and set guidelines. These committee members sought three things: a vertical element to punctuate the long, low, open pedestrian space, animation, and an historical emphasis. They wanted a clock that "would pull people off the expressway as they passed through Louisville, on their way from Chicago to Miami."[1] Says Bipen Hoon of LCA, they wanted to "reinforce the identity of Louisville."

The committee spent a year—from November 1972 to November 1973—interviewing sculptors "of established reputation"[2] from all over the world. These included George Nelson and Felix de Weldon of New York, Wen-Ying Tsai of Paris and New York, Franta Belsky of London, Francois and Bernard Baschet of Paris, Harry Bertoia of Pennsylvania, and Charles Eames of California. None produced a design that satisfied the committee. Then, in November, someone suggested Louisville native Barney Bright, a figurative sculptor well known locally for his bronzes of children and female nudes. Says Heuser of the Vogt Foundation, "Finding Barney Bright was like finding oil in your own backyard."[3] Barney Bright recalls, "The people in charge wanted something large that would draw attention to the downtown, and they wanted to say something about Louisville. They asked some artists from Europe and some artists from New York, but they couldn't get what they wanted. Then they finally came back to Louisville and found me."

The committee liked Bright's idea for a race track, but when Bright presented his preliminary design three months later and quoted a budget of $300,000, the committee sent him back to the drawing board. The committee still liked the original concept, but not the expensive design. Moreover, the Vogt Foundation had established $100,000 as their maximum donation. Wyatt searched for another sponsor for a joint public-private venture and found Jefferson County's Foundation for the Beautification of Public Property, which offered $110,000 for construction costs. The city offered to pay for maintenance costs (not knowing that these costs would reach approximately $20,000 a year). Finally the committee and the Vogt Foundation approved Bright's second model for the clock. After much technical planning, the clock was constructed between 1974 and 1976, with the help of electrical and mechanical engineers, and of Bright himself. The original budget of $210,000 for construction did not suffice, and estimates are that an additional $20,000 worth of his time and equal amounts of mechanical and electrical engineers' time were also donated.

Description

The Horse Race Clock looks like an old-fashioned, forty-foot-high metal toy. The clock itself crowns a small gazebo, housing five mechanical spectators who cheer on the animated horse race that encircles them on a twenty-six foot diameter oval track. Tilted for better visability, the track is held up by eight columns repeating the richly ornamented, Victorian style of the grandstand gazebo. Although the entire structure is made of painted aluminum alloy, the petal-shaped capitals appear to be cast iron, and the columns, spandrels, decorated lintels, and mouldings are crafted to look like turned wood.

Traditionally gracing squares and plazas in American cities, clocks providing official time used to be a popular element of municipal urban design; some became symbols of the municipalities. Bright's clock was inspired by the animated clocks of many European cities, like Bern's Zytglogge and Prague's astronomical clock, although he consciously chose to make his design "uniquely Louisville."

Starting hourly for a "paddock parade," five hand-sculpted racers and their steeds circle the race track, keeping time to music. The big race is scheduled every day at noon, weather permitting. The race begins with a trumpeted call to the post and a taped introduction of the racers. The five contestants are well-known characters from Louisville's past, including Daniel Boone, who blazed the Wilderness Trail through the Cumberland Gap to Louisville, with a galloping bear for his steed; King Louis XVI of France after whom Louisville is named, drawn regally along in a chariot; and the Belle of Louisville, a nineteenth-century steamboat which traveled the Ohio River, personified by a female figure who lunges forward atop stylized waves, propelling the steam paddle with her bare feet. At the sound of the bell the race begins, with the day's winner randomly chosen by computer control. At the finish, the winner is announced and makes a triumphant victory lap around the track.

The spectators in the gazebo are also local celebrities, including D. W. Griffith, director of the classic silent film *Birth of a Nation*; Oliver Cooke, a well-known Louisville classical and jazz trumpeter; Zachary Taylor, twelfth President of the United States, who grew up in eastern Jefferson County; Mary Anderson, Louisville's most famous actress, whose career began in 1875 in the original Macauley Theatre in downtown Louisville; and Henry Watterson, who was editor and publisher of the *Courier-Journal* from 1868 to 1918.

Not only do the riders move around the track, all ten figures have animated parts with movements reminiscent of a child's pull toy—wheels turn, arms wave, and Daniel Boone kicks his bear to run faster. Each character in the race evokes its own persona through dramatic posture and facial expression, manifesting simultaneously the drama of the race and a comic air. Bright's piece has a kind of exuberance which is often lacking in other mechanically operated figures. The artist said one of the compliments he most values came from artist Red Grooms, an internationally known maker of collage scenes with papier-mâché figures, who said, "Of anything I have seen in Louisville, this is what I like the best."

Design Impact

The Horse Race Clock ran its premiere race at its unveiling ceremonies in November, 1976. Three thousand people enjoyed the festivities, which included a performance by a local band and speeches from the mayor and the artist. The Belle of Louisville won the first race, an ironic touch, as the Belle had been the one element of the clock to incite controversy. Bright's first model included a nude and very voluptuous 'Belle' but with the disapproval of the selection committee, Bright added a bikini. Yet even this attempt at modesty proved controversial: shortly after the unveiling, letters to the editor in both Louisville newspapers—the *Courier-Journal* and the *Louisville Times*—indicated some negative public response. The artist remembers one outraged observer suggesting the clock belonged at the bottom of the Ohio River. Despite this initial reaction, the uproar soon died down, and apparently most people find the Race Clock an intriguing addition to the downtown. It is a popular lunch-time attraction, even drawing small time wagers among office workers betting on who will pick up the lunch tab.

The Horse Race Clock is featured on a promotional brochure for tourists, highlighting Louisville's attractions, sponsored by the Louisville Visitors' Bureau. A color postcard of the artwork is also available. The artist says that on some days when the Race is postponed, and a sign on the Clock tells viewers, "No Race Today," disappointed visitors call him up to complain that they brought relatives from out of town to see the race. Bright apologizes but must tell his callers he cannot help them; the city is responsible for the Clock's operation and maintenance. Sadly, the Clock suffers mechanical difficulties, and needs constant care, which has amounted to $20,000 a year. The city is not always able to devote funds to Clock maintenance, and many weeks may go by without a race.

Originally the Clock was located on a brick

and concrete platform, and the pleasant tree-shaded central pedestrian area made the site natural for performances, street fairs, and other events. However, a new attraction threatened the Horse Race Clock's fate. The Galleria—a complex of three levels of retail space, two high-rise office towers, a glassed-in atrium and skywalks connecting existing hotels and department stores—bisects the pedestrian mall and has become the new focal point of downtown. The developers of the Galleria did not want the clock in their atrium, which was built where the clock now stands. They felt the scale of the clock was inappropriate and would obstruct the open vistas and pedestrian circulation. Despite an attempt by community members to keep the Clock in its original location, the Galleria developers paid the city $100,000 to move it. It is now a block and a half away, on the same open mall, but the artist feels the new site is a less attractive architectural setting and has fewer amenities.

Louisville's latest revitalization plan for its downtown will precipitate yet another move for the Horse Race Clock. The LCA has decided that the three-quarter mile long mall is too long for pedestrians to navigate. They plan to resurrect a trolley track

which once ran down the street where the mall is, and service the mall with a trolley shuttle. Unfortunately, the clock stands directly in the proposed trolley's path. LCA hopes to find a permanent location for the clock in a prominent downtown site, and is considering an interior location to avoid the mechanical problems due to inclement weather. Perhaps the new location will do the Horse Race Clock justice and let it live up to the dream expressed by Henry Heuser when he said, "It is hoped that the racing clock will become Louisville's identifying symbol, such as the arch is to St. Louis, and the space needle is to Seattle."[4]

Firemen's Mural

Background

Inman Square's Firemen's Mural is an eye-catching group portrait painted in a style recalling the burgher guardian portraits by Rembrandt and Frans Hals. It evolved out of a competition sponsored by the Cambridge Arts Council, for the design of a public art work which would reinforce the sense of identity in a given Cambridge commu-

nity. Ellary Eddy, a young artist who lived near Inman Square, was among those submitting proposals. Contemplating the ethnic diversity of her neighborhood, which included student, working class and Portuguese communities, she concluded that the single, most unifying element was the firehouse, "flames being completely egalitarian." Although she had never painted realist

NAME: *Firemen's Mural*, Cambridge, Massachusetts

PROJECT: Wall painting on the side wall of local fire station, two stories above street level, depicting members of Fire Company Number 5 posed against a fire truck

ARTIST: Ellary Eddy

AGENCY: Cambridge Arts Council

SIZE: Approximately 30 feet by 55 feet

DATE: 1976

COST: $3000 (Materials $300, scaffolding $1700, artist $1000)

MATERIAL: Exterior enamel paint

PHOTOGRAPHY: Brian Dowley

works before, Ellary won the commission and painted the second story wall during the summer of 1976. The process was a learning experience for the artist which included more than painting:

> For the three months during which I painted, I was practically in the firemen's pockets: drinking their coffee and pop and shooting the bull. To share a cup of coffee at six in the morning with ten guys who had just been walking through flames connected me with a reality I'd never before known . . . my respect for these men was transformed from an intellectual appreciation to a visceral and soul-struck admiration. Conferring with them on the proper blue for the sky, or pondering aloud certain compositional alternatives, I think I in turn opened up another horizon for some of the men.

Description

The painting, three times life-size, on the blank side wall of the firehouse, depicts all the firefighters of Engine Company Number 5, posed against a fire truck. The fourteen firemen are joined by two famous Americans who could not resist the lure of firefighting: George Washington, a volunteer fireman, and Benjamin Franklin, a native Bostonian who started the first fire insurance company in America. Franklin, always the individualist, is sporting red tennis shoes. A rectangle of blue sky left of center presents an ethereal, graphically bold background. In deference to the building's handsome Italianate features, the unmarred natural brick is left showing on all sides of the mural.

Design Impact

The firemen, originally indifferent to the building's careful detailing, and the molded plaques of firefighting scenes over the station doors, now view the building with interest. Efforts to demolish the firehouse for a high-tech station similar to one in East Cambridge were dropped; firemen lobbied effectively for restoration funds.

Depicting the dignity of firefighting, and associating it with two founding fathers, the mural has become a source of great pride not only to the firemen, but to the community at large. Since the mural's creation, the firehouse has received over sixty thousand dollars in Community Development Block Grants for restoration. Acknowledging that the mural had become a local landmark, the city turned around the quartz street lights to illuminate the painting at night.

Not to be outdone, the Cambridge Police, in 1980, without Arts Council funds, commissioned the same artist for a painting on the station's garage doors. The painting depicted four policemen wearing uniforms from different eras—the 1900's to the present. Unfortunately the garage doors broke, and the mural was not replaced. Later in 1980, a different artist painted two officers' portraits on the front doors of the station.

The Firemen's Mural has faded somewhat, but although the face of George Washington is turning pale, he nonetheless continues to command the corner.

Waiting for the Interurban

Background

In the early half of the century, Fremont, a prosperous lumbering town, was connected to Seattle and other working class communities along Puget Sound by an interurban trolley system. With the increasing use of the automobile, the community dispersed, public transit was discontinued, and Fremont lapsed into a period of stagnation. In the 1970's, as Fremont approached its centennial, an urban revival began. Artists and other young professionals, attracted by the relatively low cost of accommodations, moved in, and Fremont was reborn as a fashionable place to live.

To celebrate Fremont's centennial and revitalization, the city announced a competition among local artists for the design of a symbolic public artwork. There were no responses. Finally, Seattle artist Richard Beyer submitted his proposal, "Waiting for the Interurban," a sculpture of five adults, one child, and a dog waiting pensively at the site of Fremont's abandoned trolley terminal for a train that will never come. Embraced at a neighborhood property owners' meeting, and approved by the town planners, the idea was brought to fruition by a group of concerned citizens. Establishing the Fremont Arts Council, they appealed to community residents and businesses for support, and raised the necessary funds and volunteer labor for the work's construction. Later, political complications slowed the reimbursement to the artist for the cost of materials, which, owing to the rising cost of aluminum, had come in at $5,000 over the original budget. Again, the community rallied, and an ad hoc group known as the Interurban Committee threw a benefit and succeeded in raising the needed funds.

Description

As models, Beyer photographed present-day commuters and composed a tableau that is intentionally ordinary: a woman chewing on a bit of food, a conservatively suited businessman, a plainly dressed woman holding a child, a workman with a lunchpail and a young man engrossed in a book. Each seems preoccupied with inner concerns; none seems to notice that beneath them peers

NAME: *Waiting for the Interurban*, Fremont, Washington
PROJECT: Life-size sculpture of five adults, one child and a dog waiting for a trolley
ARTIST: Richard Beyer
AGENCY: Fremont Arts Council
SIZE: 4 feet by 10 feet by 6 feet
DATE: Started 1976, completed 1978
COST: $35,000 (materials—$5000 construction—$12,500, labor—$12,500)
MATERIAL: Cast aluminum
PHOTOGRAPHY: Seattle Arts Commission—Charles Adler

a dog with a human face, which some have ascribed to a prominent local official. Waiting at the tracks, the group represents the shared destiny of the working people of the community, for whom the rebirth of Fremont was for a long time a dream. The sculpture ensemble is also a symbol of hope for the future and, as described in the fund appeal of the Fremont Arts Council, expresses the "neighborhood's patient expectations for a renewal of community values."

The figures are blockish and solid, with a curt, almost heavy-handed workmanship reminiscent of 1930's social realism. The group is set on a traffic island. Cast in a ghostly gray aluminum, they visually complement the setting of concrete and steel rails behind. A pergola reflecting the architecture of the old interurban station, part of the original proposal, was added a year after the placement of the sculptures.

Design Impact

While some critics have denounced the work's lack of technical sophistication, the public response has been hearty enthusiasm. People have climbed on the statues, placed flowers in the woman's hand, kissed the workman's cheek (as revealed by a smear of lipstick) and strapped a leash to the dog, as required by city law. In cold weather, the sculptures receive scarves and warm hats; on holidays like Halloween and New Year's they are decked out in masks and party outfits; and when Mt. St. Helens erupted, they were given dust masks. Pictures of the group have been used for customized greeting cards and as the advertising motif of a local supermarket. One Seattle TV station employs the figures regularly as a backdrop for weather reports. The press has labeled the work "a visible and significant symbol of Fremont's revitalization," and, testifying to its success in representing community identity, "the statute that has become Fremont's calling card." Significantly, there has been no vandalism, despite the exposed location. "Waiting for the Interurban" is an art work that has become a participant in the community's life. Said one Seattle resident: "Whenever I go by the sculpture I smile: I go by the sculpture to see what's happening."

Gasworks Sundial

Background

In the early 1970s, the city of Seattle commissioned landscape architect Richard Haag to undertake an unusual project: the conversion of a defunct, polluted industrial plant located on a jutting 22 acre peninsula on Lake Union, into a public recreational facility to be called Gasworks Park. The extensive reclamation process included the creation of a "great mound" with a spectacular panoramic view; from its summit, viewers can see the portentous black pipework of the coal plant, park visitors on the lawn below, and, across Lake Union, downtown Seattle, the University of Washington, and the snow-capped Cascade Mountains.

In 1978, the spot became the site of the Gasworks Sundial, a disc of inlaid concrete 28 feet in diameter. The dial was the conception of Haag, Greening and gnomonist John Purcell. It was the gift of an anonymous donor.

From conception to completion, the work involved over three and a half years of what

the artists termed "collective effort." Among those contributing to the project were mathematicians, the gnomonist, an architectural engineer, foundry workers, draughtsmen, park architect Haag, and the donor, who remained active throughout the project's development. Even the police department was involved, locating an alternate work place when the warehouse being used was no longer available. The final product incorporated over seven tons of material, and was officially dedicated on September 21, 1978—the autumnal equinox.

Description

The timepiece is in the shape of an open flower, contained within a disc twenty-eight feet in diameter. The moon and sun, cast in bronze, form the poles of the cosmological map, while the ram, fish, crab and other zodiacal symbols, also cast in bronze, mark off points along a circle in the center. A yin/yang symbol constitutes the center of the dial. Bronze numerals set in ray-like patterns of colored sand, mark the hours. A collection of artifacts from different geographic areas, some found in Seattle, decorate the surface. These include multi-colored sands, assorted shells, volcanic rock, diverse marbles and stones, blue cobalt por-

NAME: *Gasworks Sundial*, Seattle, Washington
PROJECT: Large concrete sundial set into summit of hill in renovated industrial park
ARTIST: Chuck Greening and Kim Lazare
AGENCY: Anonymous donor
SIZE: 28 feet in diameter, minimum thickness of 6 inches
DATE: Conceived 1974, completed 1978
COST: $20,000
MATERIAL: White cement with color pigments, colored sands and gravels, bronze, stone, tile, glass and assorted fragments
PHOTOGRAPHY: Seattle Arts Commission

celain chips, bits of old Chinese and English teapots, American, Spanish and Italian tiles, and contemporary ceramics. They allow the observer to make up a story of Seattle's geology and history. Household objects such as beads, keys, and eyeglass frames are incorporated into the design, extending the traditional concept of ornamentation. Around the chart's periphery, a meandering, multi-leveled gutter regulates the flow of rain water over the surface, and accentuates the design; the whole is surrounded by a red brick collar.

The sundial's layout is similar to those designed by ancient Greek astronomers and architects. Because it is an analemmatic sundial, the viewer serves as the shadow caster, or gnomon: by standing over a center line at a point marking the appropriate time of the year, one's shadow is cast over the correct hour. Without a participant, the device cannot function. A plaque nearby describes how to use the dial and how to adjust the measurements to tell time by moonlight.

Design Impact

On the site of what was until recently a shunned industrial wasteland, with poisoned soil and decrepit landscape, Gasworks Park has rapidly become one of the liveliest and most frequented of Seattle's twelve city parks. The landscape is magnetic; broad slabs of color compete for attention and contrast sharply with the mechanical forms of the now defunct factory equipment that was left standing, and where children now play. The Sundial is a natural extension of its surroundings. Where the sky was once blackened by industrial soot, the Sundial now celebrates the clear sky.

The artists, both Seattle residents, en-joyed the close architect-artist relationship, and the opportunity to enhance their neighborhood. Both praised the pooled effort necessitated by the scale of the work. Said Lazare, the greatest feeling was that "something could be created that singularly existed larger than any individual could have realized."

The park was temporarily closed to the public in April, 1984, because the city found hazardous chemicals in the soil, left from the previous industrial use of the site. After a period of analysis and preliminary steps to rid the site of the problem, most of the park, including the Sundial, was reopened in August of the same year. During this time, the city cleaned the Sundial, which remains in good condition.

Another site-specific collaborative project followed Mr. Greening's Sundial in 1981. The Seattle Arts Commission held an open competition for a playground entrance, which

Meridian Arch entryway by Chuck Greening for ramped path leading to a playground in Seattle, Washington, made from indigenous stones and other natural materials, such as fossils and ash from Mt. St. Helens.

Greening won. He was commissioned to create an entrance gate and stair for Meridian Playfield, adjacent to the Good Shepherd Center, a convent now converted into an arts and community center.

Given the requirement of designing a barrier-free access, Greening created an undulating Gaudi-like ramped pathway, with rock walls and built-in benches, which entered through a stone arch. The Meridian Arch and the pathway invite the viewer to explore a rich array of textures and cast details. It is like an archaeological site: Oregon coast fossils, petrified sand dollars, and Mt. St. Helens ash are embedded in strata of indigenous rocks. Greening used natural materials to achieve a level of visual-tactile complexity similar to his Gasworks Sundial.

Echo of the Waves

Background

The New England Aquarium and its large, new, kinetic sculpture, "Echo of the Waves" are centers of attraction for throngs of people at Boston's central wharf. From the birth of Boston in 1630 through the early twentieth century, her waterfront wharves have been centers of intensive activity. Vessels of many types crowded the harbor, from modest fishing boats to graceful China clippers, floating symbols of the primacy of trade in the bustling city. Later, as waterborne trade declined and shipping techniques changed, the wharves became obsolete and the city turned its back on a decaying waterfront. In the 1960's, however, the city discovered the redevelopment potential of the waterfront area. Now, in addition to the Aquarium, there are hotels, condominiums, shops, and a park along the revitalized harbor front.

Peter Chermayeff, of Cambridge Seven Associates, has been responsible for building and augmenting the Aquarium since its conception in 1962. He designed several additions to the complex, and in 1979 created an outdoor plaza to animate the space in front of the Aquarium. Concerned that this broad expanse lacked vertical elements, Chermayeff suggested that Japanese artist Susumu Shingu design a wind sculpture for the plaza. Shingu, whose work appeared until recently only in Japan, creates kinetic works which respond to the forces of nature. The artist, the architect, and representatives from the Aquarium agreed that such a sculpture would suit this windswept waterfront site where crowds visiting the Aquarium congregate. The piece was funded by Mr. and Mrs. David Bakalar, a developer and his wife, and donated to the New England Aquarium.

Description

Swaying majestically to rhythms orchestrated by the wind, two red and white wings balance on top of a thirty-five foot steel mast, moving like enormous see-saws. The thirty-five foot-wide wings are shaped like trusses, rounded at the corners. With wings vertical and fully extended, the sculpture reaches sixty-five feet; when they are at rest, the sculpture is forty-five feet high. The wings are made of carbon-fiber reinforced plastic, a relatively new material with the structural strength of steel, but of lighter weight. A small gust is enough to propel the wings into motion. Rotating vertically and hori-

NAME: *Echo of the Waves*, Boston, Massachusetts
PROJECT: A wind sculpture at the New England Aquarium Plaza on the Boston waterfront
ARTIST: Susumu Shingu, Artist
Peter Chermayeff—Principal Architect, Cambridge Seven Associates
Peter Sollogub—Project Architect, Cambridge Seven Associates
Everett Reed—Wing Design Engineer, Littleton Research
Joe Welch—Bearing and Machine Consultant
AGENCY: A gift to New England Aquarium from Mr. and Mrs. David Bakalar
SIZE: 45 feet tall (at rest)
DATE: Dedicated July, 1983
COST: $350,000
MATERIAL: Steel for mast, carbon fiber plastic for wings, concrete foundation
PHOTOGRAPHY: Steve Rosenthal

are translucent, exposing smaller wings, each fifteen feet wide, which rotate independently within the larger wings. The translucence allows shadow patterns to move across the surfaces of the sculpture and reflect onto the ground.

Artist, architect, engineer and machinery expert, with public safety in mind, teamed up to choose the materials and adjust the aerodynamics of the piece, so that it would be responsive to moderate breezes but remain structurally sound in heavy winds. Shingu's original proposal for the piece to be built in steel was rejected when structural analysis indicated that steel would make the wings excessively heavy. When the design team chose carbon fiber reinforced plastic for the sculpture, the architects and engineers were forced to make extensive changes in the design of the wings. Shingu approved the necessary changes. Design Evolution Four, a fabrication company from Ohio, was selected to build the sculpture because of its experience and innovative work with this relatively new area of technology.

Design Impact

According to Mr. Chermayeff, the artist chose the name "Echo of the Waves" because it evokes the ocean, yet resists a label, allowing free rein to the viewers' imaginations. Observers see many different images as the sculpture swings gracefully in the wind—two whales swimming side by side, boats bobbing amid ocean swells, birds flying or even a giant red lobster. In fact, though the sculpture lays claim to Boston Harbor, it could easily belong to other waterfront locales, as it captures the spirit of ocean life. Yet it serves as a visual beacon for the Aquarium Plaza, providing a focus for the wide open space, and drawing passersby to the Plaza's other features—a cascading water sculpture with a pathway of concrete stepping stones, and a pool of live frolicking seals.

Shingu has created a wind sculpture in another urban space nearby: "Gift to the Wind" at the Porter Square subway station

zontally, they respond independently to changes in wind direction and velocity. They move like two dancers interpreting the same music differently, oblivious to each others' existence, yet never colliding.

The skeleton of the sculpture is glossy red, while the white surfaces of the wings in Cambridge. In its original conception, this work would have revolved both in the bowels of the station and on the plaza above. The turning motion would have activated chimes underground responding to shifts in the wind above, giving people at the fare collection mezzanine an unusual and spontaneous concert, while persons below would have seen through a skylight the piece moving against the sky. Unfortunately, cost reductions for the overall station forced the MBTA to decrease the corridor space at the mezzanine level, where the sculpture's base would have been. The piece was therefore adapted; the chimes were deleted, and only a mast emerges from the ground outside the entrance to the subway station, where it is visible from busy Massachusetts Avenue. "Gift to the Wind" is an eyecatcher; standing forty-five feet in the air, it looms above the station's roof. Three large red "wings" made of steel and aluminum plates nod up and down as they twirl, at the whim of the wind, around their pedestal. The sculpture, administered through the Arts-on-the-Line program of the Cambridge Arts Council, and funded by the MBTA, was dedicated in December, 1984.

The Meeting of the Waters

Background

Six miles north of St. Louis, the powerful Mississippi and Missouri Rivers flow into each other to continue their course to the Gulf of Mexico. Centrally located in Aloe Plaza, across from the old city railroad terminal, is Carl Milles' fountain, "The Meeting of the Waters," which symbolizes this union. The work incorporates nineteen bronze figures in a 200 foot by 30 foot pool. Its funding culminated an eleven-year campaign led by Mrs. Louis P. Aloe, a patron of the arts who was inspired by the Swedish sculptor's work at a 1930 exhibition.

At first, support was slim. Despite enthusiasm for the idea, people balked at giving thousands of dollars to a foreigner when the Depression was depriving so many Americans of jobs. Nor did it help that Louis P. Aloe, the patron's husband and the former President of the Board of Aldermen for seven years, for whom the plaza was to be named, was a Republican. The city elected a Democratic administration after deciding to erect the fountain. In 1934, after remaining dormant for several years, the campaign collection resumed, and in 1936 Mrs. Aloe presented the city with the sum of $12,500. Later that year, the Municipal Arts Commission approved the sculpture and the contract for construction was signed, with the city supplying most of the additional funding.

There was fresh controversy when the artist revealed the plaster cast of the sculptures, showing nude figures. Responding to the St. Louis burgher's objections, the original title "Wedding of the Rivers," was changed to its present, less descriptive one. The completed sculpture was unveiled in 1940; landscaping and lighting were added in 1954.

Description

The fountain depicts the union of the rivers as a marriage procession, with the Mississippi as the male figure, the Missouri as the female figure, and a cortege of seventeen

water sprites symbolizing the tributary streams. The bronze figures are heroic in scale. Many sit astride leaping fish, as numerous jets of water shoot out in all directions. The pool is built of rainbow granite and is situated lengthwise in front of the impressive stonework of the Union Terminal. With the expanse of the pool contributing to the openness of the plaza, the fountain is visible from many directions.

Design Impact

St. Louis' central geographic location, midpoint for both the passageway from east to west and for the north-south trade in the Mississippi Valley, was crucial to the city's character and development. At the turn of the century, it was the fourth largest city in the United States. Like the later "Gateway Arch," "The Meeting of the Waters" commemorates the city's strategic geographic location. The work is well frequented. Facing Union Station, near the business district, it is a focus of traffic in the area and a popular gathering place at lunch time and

NAME: *The Meeting of the Waters*, St. Louis, Missouri
PROJECT: Fountain with allegorical couple depicting the marriage of the Mississippi and Missouri Rivers, including fifteen sculptures of sprites and fish
ARTIST: Carl Milles
AGENCY: The Municipal Art Commission of St. Louis; Mrs. Louis P. Aloe
SIZE: Pool is 200 feet by 35 feet
DATE: Started 1936, completed 1939, unveiled 1940; landscaping and lighting added 1954.
COST: $225,200 (Fountain—$150,000, Sculpture—$60,000, Lighting—$12,000, Other—$3200).
MATERIAL: Statues—bronze; pool—rainbow granite
PHOTOGRAPHY: Renata von Tscharner

after hours. Unfortunately, the drainage system has not proved adequate, and the surrounding plaza is often wet from spray or overflow. The monument has been carefully maintained, with the addition of lighting and landscaping to increase the fountain's accessibility at night. When a bronze tulip was stolen from the male figure's hand in 1966, two copies were commissioned— one as a replacement and one as a reserve.

Across the street from the fountain, the Richardsonian Romanesque-styled Union Station has been converted into a commercial center by the Rouse Corporation and includes a hotel, restaurants and boutiques.

In May, 1983, Richard Serra's *Quadrilateral* was installed two blocks from "Meeting of the Waters". It was funded by an NEA grant and matching local monies. A massive wall of eight Cor-Ten steel panels, each ten feet high, form a triangle, whose sides range from 82 to 125 feet in length.

Gaps approximately three feet wide are left between the rusty weathered panels, through which people can enter the circumscribed triangle. But there is nothing now to draw people to this empty space which is to be the centerpiece of the park for Gateway Mall. This four block-long mixed-use renewal project has been on the boards since the Roosevelt administration, and is slated to be completed by the late 1980's.

Serra's St. Louis sculpture, like 'Tilted Arc' in New York City's Federal Plaza, has received mixed reactions from the public. Some do not consider it appropriate for a public space. It also poses a peculiar maintenance problem, as no lawn mower can fit between the panels to cut the grass within the walled triangle. It exemplifies a marked contrast between the representational style of "Meeting of the Waters" executed in the 1940's, and the minimalist style of the 1970's.

River Murals

Background

When Cambridge residents discuss the Charles River, invariably someone will note what a shame it is that the once clear water should have become so polluted in the last few decades. The river, and the nostalgia associated with it, are the subject of two murals painted by local resident Lisa Carter. Characterized by bold, graphic colors, the murals are located along main arteries in Cambridge.

Description

The first mural was painted in autumn 1978, on the side of a furniture-leasing building in hectic Central Square. It depicts a turn-of-the-century couple idling calmly in a rowboat, with the busy façades of present day Massachusetts Avenue reflected surrealistically in the water around them.

Inspiring the mural, explained Carter, was the "idea of the contrast between the peaceful, quiet 1890's boating scene and the bustling street scene." Situated three stories above street level, the mural draws attention to architectural details of the square's buildings.

In executing the mural, Carter and associate, Michael Stanton, first layered the wall with a primer coat of white paint. The artists then spent two nights simultaneously projecting a pair of slides onto the surface from an adjacent rooftop and tracing the outlines. The slides, respectively, displayed a view of the square and a drawing (derived from an old photograph) of a couple rowing. Paint—largely blues, greens, browns and grays—was applied during the next few days, from atop hazardously high ladders.

Carter's second mural, painted in the

spring of 1979, is also taken from a photograph. The mural shows the Magazine Street beach in Cambridge as it appeared during the early years of the century, with a crowd of bathers wearing full-body bathing suits, and Gibson-girl skirts. In the background, the river is wide and tree-lined, unobstructed by bridges or buildings.

The work is located on the side of a small grocery store, and has a clapboard surface. With the aid of Boston photographer Jean Broughton, Carter first painted the scene in black and white, and later added the colors— green, red, and an expanse of deep blue—to evoke the sense of an old, hand-tinted photograph. The good old days referred to in the mural are still within memory for several of the older residents of the neighborhood; some even recall the raft floating off the beach which is depicted in the mural. In the words of the artist, the painting "comments on the quality of life in the city then and now, but it's a hopeful image."

Design Impact

In their color and design, the murals are bold, bright additions to gray street scenes. Yet the particular focus—nostalgia, recreation, the Charles—is what makes the works so relevant to the people of the local communities. The juxtaposition of the idealized image in the mural with the actual location strengthens the interest of each work, allowing one to compare the mural with the location that inspired it. They exemplify the initiative necessary for the execution of individually conceived artworks. The painting was done in each case with the assistance of several friends and volunteers and in each case involved two hundred hours of labor; locating appropriate sites and receiving permission required additional months of effort.

The Charles River is being gradually cleansed from its unhealthy state, and when funds become available, the public beaches will once again be opened.

Though Carter's "Anderson Bridge Crewers," painted in 1980 on an MBTA transformer building, was demolished along with the building, the image of the Charles River has been recaptured again—this time by the new Charles Hotel nearby, which commissioned paintings of the river and other highlights of Cambridge.

The artist has since created other murals in Cambridge and in surrounding communities. In 1981, she completed a trompe l'oeil for Boston's Logan Airport, depicting figures associated with aeronautics history, like Amelia Earhart, and flying machines like the Wright Brothers' 1902 model.

In 1984, Carter won the competition

NAME: *Boating in Central Square*, Cambridge, Massachusetts
PROJECT: Mural on side of furniture company building depicting 1890s couple rowing and buildings of contemporary Central Square reflected in water surface
ARTIST: Lisa Carter and Michael Stanton
AGENCY: Cambridge Arts Council; Art Army
SIZE: 20 feet by 28½ feet
DATE: 1978
COST: $325
MATERIAL: Exterior paint
PHOTOGRAPHY: Renata von Tscharner

NAME: *Magazine Street Beach Scene*
PROJECT: Mural near site of 1900s beach depicting swimmers and bathers of that time period in style reminiscent of hand-tinted photograph
ARTIST: Lisa Carter and Jean Broughton
AGENCY: Cambridge Arts Council; Cambridge River Festival
SIZE: 15 feet by 22 feet
DATE: 1979
COST: $675
MATERIAL: Exterior paint
PHOTOGRAPHY: Renata von Tscharner

rent resident and historic figures, including the former minister of the church; three breakdancers; the Honorable George Ruffin, the first black judge in New England; Roland Hayes, the first black man to sing at Symphony Hall; and sculptress Meta Fuller.

sponsored by the Neighborhood Development Employment Agency, and was commissioned to paint a mural on a wall of the Beulah Pilgrim Holiness Church, near a new pedestrian mall in the Grove Hall section of Roxbury. The mural complements an ongoing effort to upgrade the physical fabric of this district. Both contemporary and historic buildings frame a portrait of both cur-

Lisa Carter's mural (1984) in the Grove Hall section of Roxbury, Massachusetts.

Burke Building Remnants

Background

In 1971, when the Seattle General Services Administration began clearing a downtown block for their new Federal Office Building, the turn-of-the-century Romanesque Burke Building with its ornate terra-cotta reliefs was slated for demolition. While preservation groups were unable to protect the structure from the wrecker's ball, the responsive GSA project architect, Fred Bassetti, managed to salvage some of the building's most prominent features: ornaments, window and roof cornices, and the period stone entrance arch. Now incorporated into the plaza and interior of the 37-story concrete and glass tower, these isolated elements evoke a powerful sense of history while playfully complementing Bassetti's contemporary design.

Seattle's Burke Building was the last of several historical buildings on the block left standing, following the demolition of the Department of Labor and Industries Building, the Rivoli Theater, and the Palace and Stevens Hotels. At the time, there was hope that the Burke Building, considered at the time of its design in 1890 to be "a building of the most handsome features,"[1] would be spared. Preservation advocates, in the absence of an historic preservation commission or ordinance, urged that the new office be relocated, and architect Bassetti even suggested that the structure be rehabilitated and allowed to coexist on the same block with the new office bulding. However, the GSA insisted that only a clear site and free-

NAME: *Burke Building Remnants*, Seattle, Washington

PROJECT: Integration of old building remnants—including stone archway, window arches, coffered wood ceiling, terra-cotta reliefs—into design of 37-story federal office building in downtown Seattle

ARTIST: Fred Bassetti and Company, Architects

AGENCY: The General Services Administration

SIZE: Arch approximately 18 feet high; fragments of all sizes

DATE: Design started 1965, completed 1975

COST: Entire project: $22.5 million; costs of remnants included in general construction budget

MATERIAL: Fragments made of stone, terra-cotta and metal; accompanying plaza design in brick

PHOTOGRAPHY: Renata von Tscharner

standing new building would adequately represent the federal government's presence in the formerly dilapidated area. They refused to change the site or renovate the Burke Building, and the bulldozers moved in. Bassetti, however, saw the opportunity to integrate the immense tower into the surrounding neighborhood through the extensive and imaginative use of brick incorporating an arched portal and decorative fragments of the old Burke Building.

At the time the Federal Building was in the planning stages, the GSA Fine Arts Program, which allocated half of one percent of construction costs to public art, had been temporarily suspended. Bassetti nonetheless submitted a proposal to incorporate artwork, and wrote a short appeal to reinstitute the program. Largely owing to his convic-

tion, the Seattle tower was granted funds when the program was reactivated in 1972. The artworks which ensued, and which now coexist with the Burke fragments, include two sculptures by Harold Balaze and Phillip McCracken, and what was at the time a controversial $100,000 ensemble of chiseled boulders by renowned sculptor Isamu Noguchi.

Description

Clad in pre-cast white concrete, with a steel frame, the Federal Office Building is a monumental edifice, dwarfing the neighboring stone buildings in the area. The Burke remnants, though they are comparatively small fragments, have been situated along the ground floor and multi-leveled plaza of the tower where they are highly visible to passersby. The terra-cotta ornaments and metal, turret-shaped cornices adorn terraces on both sides of the building. Other ornamented panels—depicting acanthus leaves and floral motifs—frame the entrance to the underground parking area, and the stones bearing the chiseled words "Burke Building" have been inserted in the wall outside the modern cafeteria. Installed inside the cafeteria is the only interior piece saved, the coffered timber ceiling from the entrance to the Burke lobby. At the top of the plaza in-

cline, standing alone like a neatly trimmed ruin, is the Romanesque entrance arch. Rising 18 feet, and made of over 75 stones, the portal marks the entry to the plaza next to the bus stop. The arch is supported by six polished columns; low walls beside the arch serve as benches.

Near the arch, Noguchi's sculpture, entitled "Landscape of Time," is a representation of prehistoric forms, complementing the historic Burke fragments, in the plaza. The stones are massive but gentle, with a seeming aura of mystery linking both the modern structure and the 19th century remnants with the ancient past.

Design Impact

When the Federal Office Building opened in 1975, it was greeted with strong praise in architectural circles. Among the main reasons were the openness and accessibility of the building's ground level. The use of progressive levels of small plazas, the composition of the stones and the Burke fragments

all help reinforce the human scale of what otherwise would have been a stark plaza. During the late sixties, when the building was being designed, site interpretation was rare. Bassetti's design, with its references to the surrounding neighborhood and its history, can be considered a pioneering effort to add richness and layers of meaning to a large-scale public building, through its use of both artwork and salvaged pieces.

The Seattle project also seems to have contributed to several positive changes in GSA policy. It encouraged resumption of the Fine Arts allocations, openly broached the issue of responsiveness of materials used in federal buildings, and espoused the integration of private stores and restaurants into the ground floor of government buildings, an approach later officially adopted by the GSA administration.

Renamed the Henry M. Jackson Federal

Watermark Tower in Seattle, Washington, incorporates into its façade turn-of-the-century terra cotta walls of the original structure that stood on the site.

Building in 1985, the Burke fragments remain an important landmark on this downtown site. Though no other new GSA buildings have incorporated historic remnants in the area, the regional office has become involved in preserving and restoring their historic properties in Seattle and other cities in their district, as an alternative to new construction.

Just one block north of the Jackson Federal complex, a privately-owned, twenty-two story, mixed-use office complex has also recaptured fragments of the past. The new design, built by Cornerstone Development Company incorporates into its façade two terra cotta walls of the original building on the site—a low-rise structure designed at the turn of the century by Carl Gould.

City Entrances

Background

It is difficult to find a superhighway bridge with a personality. All that standard gray concrete and aluminum railing and frequent chain link fencing make most interstate overpasses look the same. But motorists on Interstate 475 looking up at the overpass bridge will see a silhouette of old Flint motor cars and a spanning arch, announcing Vehicle City. Can it be true? The bridge sign will tell the motorist that this city loves the motor car.

First, Flint was a lumber center with saw mills on the river; the hardwood soon supported carriage manufacturing, and later on, the largest carriage center in the world. A special downtown feature celebrated this development: twelve iron spandrels arched across the main street, Saginaw Avenue, from 1901–1918, and the importance of the name "Vehicle City" that topped each archway increased as Flint became an automotive center. A colorful local entrepreneur, William C. "Billy" Durant, turned his carriage business into the General Motors Corporation, and for years Flint prospered under the Vehicle City sign. But the arches disappeared between the wars, and the downtown, surrounded by a moat of interstates, slipped behind the concentric ring of suburban shopping malls in the 1960s. Along the way, Flint lost some pride, and the unemployment figures climbed to among the highest in the nation during the next decade.

The Charles Steward Mott Foundation, a local institution which is among the nation's largest, has long devoted a substantial percentage of its largess to its home city. When times were depressed in the late 1970s, the foundation performed like a community development corporation and underwrote construction of a new downtown hotel; a block away, a Disneyland for the automobile called "Auto World;" and a shopping center on the main street sponsored by the Rouse offshoot, The Enterprise Development Company. To complement and strengthen this economic recovery program, the Foundation wished to identify visual improvements which would effectively convey the image of a revitalized downtown and consulted with The Townscape Institute of Cambridge, Mass., to generate new ideas.

Four city entrances and Main Street, the face and the heart of the city, were selected for the first phase of beautification. Design

As a result of several community workshops and design review sessions, the selected option was a combination of the traditional Flint Vehicle City spandrels and a side-view of William Durant's "Flint" automobile. The flat metal cars are larger than life-size and are viewed "driving" towards the city center.

Just as the spandrels in downtown Flint used to be lit at night, the arch over the freeway bridge is designed to have the same glowing arch. The cars are sculptural elements, which are proposed to have headlights and backlights at night.

NAME: *City Entrances*, Flint, Michigan
PROJECT: Metal sculptures—arch and cars—affixed to protective mesh fence on the freeway overpass marking major entrance to Flint, Michigan; trees and berms with changing plantings complement the city entrance.
ARTIST: George Greenmayer, metal sculptor; Preliminary conceptual design: Martha Schwartz, artist; Gary Govulick and Renata von Tscharner, designers; Grant Jones, FASLA, landscape consultant; Theo Ballmer, sign designer
AGENCY: The Townscape Institute; the FEAT Foundation (Flint Environment Action Team) as local liaison; the Charles Stewart Mott Foundation, as initial funder; and the City of Flint
SIZE: Sculpture on bridge: 170 feet long and 60 feet high
DATE: Logo and berms: installation, fall of 1984; arch and car sculptures: installation date subject to permission by State Highway Department
COST: $155,000 for arch and cars (exclusive of $50,000 for fence armature which is funded by State Highway Department and City); logo and berms, $42,500
MATERIALS: Steel, landscaping
PHOTOGRAPHY: Day and night views of the Bridge—The Townscape Institute; Image of Spandrels on Saginaw Street—*The Flint Journal Picture History of Flint*, edited by Lawrence R. Gustin; Logo on Pillars—Brian Day, FEAT Foundation

guidelines for Saginaw Street and an art and landscaping plan for a key freeway access off Interstate 475 were the first results.

Description

The bridge site should be not only a city entrance for motorists coming from Detroit but also a key gateway for the eastern suburbs. It will serve both those actually entering Flint and those passing through on the interstate.

The design of the bridge improvement ex-

From 1901–1918 Saginaw Street, Flint's main street, had some twelve metal spandrels, some of which had "Flint Vehicle City" on them. None of these spandrels are left, but the image remains a strong memory for Flint's residents who remember them on postcards.

ploits and transforms the chain mesh fences common to Interstate bridge rails and fashions them into armatures for environmental art at a freeway scale. They became a partial means of financing the gateway. These ugly barriers—requested and funded by the State Highway Department to reduce the liability risk from stones and bottles thrown onto cars—cost approximately $50,000 per bridge.

The landscape design consists of double rows of evergreens along the ramp and of berms with perennials on the open parcel at the bridgehead. This traffic island, now converted into a flowering park, also announces the nearby Horticultural Center, which shares the maintenance duties for the plantings. This integration of bridge design and landscape motif grew out of an extensive participatory effort by conceptual artists, landscape designers, community groups, and a design review committee. An initial survey of appropriate images, artistic techniques, and locations resulted in recommendations to the design charrette team. After a twenty-four hour collaborative design session, the team presented a wide range of design options to the review committee and to the press.

Design Impact

A city is characterized by its entries, by the sense of expectation they generate, and by the feeling of boundaries they proclaim. While freeways around the new American cityscapes symbolize the moat and fortified walls of an earlier European settlement, few American cities have achieved, on a highway scale, the drama and immediate *significance* of the medieval gateways that marked the entrances of these walled cities. But the portals of our cities today can be landmarks, at once of celebration and of welcome, ultimately conveying a meaning over time that only memory can bequeath. This design for Flint seeks to affirm such a stature while responding to a particular heritage with its new arch and row of black Flint cars.

Brian Day, the Executive Director of the

As an additional component to the city entrances programme, this set of pillars framing the newly designed logo marks the downtown entrance. The sign is surrounded by changing flowerbeds marking also the proximity to the new horticultural center.

FEAT Foundation who coordinated both the design sessions and the community outreach, said that no previous *Flint Journal* article on environmental issues has resulted in so many calls and comments as the two proposed gateways. One showed the traditional spandrel, the other a gigantic frontal car view. The comments ranged from "grandiose" to "vulgar," "absurd" to "fantastic."

Representatives of the United Auto Workers Union expressed the wish that if any car be shown, it should be a model made in Flint. To make the gateway more significant to the Baby-boom generation, one prominent citizen suggested using the front of a 1958 Buick.

The prolonged struggle to obtain permission not only involved the regional highway department but also required intervention from politicians in Washington, D.C. It revolved around a Catch-22 situation: the issue that such a bridge addition requires a permit as a highway sign, yet what was being put up did not conform with regulations

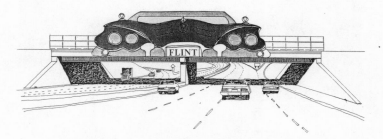

In the process of designing the bridges over the freeway, this frontal view of the "classic" 1958 Buick was considered. Many residents like the boldness; others felt it might be frightening for the drivers on the interstate.

for signs. It is the designer's hope that this struggle for an innovative approach will also benefit other communities that wish to change mesh wire fences into urban design. The downtown entrance with its "Vehicle City" arch will establish quite a precedent. Maybe that is what the Highway Department worries about as other communities seek to use it as a model for differentiating themselves.

The Newspaper Reader

Background

"The Newspaper Reader," a realistic life-size bronze, is comfortably settled on a bench in front of Princeton's Borough Hall. The designer and sculptor, J. Seward Johnson, Jr., had long been interested in public art and in 1973 founded the Johnson Atelier Technical Institute of Sculpture in Princeton. It was here that the statue was constructed, using the 'lost wax' method of casting. With a staff of thirty, and some fifty students, the Atelier is a research organization looking for superior methods of production, a school for instruction in sculpting skills and techniques of crafting metal, and a workshop for production of public art pieces. While students have a chance to experiment with a variety of techniques, the creation of public

NAME: *The Newspaper Reader*, Princeton, New Jersey
PROJECT: Realistic bronze of a professor seated on a concrete bench reading the *New York Times*
ARTIST: J. Seward Johnson, Jr.
AGENCY: None
SIZE: Approximately 4 feet by 3 feet by 10 feet
DATE: Started 1973, finished 1975
COST: $17,675. Materials—$1425, Construction—$16,000, Subcontractors—$250.
MATERIAL: Bronze
PHOTOGRAPHY: Courtesy of J. Seward Johnson, Jr.

art has always been the guiding motive behind the institution. Says Johnson, "the whole purpose is to make finished sculpture for the public less expensive . . . to get pieces of sculpture out of museums and into life, to be a part of the human experience." Johnson, a Princeton resident, donated The Newspaper Reader to his community.

Description

Johnson defines his art as "superrealistic, expressionistic, humanistic." The Newspaper Reader exhibits those qualities, and, like the rest of Johnson's sculpture, is located in an area that is a center of human traffic.

The Reader, modeled after a Princeton professor, sits casually, with one leg crossed over the other. He sports a conservative suit and a fedora. His slightly sad-looking face stares at the "Nixon Resigns" issue of the *New York Times*. Other sections of the paper rest by his side. Up close, the detail is startling: every word on the exposed pages is readable, thanks to the services of a photoengraver, and the texture of the wing-tipped shoes, socks and herringbone suit is deftly accurate—rendered by a professional seamstress. A pipe rests in one jacket pocket.

From a distance the work is illusionistic; it has gained a reputation for confusing motorists passing by at night or in the rain. Nicknamed "Everyman" by his Princeton neighbors, The Newspaper Reader is suggestive of the ultrarealistic figures of Duane Hanson, or the cool, melancholy tableaux of George Segal. Like them, Johnson honors the "ordinary man," but The Newspaper Reader shares neither Hansen's obsession with realism nor Segal's dynamically charged spaces. Its guiding concept is simpler: the statute is a monument to public life. Though the work commemorates a moment in history, Nixon's resignation, the focus remains on Everyman's reaction to the event rather than the event itself. Spot lighting, also donated by the artist, illuminates the statue at night. Sitting on a specially-cast concrete bench, in a park by a main thoroughfare, the Reader has no pedestal to separate him from the human activity on all sides. This allows for greater psychological as well as physical accessibility.

Like other life-sized public statues, The Newspaper Reader evokes public responses in the form of games and photographs.

The Johnson Atelier created copies of the sculpture for six other locations across the country—which are now located in parks in Lancaster, Penn., and Forest Grove, Oregon; the USA Today Building in Rosslyn, Va. (near Washington, D.C.); Helmerich Collection, Tulsa, Oklahoma; Lincoln Property Company, Lincoln Center, Dallas, Texas; and for a private collection in Buffalo, New York. In each of these communities the Reader is holding a copy of the local newspaper in his hands instead of the *New York Times*. Despite this connection made to each specific locale, the sculpture is essentially a generic placemaker, not making specific reference to any one place. The more it is reproduced, the more its place-making potential is diluted. Aware of this danger, Johnson will cast a maximum of seven reproductions of his sculptures, and prefers that no two castings of the same sculpture be installed in one locale.

Other works by Johnson include "Allow

The Mayor Curley statues by sculptor Lloyd Lillie on Congress Street near Faneuil Hall, Boston, Massachusetts, elicit similar responses from the public as does the Newspaper Reader, in Princeton.

Me," depicting a man holding an umbrella and hailing a cab, installed at the Pioneer Courthouse Square, in Portland, Oregon; "Double Check," portraying a businessman sitting on a bench reading a report, with briefcase in lap (purchased by the Isaacs Associates in Brea, California, as part of the Arts in Public Places Program, and installed at Birchbrook Executive Park); and "Out to Lunch," purchased by the city for the Public Library in Sunnyvale, California, with reproductions of the same statue in Georgetown Park, Washington D.C. and Rockefeller Center, New York City.

Two of Johnson's sculptures were the focus of political controversies in New Haven in 1983. Parkfriends, a private non-profit park support group, funded two temporary exhibits of Johnson's work, each to last approximately one year. With cooperation of the city of New Haven, their goal was to site sculptures in various parks and squares across the city, hoping to enliven these spaces that had suffered from vandalism and defacing graffitti. The first six sculptures, installed in the summer of 1983, were replaced by a second group of six new sculptures in summer, 1984. One sculpture entitled "Playmates," depicted three boys looking at a centerfold from a Playboy magazine. The mayor protested the inappropriateness of the placement of the sculpture,

which was located near his church in an Italian Catholic neighborhood, and had it removed. A less controversial sculpture by Johnson replaced "Playmates." Entitled "Spring" it was a seated boy and girl, reading.

With similar political overtones, the Johnson sculpture called "Getting Down" received publicity in the local newspapers. This sculpture portrayed a young black boy listening to a large portable radio. The head of the local chapter of the NAACP, who was running for mayor, wrote a letter to the local newspaper, protesting the racist implications of the sculpture. The newspaper responded with an editorial which challenged this protest. Mara Brazer, director of Parkfriends, said she considered this protest only one man's effort to strengthen his political campaign, rather than an issue raised by the community, because the protester registered his complaint five months after the sculpture's installation which coincided with election time. Perhaps the most telling expression of acceptance of the sculpture was that in its year-long residency, "Getting Down" was never vandalized. When Parkfriends removed the statue from the green, passersby and local residents expressed the wish that the sculpture remain. Both sculptures were returned, as planned, to the Johnson Atelier.

Ghost Parking Lot

Background

Like Pompeian artifacts preserved for two millennia by volcanic ash, the silhouettes of twenty asphalt-covered automobiles at Hamden Shopping Center give viewers the sensation of a moment frozen in time. One

feels part of a time warp, as if looking at a now extinct species from the twentieth century technological age, set in its appropriate habitat—the suburban shopping center. The project is located along the front edge of a parking lot, so that unsuspecting motorists driving past the Hamden Plaza, a strip mall on the outskirts of New Haven, catch a glimpse of this unique and playful response to the sameness of the standard shopping center.

David Bermant, an art buff who co-owns this shopping center among others, has experimented elsewhere with siting public art works in non-traditional locales. Bermant is particularly interested in using high technology artworks to add allure to his shopping centers. Through touches of humor and visual intrigue, he hopes to entertain shoppers, and at the same time encourage more business.

Bermant's hypothesis that locating enticing artwork in commercial settings increases sales seemed to be true, but he was never able to isolate the artwork as the key variable to measure increased business. All Bermant's previous public art projects involved integrating art into *new* shopping sites, where an increase in sales could have resulted from the location, the architecture, or the simple novelty of the site. To test his theory about public art, Bermant chose the Hamden Plaza strip mall, originally constructed in the 1950s, where sales had remained static for the previous seven years.

If keeping constant all other factors (tenancy, architecture, location), and giving the site highly visible outdoor artwork resulted in increased sales, then Bermant felt his theory would be proven valid. With this scheme in mind he attended the first World Art Conference, sponsored by *Artnews*, where he met James Wines from SITE (Sculpture in the Environment), a New York City design group. Wines showed him SITE's project for BEST Products, called "Falling Facade"—a pile of bricks in front are carefully designed to give the illusion of a collapsed

---

NAME: *Ghost Parking Lot*, Hamden, Connecticut
PROJECT: Twenty automobile bodies buried at various levels and covered with asphalt, "parked" in the Hamden Plaza Shopping Center.
ARTIST: James Wines and Emilio Sousa of SITE (Sculpture in the Environment)
AGENCY: National Shopping Centers, Inc., Rye, NY
SIZE: Approximately 2000 square feet
DATE: 1978
COST: $125,000
MATERIAL: Discarded automobiles, concrete, "Bloc Bond"—a sealer, asphalt
PHOTOGRAPHY: SITE

entry. Bermant was instantly intrigued by SITE's objective of altering people's psychological and visual orientation with architectural designs and commissioned SITE for the Hamden Plaza "experiment."

Bermant requested that the artwork be located along the front edge of the site for two reasons. First, Bermant wanted to avoid possible lawsuits by his tenants, one of whom had threatened to sue him earlier when Bermant hired two local artists to paint a mural on the exterior wall of the building. Second, and more important, Bermant wanted the piece to "call attention to the Center . . . I want the whole city of New Haven to look at it." Bermant heartily approved SITE's model of the Ghost Parking Lot, chosen for its success as a visual landmark and for its relation to the American merchandising ritual, which is so strongly connected to the automobile.

Description

The Ghost Parking Lot takes the two predominant elements of a suburban parking lot—automobiles and asphalt—and has them change places. Twenty junked cars are enveloped in asphalt, submerged beneath the surface at varying heights. Some are sunk almost completely, others reveal the silhouette of complete cars. The ghostly image relies on its context for full visual impact. With no eye-catching materials or colors, the piece uses "the unexpected" in a familiar setting to attract people.

Cars for the project were purchased from local dealers and individuals, and sent to a Hamden warehouse where interior fixtures and exterior paint were removed. Window areas were reinforced to accommodate an infill of concrete. Transported to the parking lot of Hamden Plaza, the cars were placed in a row of excavated 'graves' along Dixwell Avenue. Next, the cars were filled with concrete, the land adjacent to the cars was modeled to create continuous contours, and the exposed metal surfaces of the cars were sprayed with layers of Bloc Bond to seal them and create the desired "skin" effect. The last stage included covering the entire project with a layer of asphalt, and repainting parking lines, to visually connect the Ghost Parking Lot with the rest of the parking area.

Design Impact

The Ghost Parking Lot made front page news in the *New Haven Register*, with a headline that read, "Graves Readied at Plaza." David Bermant remembers that the work became an overnight attraction, with responses ranging from laughter to "They call this stuff art?" Articles appeared in journals from all over the world, such as Italy's *Bolaffiarte*, England's *Building Design*, and U.S.A.'s *Art Express*. City officials, including the Mayor, shunned the piece when it was installed, and some have never changed their opinions.

Immediately following the installation of Ghost Parking Lot, Bermant reported an upswing in retail sales, and tenants applying for space represented an upgrading of the quality of stores. Bermant and the artists from SITE believe that the artwork adds a novel and memorable experience to a retail locale, increases consumer traffic, and contributes to higher sales figures. Bermant links economic strategy with visual strategy. "I am trying to give my centers an identity."

SITE, the New York City design firm, bases its work on shocking people's psychological and physiological responses to conditions in a given context. The designs seek to expand viewers' perception and experience of the ordinary. In an ironic twist, Ghost Parking Lot attempts to make something out of nothing. It finds inspiration from the mundane anonymity of shopping malls or strip development, and forces viewers to notice them. Banal commercial contexts are transformed by treating the facades in an unorthodox manner. Another example of SITE's work is the Forest Building in Richmond, Virginia, where a forest of indigenous trees cuts the showroom apart, creating a vision of nature overthrowing man's handiwork. These pieces represent a particular kind of placemaking where, instead of reinforcing the threads of historic or social fabric, SITE embellishes the holes, poking fun at the threadbare places in our cityscape.

Since Ghost Parking Lot, Bermant has commissioned more than twenty-five novel artworks in his shopping malls; no two pieces are alike. Since its installation in 1978, only minor repairs in the asphalt have been necessary to maintain the Ghost Parking Lot.

He plans to add other art works to Hamden Plaza in the near future. Bermant predicts that fifty years from now, despite its controversial infancy and continued grumbling from city officials during its adolescence, members of the community will be asking the city to preserve Ghost Parking Lot as an historic site. Then, people will want to view these 'vintage' relics of a bygone era.

Judge's Bench

Background

Like the figurehead at the bow of a ship, the face carved in the Judge's Bench in Pemberton Square sits proudly before the handsome Second Empire Courthouse. Pemberton Square is a modern plaza located on the edge of the massive Government Center urban renewal project of the 1960s. Situated at the top of a flight of stairs, it is tucked between the granite Beaux Arts Suffolk County Courthouse, built between 1886 and 1893, and the curving cast concrete facade of the 1960s Center Plaza Office Building. This crescent shape is the only reminder of the elegant nineteenth-century residential square once situated here. The space was designed as a "pedestrian plaza" in the 1960s when such a term often meant a formal pattern in the pavement that was best appreciated in a bird's eye view. Two-tone brickwork surfacing in large abstract patterns, bulky bollards, and several stark pillboxes containing seating areas and disguised air vent tunnels to the garage below were not enough to encourage pedestrians to linger in the barren windy plaza. It is cast in shade during the middle of the day by an adjacent corporate tower.

A bomb explosion in 1974 dramatically limited the pedestrian flow through the plaza, as tightened security allowed only people with official identification to travel through the Courthouse hall, previously a popular shortcut linking the State House and City Hall.

The barren urban plaza of Pemberton Square, Boston, Massachusetts, is the setting for the Judge's Bench.

In 1981, the Bench and Bar Task Force, a group of lawyers originally organized for Boston's 350 Jubilee, decided to pursue earlier plans to enliven the Plaza, which they envisioned as Boston's 'courtyard.' They commissioned The Townscape Institute to develop a public art and intrepretation strategy for Pemberton Square. The goals of the strategy were to create an ensemble that relates to the central theme of law and to make Pemberton Square a more livable space. The Judge's Bench—a sculpture and speaker's rostrum—grew out of this plan to animate the plaza. A local sculptor and teacher at Harvard, William Reimann, was awarded the commission as a result of a limited competition among four artists. The artist's task was to create an element that satisfies both aesthetic and functional needs. The project received financial support from the City's Browne Fund, a privately endowed fund "for the beautification of Boston."

Description

William Reimann's winning entry is the top of a huge limestone column with a richly

decorated ionic capital, found by the artist in a local salvage yard. The column is reputed to have come from a nearby site which was destroyed by urban renewal. Reimann hollowed the column out and transformed it into a speaker's rostrum which he carefully integrated into the staircase. The leafy motif of the scrollwork on the capital is similar to the scrollwork of the same motif on the pediments of the classical Courthouse building. The piece alludes to the classical origins of law and to the architectural style of the Courthouse. Robert Campbell, architecture critic for the *Boston Globe* called the Judge's Bench a "snapshot that collage(s) the present against the past."[1]

Design Impact

The Judge's Bench is designed as a lectern for swearing-in ceremonies; and for theatrical re-enactments of trials. Television newscasters regularly use the lectern to cover court activities, since they are not allowed to televise court proceedings. The Judge's Bench is only the first element in the animation and enrichment plan developed for the plaza. Proposed plans include interpretive panels about the legal history; benches crafted to match the rich architectural vocabularly of the Courthouse; and figurative sculptures of great Boston jurists—Theophilus Parsons, John Adams, Lemuel Shaw, Oliver Wendell Holmes, and Louis Brandeis.

NAME: *Judge's Bench*, Boston, Massachusetts
PROJECT: A portion of a salvaged limestone column and its capital crafted into a speaker's rostrum for ceremonial events commemorating the judicial history of Boston
ARTIST: William Reimann
AGENCY: Bench and Bar Task Force, The Townscape Institute
SIZE: Approximately 4 feet wide, 3½ feet high
DATE: Inaugurated October, 1983
COST: $30,000
MATERIAL: Limestone
PHOTOGRAPHY: The Townscape Institute

The proprietors of the abutting office buildings are also contributing to the beautification of Pemberton Square. The Beacon Companies, which own Center Plaza, have redesigned the stairs and lobbies and are financially supporting the efforts of the Bench and Bar Task Force. The Prudential Companies, of One Beacon Street, have plans for enhancement that include the landscaping and sculptural enrichment of the sunny sitting area that extends over the Beacon Hill Cinemas on the east side of the square.

Though the implementation will be incremental, each piece forms part of a larger plan to enrich the meaning, increase the animation, and strengthen the contextual relationships among the art works. As critic Campbell says, "The lesson of Pemberton Square is a simple one. If you want a city of lively outdoor rooms, you must do more than create rooms. You must also furnish and program them with activities."[2]

Tribune Stones

Background

Embedded in the base of the Chicago Tribune Tower, at the intersection of Michigan Avenue and the Chicago River, are over one hundred and twenty stone fragments from around the world. The museum-quality collection of carved or otherwise distinguished stones is the most striking example of the eclecticism which characterizes this 1925 building. The design process for the structure was as extraordinary as the final result. In 1922, finding itself rapidly outgrowing its original offices, the *Tribune* announced an international competition for the design of a new building which aimed to be "the most beautiful . . . in the world." Over 250 submissions were received; entrants included famed Bauhaus architect Walter Gropius and Finnish architect Eliel Saarinen, whose visionary modernist plan received second prize. First prize was awarded to John Mead Howells and Raymond Hood, a team of New York architects, for the 36-story Gothic monument that stands today. Crowned with an octagonal tower and eight flying buttresses, and an equally ornate Gothic facade on the bottom floors, the building resembles a high rise cathedral. Deep-set windows, separated between floors by rectangular lead spandrels, contribute an Art Deco flavor. The historical stones were acquired and mounted mostly in the period from the building's completion until 1955, although a few have been added since.

Description

The concept of embedding stones along the tower's base was the inspiration of Col. Robert R. McCormick, *Tribune* publisher and editor, for whom the study of history was a life-time pursuit. The *Tribune*'s network of foreign correspondents provided the publisher with a dauntless stone-collecting force. McCormick gave instructions that only "honorable means" be employed in the acquisition. Now set in 26 panels along three sides of the tower and its adjacent building, the stones are on continual display, each identified with a marker. Their origins are as disparate in time period as in location. Among the most famous structures represented are the Great Pyramid of Cheops, the Taj Mahal, the Cathedral at Reims, the Great Wall of China, the Kremlin, the Coliseum, and the Houses of Parliament. Some stones derive significance through association with people or events, such as a brick from the Abraham Lincoln home in Springfield, and tiles from the Baths at Pompeii. Others, like those from the Petrified Forest in Arizona and Yosemite National Park, exemplify great places of beauty. Of most religious value in the group are the few fragments from the Cave of the Nativity of Nazareth. The literary past is represented by a rock from the Mark Twain Cave in Missouri, supposed hiding place of Injun Joe.

Varying from concrete chunks out of WWII fortifications to stone carvings worn smooth over centuries of erosion to tiny colored tiles, the stones of the display encompass a diversity in size, design and texture. Each physically contrasts with its neighbors; together, implanted in the masonry at the base of the tower, they invite close inspection.

Other ornamentation is woven into the Gothic fabric of the building; most noticeably that clustered around the archway to the main entrance: a large stone screen narrating Aesop's fables; a carving identifying the "four elements"—wind, fire, earth and water—with American animals; and, appropriately, two heads representing news and rumor. Gargoyles illustrating the good and evil traits of man decorate the fourth floor façade.

Design Impact

The combined effect of these eclectic displays would be overwhelming, except that, in the tumult of urban activity around Tribune Square, even odd and exaggerated decorations are unobtrusive. The Tribune

NAME: *Tribune Stones*, Chicago, Illinois
PROJECT: Stones gathered from historic structures and sites around the world, displayed in street-level masonry of Chicago Tribune Tower
ARTIST: John Mead Howells & Raymond Hood, Architects; Col. Robert R. McCormick, *Tribune* editor and publisher, Project Coordinator
AGENCY: The Chicago Tribune
SIZE: From over a foot to under two inches across
DATE: Tower—designed 1922, completed 1925
COST: Unknown
MATERIAL: Variety of stones, bricks, fragments
PHOTOGRAPHY: Chicago Tribune, Barabe Kauffmann-Locke

Stones, unintentionally humorous in their excess, provide a free museum for the urban pedestrian. The variety of the stone display allows it to be continually surprising; its accessibility invites exploration of the different surfaces. The stones present history as a procession of landmarks and monuments, and are representative of an era when this type of collecting was commonplace, as a means of bringing the best of the world to the feet of Americans. Although no stones have been added in the past few decades, the installation of stones in the 1930s and 1940s provided exciting occasions for public gatherings. The dedication of the Alamo stone was arranged to coincide with the Chicago Century of Progress Exposition in 1933.

California Street People

Background

A woman walking a pelican on a leash, a boy fishing the grill of a post office window, a nun flying a paper airplane from the balcony above a gift shop: these unusual characters are three in a series of nine pedestrian portraits painted by Palo Alto artist Greg Brown. Lifesized, realistically rendered, and dispersed throughout the downtown area, they comprise a witty homage to urban street life, and represent a major public art project in Palo Alto.

The arts got their first major boost in the city in 1970, with the conversion of what was then City Hall into an extensive Cultural Center. In 1975, the city expressed interest in a formal public arts program. Using as a model the WPA Program of the 1930s, and the contemporary art policies of several West Coast cities such as San Francisco, the Director of the Arts Department applied for federal Comprehensive Employment and Training Act (CETA) money to hire a full-time artist. Greg Brown, a native of Palo Alto who had a year of study in London after graduating from Palo Alto High School, was chosen out of the nine applicants interviewing for the position.

While investigating the possibilities of involving students in community arts projects, and scouting locations for public sculptures, Brown searched for a large wall surface that could accommodate a mural of his own. But, said Brown, "I wanted to keep my hand in paint," so he persuaded a drugstore owner to let him paint the wall of his establishment, facing a sidestreet. Here he painted his first so-called "pedestrian," a Bogart type in a trenchcoat. Despite the fact that he also painted a bird nesting in the figure's hat, the menacing figure provoked immediate trouble, frightening several local residents, including a City Councilman buying a paper late at night. A less menacing portrait was added—a man pushing a cat in a stroller—and soon other merchants approached the artist offering their storefronts and walls for painting. Finding the right sites, slowed by bureaucratic red tape, often took weeks; painting usually required no more than twelve hours for each work. From May to November, the artist continued adding characters, and by the time he left the CETA position, there were nine figures in all.

Description

Each image in the series is arresting, combining realistic imagery with unusual subjects. Among the most dynamic in the series is the pair of cat burglars lowering themselves on the metal awning of a clothing shop on University Avenue. Several murals play off their architectural context, such as the nun leaning over the balcony with the paper airplane. A few depict members of the artist's family. A woman gardening with a bird perched on her watering hose is Brown's grandmother; a garbage man approaching a trash bin is his brother-in-law; the cat burglars are in fact the artist and his wife, Julie. When the rest of the family began clamoring for immortality, Brown noted, he had to stop painting relatives. Each figure is painted a few inches larger than life, to balance the diminution occurring with perspective.

Design Impact

The only vandalism inflicted to date has been to the man pushing the cat in a stroller, who is occasionally mistaken for Spiro Agnew. Otherwise, the city has warmly adopted the murals, and as the artist admits, popular reaction has been "fortunately an incredibly positive thing." Located throughout the town, they are equally accessible to all, yet unlike a single large mural, require time and effort to be discovered—thus, in a sense, they belong more to the residents who know the city well than to visitors. This is reinforced by the pedestrian orientation of the murals. Unlike the many large murals that emblazen the roadsides of southern California, which are best viewed from behind the wheel of a car, these are designed to be explored on foot, and so emphasize the human scale in the city's downtown area. Perceived singly as popular landmarks, their cumulative effect in the mind's eye is an associational network—connecting various locations throughout the city.

While Palo Alto has continued to expand its Public Arts Program, with a second hired muralist and new sculptural acquisitions, the "Pedestrians" series provoked a comprehensive discussion on the regulation of public art. Because the murals involved federal money, city initiative, private property and the creativity of a single individual, their legal ownership seemed to include everybody. The City Assembly put weeks of deliberation into an 80-page document on public art that was passed as law and repealed shortly thereafter as being too burdensome. As it now stands, the city maintains the copyright, while the artist keeps the license to use the images as he will.

The City of Takoma Park, Maryland, a suburb of Washington, D.C. achieved an effect similar to the Palo Alto artwork by adding a trompe l'oeil mural to a roadside commercial area on the edge of the business district. The Takoma Junction Revitalization Steering Committee sponsored a competition in 1984, and selected local artist Saundra Philpott because she best fit their criteria for creating a work that would, "relate to the unique historic, cultural, or geographic character of the site and/or of Takoma Park." Painted on the side of a convenience store, Philpott completed the 14 x 16-foot wall painting in early 1985. It depicts a turn-of-the-century streetcar crossing in Takoma Park, recalling Takoma's position as the first railroad suburb in the metropolitan area. Next to the large mural are five 3 x 3 foot trompe l'oeil portraits of noteworthy Takoma residents. Painted

NAME: *California Street People*, Palo Alto, California

PROJECT: Series of nine illusionistic murals in dispersed spots around downtown Palo Alto, representing imaginary street characters

ARTIST: Greg Brown

AGENCY: The City of Palo Alto; CETA (Comprehensive Employment Training Act of the Federal government)

SIZE: Slightly larger-than-life

DATE: 1976

COST: $6000

MATERIAL: Acrylic latex exterior paint, lacquer varnish

PHOTOGRAPHY: Jane Lidz

on masonite panels, they are placed in formerly boarded up windows. The portraits include actress Goldie Hawn, and one of the city's newest residents—Ty Eam, a schoolgirl from Cambodia. The murals were commissioned at a cost of $3900.

The Arts in Public Places Program in Palo Alto, no longer funded by CETA, receives an annual allocation of $15,000 from the city's Capital Improvement Project Fund. Aware of the potential controversy arising when public art is acquired *for* the public without their consent, which is often the case, Palo Alto has initiated a novel approach to involve the community in the selection process. The City Council appointed a Visual Arts Jury, staffed by people from the community who have visual arts expertise, to choose public art for the community. To obtain a broader range of opinion, an outdoor sculptural exhibit took place in the summer of 1982, when upon invitation by the Visual Arts Jury twenty-one sculptors exhibited their work. The public was encouraged to view the exhibit and then vote for their three favorite works, the winners of which would be placed in various locations in the city. Ballots were collected in libraries, community centers, and the Civic Center. Based on the public's responses the three most popular sculptures were installed in June, 1982. Two non-representational sculptures installed are "After the Fall", by Bruce Johnson, a work made of a redwood burl, located in Mitchell Park, and "Albequerque" a painted steel piece by Gail Wagner located outside the Cultural Center. The third artwork chosen is entitled "Push" and depicts a woman pushing a large barrel. Fred Hunnicut created this Cor-Ten steel sculpture installed in Mitchell Park.

As a safeguard of its popular investment, the city has decided to lacquer the paintings, and repaint them regularly. Greg Brown last refurbished the murals in November, 1984.

BOSTON, MASSACHUSETTS

Swan Boats

Background

Idyllic reminders of Boston's Victorian era, the Swan Boats in the Public Garden lagoon have been guiding passengers on leisurely rides for over one hundred years. In 1980, the original wood and sheet metal swans

were replaced by finely sculpted fiberglass models—to ensure that this Boston tradition would be perpetuated into the next century.

The boats had their origin in 1870, when Robert Paget, an English boatmaker who had just immigrated to the United States, acquired the rights to construct and operate boats for rides in the Public Garden lagoon. The first fleet consisted of a half-dozen row-boats, steered by lanky young oarsmen; rides cost a nickel. The swan design was inspired by a viewing of Richard Wagner's opera "Lohengrin," based on a medieval German tale in which the hero crosses a river in a boat drawn by a swan—a "Schwanboot"—to defend the innocence of his beloved. Paget combined this vision with pedal propulsion, which he had developed with the aid of a bicycle manufacturer, and in the summer of 1877 launched the new series. They were an immediate success. The small boats, each carrying four to eight passengers, were soon replaced by larger vessels.

After Paget's death only a year later, his wife Julia assumed control of the enterprise and continued its development. Over the next decades, numerous folk heroes, leaders and celebrities—most notably Admiral Richard E. Byrd and child actress Shirley Temple—have made celebrated public trips with the swans.

Today the founder's grandson, Paul Paget, is in charge of the operation. In 1977, the boats marked their centennial anniversary, and in 1980, Paget commissioned sculptor Vincent Ricci to create six new swans, to ensure that they would remain permanent Boston monuments. The new design is not a replica but retains the overall character of the original swan boats.

Description

From afar, there is little change between the old swans and their successors. "A little more stomach, a little fuller breast, maybe, but that's all," explained Paget. "You'd never know the difference." From up close, however, several changes are apparent: a newly detailed face and head, a longer neck, and a fuller, sharper plummage—with each feather created and set separately. Individually signed and numbered by designer Ricci, each swan is sparkling white.

The swans are approximately five feet high and six feet long, and are situated at the rear of the tour boats and contain the pedalworks and seat for the driver. Crafted from fiberglass (through the use of clay models and rubber molds), the birds will be able to withstand years of rough weather without deteriorating.

Since 1981 the flotilla consists of six boats. The scenic rides, which last for fifteen minutes, cost 60¢ for adults and 40¢ for children.

Design Impact

The Swan Boats of Boston are a unique

NAME: *Swan Boats*, Boston, Massachusetts
PROJECT: Fleet of six pedal-powered boats, each decorated with a large white swan, offer leisure rides during the warm season in Boston's Public Garden
ARTIST: Original Designer: Robert Paget
Replica Designer: Vincent Ricci
AGENCY: Paget family
SIZE: Swans measure 5 feet in height, 6 feet in length; Boats carry 12 to 20 passengers at a time
DATE: Conceived 1871; first boat launched 1877; replicas produced 1980
COST: Reconstruction in 1980 cost $8000
MATERIAL: Original swans made of wood and sheet-metal; replacements made of fiberglass
PHOTOGRAPHY: Renata von Tscharner

part of that city's culture, and in the words of Oliver Wendell Holmes, "are as fully native as baked beans." They are an unofficial symbol of the city, used on leaflets, posters, and other tourist information; understandably, when New York City petitioned Boston for the right to reproduce the swan boats in Central Park, the answer was a flat "no." A large celebration commemorated the swans' one hundredth birthday, and they are featured every other year during the Victorian Parade, as tableau carriers for ladies and gentlemen dressed in period costumes. Two children's books, *Trumpet of the Swan* by E. B. White, and *Make Way for Ducklings* by Robert McCloskey, have brought the swans national recognition.

SALISBURY, NORTH CAROLINA

Crossroads Mural

Background

Matching Michelangelo in scale, medium, and difficulty of working conditions, Cynvia Arthur has created her own masterpiece—an enormous 6,120 square foot exterior mural in her hometown of Salisbury, North Carolina. For three years she painted a three-story, 148-foot-tall, brick wall, often perched atop scaffolding, in temperatures ranging from 40 to 100 degrees Fahrenheit.

The mural, entitled "Crossroads—Past into Present," is a fantastical melange of the nineteenth and twentieth centuries. Arthur plays havoc with the fixed dimensions of space and time. It is as if by some stroke of magic, the artist plucked landmark buildings from their sites all over the city and conjured up other bygone buildings, as well as the ghosts of a fountain and a trolley car, and re-assembled these entities into one imaginary locale. With the same magical wand she peoples this conjuration with over 100 contemporary Salisburians, but instead of their normal apparel, all are outfitted in turn-of-the-century costumes. The result is several layers of local history superimposed—

transfixing space and time into a permanent portrait of Salisbury. This town has retained much of its rich architectural heritage; the oldest restored building, the home of General John Steele, dates from 1799. However, most of the historic buildings date from 1820–1920, and no one architectural style predominates—there are examples of Federal, Greek Revival, Italianate, Spanish Mission and Classical Revival.

In 1976 the North Carolina Department of Cultural Resources chose Cynvia Arthur as one of five artists to participate in the Third Century Artist Program, a CETA-funded program of artists residing in different North Carolina communities. Earlier that year the city planning commission suggested that the Rowan Art Guild sponsor a mural in the downtown area as part of revitalization activities. The Rowan Art Guild, a private non-profit organization of artists in the county, sponsored Cynvia Arthur's mural and helped choose the site. When CETA monies dried up, the foundation raised funds from individual donations and foundations and encouraged local businesses to donate supplies, scaffolding and other services and equipment. Arthur and members of the Guild spent one full year planning the mural. Rowan Art Guild obtained a five-year lease from the building owner in 1984 to ensure that the wall where the mural is located would not be repainted.

Though Arthur had some experience with large exterior murals, having painted one in Ashboro in 1977, the Salisbury mural had special significance for her because it would have the distinction of being the largest outdoor mural in North Carolina, and she was a hometown artist!

Arthur is interested in documenting the historic flavor of the locale where she works and used this as the central theme in the Ashboro mural and in the one she designed for Salisbury. The Salisbury mural stands one block from the heart of downtown, in an area where twenty-three blocks were designated a historic district on the National Register of Historic Places in 1975. Within this district, a thirteen-block residential area is protected by the local Historic District Commission, which approves any exterior changes. This community concern for preservation was augmented in 1976 when Salisbury participated in the initial stage of the Main Street Program sponsored by the National Trust for Historic Preservation. The program promotes the revitalization of downtown centers of selected cities, giving technical aid for facade restoration, economic restructuring and management techniques for organizations involved, as well as some financial assistance. Subsequently, since 1980, the private sector has invested some seventy million dollars in restoring Salisbury's central business district. Cynvia Arthur's mural was warmly accepted in this preservation-minded community, which has succeeded in conserving much of its nineteenth- and early twentieth-century commercial and residential architecture in the downtown. Unlike some murals which chronicle lost chapters in a town's architectural evolution from landmarks to parking lots, Arthur's mural is a kind of congratulatory message to Salisbury for having retained a rich sense of place over time.

Description

One of the most impressive features of this mural is the extreme depth of field that

---

NAME: *Crossroads—Past into Present*, Salisbury, North Carolina

PROJECT: A mural depicting existing and lost Salisbury landmarks and portraits of over 100 citizens, located in the historic downtown area.

ARTIST: Cynvia Arthur

AGENCY: Rowan Art Guild

SIZE: 6120 square feet

DATE: Begun 1977. Completed 1983

COST: Approximately $34,000; additional $40,000 in services donated

MATERIAL: Latex enamel paint, "Plastic Shield" sealer

PHOTOGRAPHY: James P. Barringer, *Salisbury Evening Post* staff

she achieved, counterbalancing the 127-foot-long horizontal orientation of the wall. The mural depicts two main streets of Salisbury, Main Street and Innes Street, as intersecting in a very wide angle, which gives Arthur the advantage of extending views down both sides of two very long avenues. Two one-point perspectives are placed side-by-side, offering the viewer an almost baroque display of multiple vistas. Historic landmarks painted in the mural include the Meroney Opera House (1905), the Presbyterian Bell Tower (1892), a confederate statue (1908), the old Post Office (1911), the Wallace Building (1910), the old fountain on the Square (1888), the Mansion House (1822), old Purcell's Drug Store (1855), the old Wachovia Bank Building (1900), and the old Courthouse (1856). The ends of the streets continue indeterminate. This extreme depth of field, which serves as a bountiful showcase for numerous architectural landmarks, coupled with the animation of her figures, enlivens this long expanse of wall.

The mural caused a sensation in the town of 26,000 citizens, where people know each other well enough to recognize many of the 100 local citizens painted on the wall. The figures represent a cross-section of local celebrities from community leaders—doctors, lawyers, teachers and politicians, to more modest participants—a worker at the bank downtown, and a paper boy. Others include people who work in the Waterworks Gallery—a facility of Rowan Art Guild, where the artist had her studio. The woman merrily dancing in the right foreground is a potter who worked at the gallery. The man with the ice wagon is another artist who helped Arthur paint the base coat. In the lower right hand corner the artist painted herself, holding a basket of red and yellow flowers.

To achieve the level of historic and technical accuracy for such a mural, Cynvia Arthur followed a painstaking process. She spent the fall of 1978 researching the history of the buildings and period costumes and making preliminary sketches. She took photos of each person posed in costume and worked from these for many hours in her studio, drawing figures to scale so that each would be appropriately sized according to their position in the painting. She progressed from a first draft in ¼" scale to a 1" scale drawing. Next she lined the wall with 1 foot square chalk lines, and sketched the mural to scale. She began painting in mid-1979, after the Fire Department voluntarily hosed down the wall.

The most difficult part of the process for Arthur was trying to paint fourteen newly bricked-up windows in the wall. She painted and then chiseled away the same layer of paint five times, but the paint would not adhere to the new bricks until they were sandblasted, reprimed with grey paint, and coated with a water-based enamel. The entire mural was then painted in latex and covered with a layer of sealer to prevent chipping.

Design Impact

Because of the support and approval by community members during the three years, Arthur became a kind of fixture along Fisher Street, and it was no surprise that the mural was well received by the community. Before its completion, 500 people helped celebrate "Cynvia Arthur Day" in November 1980 to honor the artist and her work. Except for a layer of sealer, the mural was finished in 1982. A long search by the Rowan Art Guild produced a clear sealer called "Plastic-shield" which could be reapplied over patched areas; the sealer was added in 1983, donated by the city. Minor peeling occurred before the wall was sealed and will need to be repaired when the artist returns to Salisbury.

The mural generated arts activity as well as more general community interest. A fund-raiser at the base of the unfinished mural turned into a lively party with other artists selling their wares. The *Salisbury Evening Post* devoted a two-page spread to the project, including a contest to see who could name most of the costumed Salisburians portrayed in the mural. The winner received a color photograph of the mural.

Avé S. Cadwallader, President of the Rowan Art Guild at the time of the project, recounts overwhelming positive response not only from the area residents but from visitors to Salisbury as well. Local artists praised the work, especially lauding the "adaptability to its location, history, and needs of the city."[1] Mrs. Cadwallader received letters of praise ranging from Maine to Philadelphia, from people who wanted Arthur to paint a similar rendition in their town centers. Visitors who return to Salisbury from as far away as Germany still contact the Guild to explain why they have come back to see the mural, completed.

Arthur chronicles the evolution of one place over time in her murals. Her desire to capture the flavor of a particular locale has been an instrumental factor in strengthening the existing preservation movement in Salisbury, says Ann Williams, executive director of the Historic Salisbury Foundation. She feels that projects like Cynvia Arthur's mural, which include both lost and restored buildings, remind people of the continuing need to care for their architectural legacy.

The Krewe of Poydras

Background

In New Orleans, a new Krewe has joined the roster of the social organizations which host the resplendent balls and boisterous parades of Mardi Gras. But the members of this Krewe do not take off their colorful costumes at the end of carnival season. The "Krewe of Poydras" is a permanent sculpture group designed by New Orleans artist Ida Kohlmeyer for the entrance to the 1515 Poydras building located on the edge of the business district, across from the looming Superdome. The firm of Skidmore, Owings and Merrill (SOM), the architects of the twenty-seven story, hammered white concrete office tower, wanted a dramatic accent at the building's courtyard entrance. Envisioning a series of flags or banners that would add color, movement and sound to the ground level, SOM invited five local artists to submit designs. Ida Kohlmeyer is a New Orleans painter of national recognition, known for her canvases of colorful abstract notations, who had no prior experience with large scale public art. Yet Kohlmeyer's entry, surpassing the original concept of flags or banners, won the competition.

Description

The Krewe of Poydras is a grouping of five kinetic sculptures soaring forty to fifty feet off the ground, located in an arcaded courtyard open to the street. The sculptures' painted poles stand at equidistant points in the grid-patterned pavement of the courtyard—a row of three poles placed behind a row of two. Large hieroglyphic-like symbols, some reaching fifteen feet in width and stacked vertically on the poles, rotate as the poles sway in the wind. Each pole is composed of a unique set of symbols, simultaneously resembling forms from an ancient past and some far-off future. A red cross-hatched arrow, polka-dotted wings, a large hand, and a golden sunburst play off bold geometric designs. Set against the white surface of the Poydras Building, the painted totem-like poles show off a richness of shapes, surface pattern, and color, ranging from vivid primaries to soft pastels.

NAME: *Krewe of Poydras*, New Orleans, Louisiana
PROJECT: A group of five kinetic sculptural poles set in a courtyard entrance, designed as part of the original plan for a 27-story office building on the edge of the New Orleans business district
ARTIST: Ida Kohlmeyer
AGENCY: Skidmore, Owings and Merrill (architects)
SIZE: 40–45 feet high
DATE: Dedicated January, 1983
COST: $36,000
MATERIAL: Sheet steel painted with catalyzed polyurethene enamel
PHOTOGRAPHY: Courtesy of Skidmore, Owings and Merrill

Although the sculptures are three-dimensional, their shapes and color are reminiscent of Kohlmeyer's paintings. They seem as animated and flamboyant as costumed guests at one of the legendary Mardi Gras Balls, or as the large decorated mannequins carried in carnival parades. Kohlmeyer originally rejected such images for her inspiration, but, she says, "Maybe one's locale seeps deeper in than one is aware of, because now even I sense it, the Carnival spirit."

For maintenance purposes and in case of inclement weather, the poles can be removed and placed within the above-ground parking garage at the base of the building.

Design Impact

The Krewe of Poydras fulfills SOM's desire to animate the open courtyard fronting street-level commercial space in this high-rise office building. Roger Green in the *Times Picayune* cites the building as one of the first commercial structures in New Orleans to integrate outdoor artwork in the original design.[1] Since the Krewe, a number of new buildings have incorporated public art in their plans. The Hotel Intercontinental installed a musical garden, a collaborative effort by musicians, artists and mathematicians. A high-rise complex called the Energy Center included a large abstract tower fountain designed by local artist Arthur Silverman.

Theodore Wolff, art critic of the *Christian Science Monitor*, speaking at the dedication ceremony in January 1983, called the Krewe public art "that is purely and simply celebratory, that enchants and delights us, that causes us to smile and feel good."[2] Dana Standish of New Orleans' weekly newspaper *Gambit* says of the Krewe that "like people, each has its own character, separate from the others, an independent spirit. . . . The average person who knows nothing about art but who has to pass the building on the way to work every day can look up and see sculptures and not feel obligated to understand anything, they can appreciate them for their bright colors, their lively stance, their energy."[3] Kohlmeyer's paintings are praised for similar reasons and have won national recognition, exhibited in museums such as the Brooklyn Art Museum, and the San Francisco Museum of Modern Art. Her earlier work, labeled grid or cluster paintings, often depicts rows of letters from the alphabet or familiar symbols such as checks and arrows. Says one critic of the Krewe, "Indeed, they turn a lot of heads on that colorless stretch of Poydras (Street), and are a lot like her paintings; fun, upbeat, triumphant."[4]

Church Court Angel

Summary

Mt. Vernon Church sat open to the sky for years, a solemn reminder of the 1978 fire which destroyed the building's roof and nave. Six years earlier, a declining congregation had left to merge with another church. It appeared that the historic neo-Romanesque structure, located in Boston's elegant Back Bay, was doomed, until architect Graham Gund bought it from its membership in 1979. Gund made the building an award-winning condominium complex, which incorporates the remaining late 19th century masonry

NAME: *Church Court Angel*, Boston, Massachusetts
PROJECT: A life-size bronze angel sits atop a wall of a ruined church, transformed into a luxury condominium complex
ARTIST: Gene Cauthen
AGENCY: Graham Gund Architects
SIZE: 5'9"
DATE: 1983
COST: $20,000—standing figure
MATERIAL: Cast bronze
PHOTOGRAPHY: Steve Rosenthal

structure into a new polychromatic brick building. The ornamentation of nearby Victorian townhouses inspired Gund's controversial design, which includes bold brick patterns and bright green window frames, and angelic sculpture.

A bronze angel, 5 feet, 9 inches tall, perched on a wall above the courtyard contemplates passersbys on Massachusetts Avenue. The Angel's back is turned toward the private courtyard enclosed on the other sides by new walls. The head and torso of a second angel graces the entrance lobby, which bridges the old and new sections of the complex.

Artist Gene Cauthen follows the Beaux-Arts tradition of William Morris Hunt and Augustus St. Gaudens, who contributed figures to Boston's nineteenth-century heritage of public sculpture.

Cauthen's Angel gives opinionated Bostonians something to ponder. Is she coming in for a landing or taking off in flight? Is she blessing an innovative restoration of an architectural ruin, or looking wistfully away from the gutted church? And if angels are reputed to be sexless, then this full-bosomed creature is certainly an exception to the rule. Gund likes to leave interpretation to the viewer. For him, the piece simply stands as a reminder of the building's previous life.

ATLANTA, GEORGIA

Aluminum Subway Bands

Background

In 1973, Atlanta broke ground on its new subway network—MARTA—planned to eventually encompass 53 miles of rail spread throughout the city to be completed in 1995. What is distinguished about the MARTA system is the lack of a single, uniform station design. Each station is designed by different architects to blend with the character of the local community, and each includes an artwork. The West End Station, opened in early 1982, displays a conspicuous addition: two aluminum bands stretching across the station depicting neighborhood residents carved in relief. It features several famous men who grew up in the area including home-run champion Hank Aaron and Secretary of State Dean Rusk. The others are local characters, unknown outside the neighborhood. Created by Pastor Martelino, Jr., of Smyrna, Georgia, the relief bands relate the modern subway station to the neighborhood, while emphasizing that it is the citizens who define the character of a community.

Martelino's first community-inspired project was a 25-foot tall wind chime of concrete and cast metal, placed in a small office park, which included relief portraits of people who worked in the surrounding offices. The concept behind the West End artwork, according to the artist, was roughly the same:

> . . . to take plain ordinary folk involved with the project or neighborhood and employ them into the sculpture as a more personal, relevant aspect in an overall aesthetic design. What I am saying is that the average person is more likely to respond to a work of contemporary sculpture if, in addition to abstract forms, there is something he can directly relate with such as faces or images that he recognizes. These can be famous people . . . or someone who looks like 'Aunt Gertrude.'

NAME: *Aluminum Subway Bands*, Atlanta, Georgia
PROJECT: Two decorative aluminum bands, installed in new subway station, depicting people, places and scenes of the West End neighborhood
ARTIST: Pastor Martelino, Jr.
AGENCY: Metropolitan Atlanta Rapid Transit Authority (MARTA)
SIZE: 16 inches tall on the average, 150 feet long
DATE: Conceived 1978, completed 1982
COST: $47,000 (Materials and construction—$20,000, artist—$20,000, other expenses—$7000)
MATERIAL: Aluminum
PHOTOGRAPHY: The Townscape Institute

After receiving the MARTA commission, Martelino spent several months in and out of the neighborhood, photographing and interviewing people around their homes and businesses, to get a sense of the community.

Description

Martelino used a 1980 public art piece, located in the foyer of the Decatur Building in Atlanta, as a test vehicle for the MARTA project, employing the same materials, procedure and approach. The sculpture, also an aluminum relief, depicts scenes of industry and government relevant to the businesses represented in the building. Boldly marking the center of the design are faces of employees, set off in high relief. The West End panels, though similar in technique, are on the average only 16 inches tall, and 150 feet long, stretching like veins of unmined ore over the two concrete walls that stand at the entrance to the station. Widening at places, and sharply sloping at other points, the bands use complex, organic forms, contrasting with the geometric architecture surrounding them. As the subject of the artwork, residents of the neighborhood—over a hundred of them—are depicted in portraits and in scenes of day to day life. Incorporating details of buildings, local landmarks, and typical local characters. The scenes attempt to express the vitality of this century-old Atlanta community.

Design Impact

Because they are bands, the panels make strong use of the open space around them: spanning the breadth of the station, they can be explored by dozens of people simultaneously. Located just above eye-level, they are immediately noticeable to passersby. Their intricate form, tactile surface, and soft, reflective sheen all help the bands to stand out from their environment, and to visually enliven the station area.

Although the outdoor location provides open space and natural light, it is unfortunate that panels are not similarly placed below: opposite the tracks, they would be efficient as well as aesthetic, helping to relieve the tedium of waiting for a train.

Spirit House

Summary

Spirit House, by the New York sculptor, Hera, is both art and shelter. Standing on the site of an old Marewieck Indian trail in Brooklyn, it is a steel frame built in the shape of a beehive and resembling a wigwam structure. Spirit House stands in a small parklet on the edge of Cadman Plaza. Once the galvanized steel tubes of the structure are covered with vegetation, the work becomes an outdoor room. Conceived as a temporary structure, the piece was sponsored by the Brooklyn Botanical Gardens and partially funded by the New York State Council on the Arts.

Although the artist designed Spirit House to support the tendrils of clinging plants, in the absence of any other playground equipment in the area, local children have trampled the vines into the ground and have enthusiastically adopted this piece as a Jungle Jim. The arbor's functional character and lyrical shape caused a critic from *Progressive Architecture* magazine, Johanna Wissinger, to write "Spirit House" (and Hera's similar project called "Vaulted Arbor") helped redeem the bad rep public art has recently acquired."

When Hera designed this piece, she wanted to acknowledge the original Indian inhabitants of the area who are seldom remembered. At the dedication, Floyd Hand, a grandson of two distinguished Indian chieftains, Red Cloud and Crazy Horse, and a spiritual leader in his own right for the Black Hills Sioux Treaty Council, conducted a smoke ceremony for Spirit House. But beyond the geometry that suggests the Indian wigwam, Hera's planted structure serves as a meditative space, and casts allusion to formal 19th-century garden arbors. In 1987 Spirit House found a permanent resting place in the Laumeier sculpture park in St. Louis.

Prior to building arbors like Spirit House, Hera did planted environmental pieces that make reference to particular places. Hera has designed blossoming mazes, among them "Stormflower," in New Orleans, the "Snail Shell Maze," in Boxford, Massachusetts, the

NAME: *Spirit House*, Brooklyn Heights, NY
PROJECT: Steel arbor structure in wigwam form, placed in little park in Cadman Plaza on Marewieck Indian Trail, Brooklyn Heights, New York
ARTIST: Hera
AGENCY: Brooklyn Botanical Gardens, NY State Council of the Arts, NY City Department of Parks and Recreation
SIZE: 11 feet high, 18½ feet diameter
DATE: 1985
COST: $15,000: $10,000 NY State Council on the Arts; 3,000 private donations; $2,000 Artist's contribution
MATERIAL: Galvanized steel pipe and "U" channels
PHOTOGRAPHY: Hera

"Bear Paw Maze," in Yonkers, New York, and a maze for the State University of New York's campus at Purchase. "Stormflower" is perhaps the most dramatic of these other works; planted primarily in azaleas, the maze fans out spiral arms to a diameter of 160 feet, evoking the form of a hurricane. She installed it at the University of New Orleans, with the assistance of art students there, in June 1980.

Dublin Spring Monument

Conceived by Alexander Hamilton in 1778, Paterson, New Jersey, was the first planned industrial center in the United States. By the beginning of the 1900s, it had earned such nicknames as "the Cradle of Industry," and "the Industrial Florence of America." Situated on the Great Falls of the Passaic River, it was among the centers of a thriving locomotive industry, the home of the nation's largest silk mills, and the scene of one of the International Workers of the World's major labor disputes—attracting the leader of the union, Big Bill Hayward himself, to rally the workers. To its residents the city was famous as the site of Dublin Spring, a natural spring that was a center of social activity in the blue-collar neighborhood near the mills.

The decades following WWI saw the wane of the silk industry, and with it the decline of Paterson: mills and plants were shut down or converted to accommodate other industries, population dropped off, and in 1922 the spring was closed because of suspected pollutants in the water. But residents refused to let this particular tradition die, and a commemorative statue was erected in 1931. The Dublin Spring Monument has since become a landmark in its own right, an evocative reminder of the city's buried history.

The statue stands directly over the site of the spring, in the center of what had long been a thriving Irish immigrant neighborhood known since 1811 as "Dublin." Situated at one of the city's major crossroads, the spring was six feet below street level, reachable by a flight of stone stairs. A source of water for the residents, the spring was the scene of activities varying from political rallies to children's horseplay. Just prior to the Civil War, a pump was installed. Soldiers traditionally sipped from the spring before leaving town, as the water supposedly insured the drinker's eventual return to Paterson—a widely recognized superstition that became incorporated into Paterson folklore. Local poets were among those referring to it, as in this typical 1898 stanza:

I've wandered far and wandered wide
But no power I could bring
Could keep me long from this good town
And dear old Dublin Spring.

As industrialization spread, the spring became a source of refreshment for workers in the nearby machine works and mills. By the late 1890s, however, typhoid and cholera epidemics affected the city, and the springs were blamed. Dean McNulty of St. John's Church challenged several times in the 1900s and the 1910s the municipality's decision to close the spring because of its alleged unhealthy condition. He sought to provide the continued supply of water from the spring for his parish. As a result, during that period, the spring was closed and re-opened often. When the spring was closed permanently in 1922, a citizens' committee called the Dublin Springs Association was formed to commemorate the site. Raising money from members of the community, they commissioned a work from Paterson's most recognized sculptor, Gaetano Federici.

Description

The design for the monument underwent several changes during the negotiations between artist and committee. Early proposals for the work included an allegorical female figure representative of the Irish "race" with an Irish harp by her side, and later a sculpture of gushing water and a Triton, reminiscent of Italian Renaissance fountains. Ultimately, the more understated smiling lad with a canteen emerged. The figure is depicted from the waist up, in simple, realistic detail, leaning forward slightly as if to fill the canteen from the spring. It is believed that the model for the figure was Charles Conti, a boy whose family owned a grocery store near the site of the spring. The oval canteen barrel is actually a distortion of the round shape that would have been popular at the time, probably included to improve the composition of the piece. Below the figure is a roundel with the face of a small, thirsty bulldog looking up toward the canteen, surrounded by a traditionally Irish motif of shamrocks. A five-and-a-half-foot pedestal brings the statue to just above eye-level; across the front of this base are the words "NO MORE," a lamentation for the loss of the water supply.

Design Impact

The peak of Paterson's prosperity coincided with the height of the ornate Beaux-Arts style of architecture, and so public monuments in the city were in high fashion during the early years of this century. Gaetano Federici, an Italian-born immigrant, was a versatile artist who virtually became Paterson's biographical sculptor. The city's leading political, religious and social leaders all found their immortality through Federici's talents. Between 1903, when the artist opened his first Paterson studio, to his death in 1964, Federici created more than a hundred pieces of public statuary art, over thirty-five of them in the vicinity of Paterson alone. The Dublin Spring Monument is the only public artwork included in the city's booklets on highlights of the historical area and is generally considered Federici's best known and most popular work. It is the one statue commemorating a community landmark rather than an individual; its simple, unpretentious design lends it additional appeal.

NAME: *Dublin Spring Monument*, Paterson, New Jersey
PROJECT: Bronze torso and bust of boy holding water canteen, set atop pedestal, commemorating historic spring
ARTIST: Gaetano Federici; Dublin Springs Association
SIZE: Life-size; pedestal approximately 5½ feet tall
DATE: 1931
COST: Approximately $5000
MATERIAL: Bronze
PHOTOGRAPHY: Ronald Lee Fleming

Paterson has changed much since its heyday—the "Dublin" neighborhood is now largely Hispanic—and today the array of public monuments contrasts with the deteriorated condition of the city. In marking the loss of a popular tradition, rather than the loss of the grandeur that was once Paterson, the Dublin Spring monument is exceptional, and poignant.

The Paterson sculpture is somewhat akin to Savannah's "Waving Girl", which also commemorates an historic 'slice of life,' rather than a legendary hero. The statue is a tribute to Florence Martus, a local woman who for the forty-four years between 1887 and 1931, kept a vigil outside Elba Island's Lighthouse. According to local lore, Martus lost her beau at sea, and yearning to be the first person to see him when he returned, she greeted every ship, waving her white cloth. Today, ships still salute her bronze statue at the port's edge, with a blast from their foghorns.

Waving Girl Statue, Savannah, Georgia.

People Wall

Background

People Wall in Corning, New York, is an eye-catching collection of 150 photographs and portraits of Corning citizens, a profile of the city as it was during the Bicentennial year. On permanent display through the glass wall of the City Hall, it had its genesis in an urban renewal program which was activated in 1972 after Hurricane Agnes floods devastated large areas of the city. In the wake of that disaster, the city proposed a new civic center, funded in part by government aid, with architectural fees coming from the Corning Glassworks Foundation, representing the city's largest employer. Under the terms of the grant, one percent of building cost was allocated towards art.

City officials conceived of the artwork as a series of photographic montages, both color and black and white, to brighten the empty concrete walls and glass panels of the otherwise barren lobby. As envisioned, the photos would depict the institutions, landscape and residents of Corning. When the city commissioned the artist Elliott Erwitt, a photographer noted for his personality portraits, the project shifted focus. With the encouragement of the mayor, Erwitt changed the concept of the work to define the community in terms of its people alone—pho-

NAME: *People Wall*, Corning, New York

PROJECT: Photographs of 150 residents of Corning, taken in tableaux depicting their roles in the community, reproduced life-size on fabric and permanently displayed in the lobby of new City Hall

ARTIST: Photographer: Elliott Erwitt; Graphic Designer: Norman Gobarty

AGENCY: Corning Glassworks Foundation; The City of Corning

SIZE: Three walls, approximately 3000 square feet

DATE: Started 1975, completed 1976

COST: Approximately $35,000

MATERIAL: Photographs, fabric

PHOTOGRAPHY: Kellogg Studios

tographs including as wide a social, economic and ethnic spread as would realistically represent Corning's population. He engaged a graphic artist, Norman Gobarty, to arrange the figures into a coherent mural, then photographed over three-hundred-and-fifty people in tableaux of various sizes. The best photographs were chosen from the lot. Then, using a recently developed technique called Scanachrome, he blew up the prints to life-size on panels of fabric, and mounted them onto the wall in sections, like wallpaper. Mayor Nasser of Corning, for whom the new plaza was named, dedicated both City Hall and the mural on June 21, 1976.

Description

The People Wall is composed of eighty different panels, which include 150 people and animals. Like photographs by Richard

Avedon, the figures are pictures against a stark white background, and almost always face the camera. Whereas Avedon is harsh, however, Erwitt is playful, focusing on the most revealing characteristics of each subject. The people, photographed singly, in pairs, and in small groups, each carry a pose and costume appropriate to his or her most recognizable role in the community. Shots include: a dance teacher posing, mimicked by her four-year-old student; a high school cheerleader and hockey player, a Lions, Rotary and Kiwanis club member standing in a row, smiling in natty, conservative three-piece suits; a somber Salvation Army major and his wife; and a postman, arm extended, in the act of delivering a letter. Since the individuals do not interact with each other outside of their separate panels, the effect of the work as a whole is not so much a mural, as a composite town portrait. The People Wall spans the length of the lobby on both ground floor and mezzanine level, and is visible in its entirety from across the civic center plaza through the building's greenhouse glass front.

Design Impact

Originally, it had been suggested that a statue of Baron von Steuben, the Revolutionary patriot for whom Steuben County was named, decorate the new plaza. Compared to the more traditional public monuments and the more conventional Bicentennial displays, the People Wall presents a dramatic change of focus. The concept fits the scale of the city well; because Corning is so small (approximately 15,000), it can actually select a representative group of one hundred and fifty citizens without being overly general, or excluding large segments of the population.

The tone of the work is much more personal than most government murals, bringing humor and slight irreverence to the prosaic business of municipal government while preserving a very serious pride in its citizenry, and a rational order to its display. Photographer Erwitt commented on the

thematic relevance: "I think it's appropriate that City Hall should be filled with citizens at all times, particularly since the interior of the new building is visible from the exterior public area. Also, I liked the idea of a permanent reference point to 1976."

The use of photography as the medium of a permanent city hall artwork is itself an innovation. Whereas earlier decades might have preferred a single portrait of a town leader gracing the interior of a city hall, photography has democratized the portraiture process. It is a colorful and inexpensive way to portray large numbers of people, and it records not only specific individuals but the culture of the time. The result coincides with the goal stated by Corning's mayor—"the story of a small town USA at the time of the nation's bicentennial." Coated with a preservative and permanently affixed to the wall, the Corning of 1976 can remain intact and open to study for the next generation. Cleaned every four years, the mural remains in good condition.

Man Slopping Pigs

Summary

"Go down Broad Street and stop at the next set of hogs" is a strange but absolutely accurate set of directions to Don Beyers' Volvo Dealership in Falls Church, Virginia, where a cast aluminum sculpture of five hogs and a farmer stands at the entrance.

According to artist Richard Beyer, Falls Church was once the hog capital of Virginia. Like many other small towns on the edge of metropolitan areas before the rise of interstate trucking, it provided the Washington, D.C. market with a necessary product. Today Falls Church is an integral part of Washington's suburban web, a middle-class residential area supplying government professionals rather than pork to the city. The artist's nephew, Donald, the owner of a Volvo dealership, commissioned the piece located in front of his agency. It is a humorous sculpture entitled, "The Man Slopping Pigs," recalling one of Falls Church's past livelihoods as remembered by the artist and his brothers, who grew up in the nearby community of McLean, Virginia, from the 1920s to the 1940s when Falls Church was still hog country.

Description

Five sturdy hogs surround a farmer pouring their food into a trough. One pig pushes between the farmer's legs, another rears up to the slop bucket, a third, trying to appropriate everything for himself, sits in the trough. Passing suburban traffic sometimes supplies the squeals and grunts of real pigs and the curses of a real farmer. The sculpture is screened from the auto business by flowers, which allow the public to enjoy the sculpture without feeling they are interfering with the dealership. It is lit by ground lamps at night.

Design Impact

Though ostensibly a memorial to a bygone industry of fifty years ago, the sculpture has greater significance: a business expressing its appreciation to the community with a gift of public art. Businesses most often show community support through charitable donations or participation in social activities. Don Beyer, Jr., president of

NAME: *Man Slopping Pigs*, Falls Church, Virginia
PROJECT: An aluminum sculpture of a farmer feeding five pigs located in front of a suburban auto dealership
ARTIST: Richard Beyer
AGENCY: Don Beyer, Volvo, Inc.
SIZE: Life size
DATE: May, 1984
COST: $20,000
MATERIAL: Cast aluminum
PHOTOGRAPHY: Richard Beyer

the dealership, explained his own benefit from the sculpture: "A central reason for erecting the sculpture was to position the dealership in the public consciousness as a unique business, concerned with community and art, and unafraid of being different. This has been singularly well accomplished. Daily, people will call, drop by, and write to express their pleasure with the sculpture and their surprise that a dealership would be its sponsor."

Don Beyer also believes he is filling an artistic void. Falls Church has no tradition of public art, not even a lone confederate soldier on a pedestal facing toward Richmond. Says Beyer, "The pigs have become a major Virginia landmark, used for giving directions to hundreds of travelers every day. This has helped make the dealership a readily identifiable place to do business . . .[It] has clearly benefitted Don Beyer Volvo financially . . . Finally, the sculpture has greatly improved the warmth and sense of place of our western Falls Church community. The surrounding blocks are typical suburban sprawl, lots of gas stations, and asphalt and little humanity. The pigs surrounded by flowers and climbed over by kids, relieve the state highway monotony, startle us, make us laugh, make us stop to look and touch and wonder."

The artist Richard Beyer calls his body of public sculpture "Urban Folk Art," defined as work that would lose nothing in popular esteem if anonymous. His sculptures are in Denver, Portland, Seattle, and other smaller western towns. These include City Hall murals in Kent, Washington, which are small vignettes carved in brick, and "Dancing Around the Tree to Make It Green Again," a sculpted tree trunk in a suburban Seattle playground. The dealership displays the artist's unveiling speech on the wall of the showroom. For people who ask, "What does the sculpture mean?" he points to Beyer's statement—"We, each of us, I see as pig farmers: our elemental desires are like greedy animals pushing and squealing, but we ourselves, in our family and community responsibilities, stand over them, providing for them, caring for them because they are ourselves."

Manhole Cover Maps

Background

Seattle's innovative "Bhy Kracke" gift program, was initiated in 1977 to involve citizens personally in the beautification of their urban landscape. The program supplied a list of items that citizens could donate to the city including medallions for lampposts, manhole covers, trees, drinking fountains, kiosks, benches, and ornamental street clocks, at a cost of $25 to $50,000. The program aimed to reduce the usual red tape associated with making gifts to the city.

More importantly, it created an institutional vehicle for channeling generosity from citizens to the municipality. Donors could choose from the gift list, write a check, and leave the implementation to the appropriate city department.

When Mayor Wesley Uhlman created "Bhy Kracke," which was named for local philanthropist Warner Bhy Kracke, he commented, "As Seattle passes from its youth into maturity, its continued success will depend increasingly on attention to aesthetic detail. The view of the mountains won't be enough to compensate for barren, inhospitable streets."

Description

One item on the gift list was a specially-crafted manhole cover created by urban designer Ann Windus Knight. Nineteen such covers have been installed prominently on Seattle's sidewalks. Each displays a downtown street grid with such Seattle attractions as the Space Needle, Freeway Park, and the Pike Place Market, and each has a shiny, stainless steel button imbedded in the map pinpointing the cover's location in the city. The design is cast in three levels of relief, so that the most salient features of the map have been quickly burnished by pedestrian traffic, enhancing their appearance. The police insisted that the covers be placed only on sidewalks, to prevent accidents caused by people staring at them in the middle of the street. The manhole covers are located so visitors can chart their way through the city.

A second manhole cover design has also been made available to donors. These discs, created by Nathan Jackson, display semi-abstract Native American animal designs. With both series, a donor could have his name engraved on the cover for a few extra dollars, making the gift a personal one to the city.

Design Impact

The Seattle Bhy Kracke Program was the brainchild of a former mayor; when his term

NAME: *Manhole Cover Maps*, Seattle, Washington
PROJECT: Series of manhole covers, donated by residents through city gift program, depicting stylized city street maps
ARTIST: Ann Windus Knight
AGENCY: Seattle City Light, Seattle Department of Community Development; Bhy Kracke Gift Program
SIZE: 36 inches and 38 inches in diameter
DATE: Started 1977
COST: Fabrication of mold—$4000; cost to donor for each individual manhole cover—$200
MATERIAL: Cast iron
PHOTOGRAPHY: Renata von Tscharner

ended, so did the program. Unfortunately, the new mayor discontinued this successful program, as it was identified with the previous administration. In 1985, approximately eight years later, the city of Seattle adopted a similar program so that citizens can choose to donate items such as park benches, drinking fountains, and murals, selected from a published catalogue. Manhole covers are not listed. However, the Seattle Water Department is funding its own custom designed manhole cover project. The Seattle Arts Commission has chosen an artist, whose design will replace the nine standard cover designs found in the downtown and other areas of Seattle.

Louden-Nelson Community Center Scene

Background

As work approached completion on the trompe l'oeil mural on the Louden-Nelson (formerly the Laurel) Community Center, designer Jeff Oberdorfer was asked what had motivated his effort. The artist replied: "Whether I am working on a mural or buildings I orient my work to the community." The Louden-Nelson mural is a community tribute depicting randomly selected local residents against a background of Italianate balconies.

The concept of the mural arose during a series of public meetings held to discuss the unused open space at the rear of the community center. Jeff Oberdorfer, who lived a block away from the center, had already gained a reputation for trompe l'oeil murals with a community-inspired wall painting in Cambridge, Massachusetts. Seeing an opportunity to employ his experience, he submitted a proposal for the wall. The design, simulating an arched porch populated by members of the community, was immediately accepted by those attending the public meetings. In addition, Oberdorfer was hired to organize workshops on the design of the adjacent lot, which was to be used as a play area.

Several sources of funding and various artists contributed to the mural. The City of Santa Cruz loaned the Center $2,500 towards the painting; services were provided by a CETA worker, a Youth Employment Services worker, and many community volunteers. Various artisans—air brushers, portraitists, painters—contributed specialized skills. The mural was completed in mid October, 1979, after ten weeks of painting.

Description

While the mural ignores the building's Mission Revival style in favor of opulent Italianate arches, it incorporates features of the Community Center building in its fanciful scheme. In several places pilasters and cornices were integrated into the mural design. Architectural details were borrowed from other parts of the building, such as the arches, which were copied from the arched doorways in the front. The scene recalls the balcony sections inside a theater—appropriate because it relates to both the sense of play in the park outside, and the activities

NAME: *Louden-Nelson Community Scene*, Santa Cruz, California
PROJECT: Mural on rear wall of neighborhood community center depicting local residents against background of arched Italianate balconies
ARTIST: Jeff Oberdorfer
Assisting artists: Julie Heffernan, Ray Ginghofer, Dennis Marks, Sarah Lovett, Laurie Thomas, numerous volunteers
AGENCY: Laurel Community Center; City of Santa Cruz
SIZE: 26 feet by 45 feet
DATE: Started 1978, completed 1979
COST: $7500, plus estimated $4500 in volunteer labor plus Youth Employment Services and CETA (Comprehensive Employment and Training Administration) salaries
MATERIAL: Acrylic latex exterior paint
PHOTOGRAPHY: Jeff Oberdorfer

of the mural was painted in exterior house paint, and the fake tiles were covered with urethane which yellows as real tiles would.

Design Impact

The portraits evoke the most popular response—since the subjects are recognizable figures from different segments of the community. Among the most frequent suggestions made by viewers is that a tape recording be installed alongside the portrait of Joe, a popular, highly talkative older man represented in the mural.

The trompe l'oeil has had a significant impact of its own. When the Community Center was renovated a short time after the mural's completion, the new color scheme and architectural additions were coordinated to match those in the mural.

The artist reports that the mural is a constant source of amusement for those whose portraits are displayed on the wall, who frequently bring friends and relatives back to see their former images. The artist, who still lives nearby, has touched up the mural every year, and patched minor cracks in the stucco.

California's acceptance of Proposition 13 during the early stages of the work put much

directly inside the community center, as the painting is located on the back of the auditorium.

The fifteen life-size figures—infants, parents, and grandparents—look down from the balconies. They are so realistic that passersby have been known to wave at them. All depict actual community members, who passed through the play lot behind the center.

Care was taken to use materials which would simulate architectural elements. The portraits were painted in acrylics, the rest of the responsibility for funding the mural on the community. Donations by neighborhood residents have repaid most of the city council's expenditure.

Because paints can now last up to 100 years, murals are no longer temporary decorations, but permanent neighborhood landmarks. The Community Center mural, with its wide popularity, has set a precedent for future murals in Santa Cruz. A year later, two artists who worked on the Community Center mural, Dennis Marks and Julie Heffernan, painted a similar site-responsive trompe l'oeil on the back wall of a school, facing a playground. Featured are architectural elements of the building and portraits of the building contractor, the principal, teachers and students.

Sonja Henie Memorial Fountain

Background

During the winter of 1932, in the tiny hamlet of Lake Placid, New York, a young Norwegian awed the crowds gathered for the Olympic figure skating competition. Sonja Henie easily won the second of her gold medals that day, skating with a combination of skill and grace which set the standard of excellence in the sport for over a decade. When the Winter Olympics returned to Lake Placid in 1980, a group of Norwegian-Americans, assisted by the Norwegian Government, funded a memorial to the event which took place forty-eight years before.

On Main Street they erected a fountain which functions all year. While most of the year water flows from its spouts, on sunny winter days it becomes a brilliant configuration of ice crystals, the medium Henie used to sculpt her award winning figures. It is located in front of the Olympic Center, which combines the 1932 skating arena and two additional skating arenas added later to make a single structure for the 1980 Olympics. Carl Nesjar, the Norwegian artist who created the fountain, is known primarily for his long collaboration with the late Pablo Picasso; Nesjar assisted this master in the production of large concrete sculptures and murals. His own more recent work often explores the sculptural qualities of water. Says Nesjar:

> In Northern cities fountains are shut off in late autumn when days get short, dark and cold, leaving dead and meaningless spaces . . . Yet, late autumn is precisely the time of year when people have an emotional need for things—bright, sparkling and lively.[1]

The Sonja Henie Memorial is the first American example of Nesjar's fountains, which involve a boyhood fascination with "the play of water on the rocky Norwegian coast near his home,"[2] where he liked to watch the spray of water in the summer and the ice formations in winter transform their contexts.

He interprets this memory by building structures which drip or spray water on the surface of the structure. This creates a gentle glistening effect in the warm months, but with freezing temperatures the sculptures

105

NAME: *Sonja Henie Memorial Fountain*, Lake Placid, New York
PROJECT: A fountain functioning year round in front of the Olympic Arena, honoring 1932 gold medalist Sonja Henie
ARTIST: Carl Nesjar
AGENCY: Norwegian American Society, Lake Placid Olympic Organizing Committee
SIZE: 25 feet high
DATE: November, 1979
COST: Approximately $60,000 for production and installation. Materials donated by ALCOA (the artist received no fee)
MATERIAL: Stainless steel and aluminum for the sculpture, granite base
PHOTOGRAPHY AND DRAWING: Carl Nesjar

become a mass of ever-changing ice forms, providing, as the artist observes, much needed "light, color [and] movement" for northern cities "in their cold winter environments."[3]

Description

The aluminum fountain in Lake Placid is an abstract interpretation of a figure skater's spiral inspired by an old postcard of Sonja Henie that the artist found in Oslo. He says, "I had an idea I wanted to use two main lines at an angle resembling a skater on one toe. One day at the Henie-Onstad Art Center in Oslo, I saw an early photograph of Sonja Henie in blousy bloomers, in exactly the position I'd been thinking of. From there the idea fell into place."[4] The pose captures the dynamics of speed and static in figure skating. The athlete achieves a swift graceful gliding motion with little apparent effort. Five spheres, representing the five rings of the Olympic flag, range around an angled beam rising twenty-five feet in the air. The spheres and beam form an abstraction of the skater's pose. At its base of Norwegian black granite a simple plaque describes the memorial and its sponsors.

The aluminum tubing which coils around the struts of each of the five spheres provides a route for the descending water flowing from the top of the sculpture. The circular motion of the water drops make the spheres appear to rotate in the summer sun. In the winter these same coils are the framework from which legions of icicles hang. Evolving throughout the season, one day might find it melting in a mid-winter thaw. Illuminated from within by propane flames, at night the work becomes a beacon for the arena; in Nesjar's description it resembles "a big, glittering jewel."

Design Impact

The Sonja Henie Memorial Fountain was not the only artwork acquired by the village of 2,000 in the course of the Olympic Games. The Lake Placid Olympic Organizing Committee found that sponsoring a modern Olympiad entails more than constructing new ski jumps and bobsled runs. Cultural

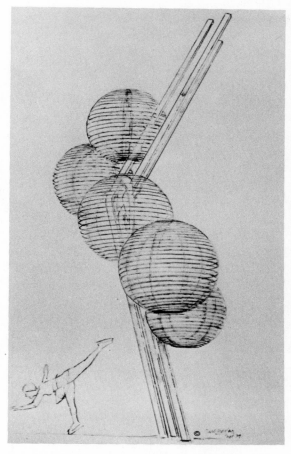

Artist's sketch of skater's pose and the sculpture it inspired for the Winter Olympics at Lake Placid, New York.

during the games, and besides Nesjar's fountain, five permanent artworks remained after the closing ceremonies.

The five other permanent artworks commissioned for the Lake Placid Olympics include three sculptures, one mural, and one relief. "All aspire to monumentality without direct reference to physical context or historical circumstance," according to Christian Hubert in *Art at the Olympics— A Survey of the National Fine Arts Program—1980 Winter Olympics*. In an article on the art at the Olympics in *Artforum*, the Sonja Henie Fountain was described as the most outstanding piece of celebratory art, compared to the other permanent artworks commissioned for the winter games. Kathleen Kinsella of the Lake Placid Olympic Organizing Committee said that in spite of some initial grumbling about its abstract qualities, people in Lake Placid agree the Ice Fountain "is a unique artwork, and is a centerpiece of art for the front of the Olympic Arena."

Although few are old enough to remember Sonja Henie's medal-winning performance in 1932, the townspeople are proud of her success, and in 1984 officially named the rink where she skated in her honor. The fountain establishes a connection between the two Olympic games at Lake Placid. It visually commemorates the tradition of world class competition in this winter sports center and also creates a point of continuing visual interest adjacent to Main Street.

and artistic events are now an important part of the festival, with large budgets and influential committees. Dozens of works were placed in the environs of Lake Placid

Asaroton 1976

Background

Mags Harries' "Asaroton 1976," lauded by *ARTnews* as "the most successful piece of

public art in Boston," and by the Boston *Phoenix* as "the finest piece of contemporary art in the city," is a humorous, unpre-

tentious, community-inspired public monument. Situated in the Haymarket, Boston's bustling outdoor vegetable market near the Italian North End, the work consists of bronze replicas of the everyday debris of the market set into the crosswalk. The unconventional piece arose from a competition sponsored by several government organizations to commemorate the national Bicentennial in Boston. The judging panel was wary of the impersonal standardized design attitudes that largely had characterized Bicentennial displays, and according to one of its members, Kenneth Baker:

> agreed early on that a conventional public monument, however stylized, would be an inappropriate choice for an occasion whose celebration was already inflated and programmed to the point of propaganda.

With this value in mind, Mags Harries' proposal was selected from a small group of atypical contenders. Initially, there was some fear that the submission might encounter resistance from some level in the city bureaucracy, since Haymarket was not within the designated Bicentennial site, and the

NAME: *Asaroton 1976*, Boston, Massachusetts
PROJECT: Realistic bronze replicas of fragments of garbage set in the pavement at the Haymarket, North End
ARTIST: Mags Harries
AGENCY: Massachusetts Bicentennial Commission; Boston 200; Bicentennial Sculpture Commission
SIZE: 55 feet 5 inches by 10 feet
DATE: 1976
COST: Approximately $10,000
MATERIAL: Bronze
PHOTOGRAPHY: Renata von Tscharner

work was inherently anti-monumental. When Harries' proposal met approval, another problem presented itself: the artist found her estimated cost of installation too low. The difficulty was overcome when a local construction company donated its services: Asaroton was installed according to schedule, in late summer 1976.

Description

Asaraton 1976 derives both title and inspiration from a second century mosaic floor in the Roman villa at Aventine. The original

"Asaroton," the ancient Greek word for 'unswept floor' is a tile still life of meal remnants. The North End sculpture similarly attempts to evoke the experience of a place through a symbolic carpet of garbage underfoot. The debris in Harries' work is particularly native to the location: cabbage leaves, rotten fruits, pieces of a discarded shopping bag, shreds from a newspaper, a half-eaten crust of pizza, a single green olive. The objects are bronze and life-size, set into a strip of concrete connecting two street corners. The realism is enhanced by careful relief—and the fact that three days out of the week, real garbage spills over from the Haymarket to camouflage the bronzes. Spread over an area 55½ feet by 10 feet, the sculpture accompanies pedestrians as they cross the intersection.

Designed to be accessible to walkers, not to drivers, the work personalizes an otherwise ordinary street crossing. Baker concluded his appraisal of the work by emphasizing that it provoked a positive response to an alienating urban scene, noting:

A sculpture that commemorates refuse by definition sanctions everyone's ambivalent feelings toward the street life that the modern city makes inevitable.

Set in a specially-poured concrete crosswalk, exposed to pedestrians and automobiles, the sculpture will be worn down and buffed by constant wear; over the years it will gain in luster what it might lose in realism.

Design Impact

Fortuitously located downtown, along Boston's Freedom Trail, Asaroton receives heavy exposure. Its placement near two subway stations makes it a starting point and terminus for sight-seeing trips. However, Harries' artistic license finally did conflict with the mores of city administrators, who objected to the inclusion of a newspaper scrap with the headline "15 Students Seized at South Boston High": Officials did not wish

to be reminded of Boston's racial problems. For this reason, Harries maintains, the artwork was denied an official dedication; an unofficial ceremony was held instead. Harries' more recent works have also explored realistic street imagery in public places. Among these is a collection of objects installed in Chelsea's Bellingham Square in

NAME: *Glove Cycle*, Cambridge, Massachusetts
PROJECT: Series of small sculptures for the new MBTA Red Line Station in Porter Square, consisting of discarded gloves, arranged individually in clusters and piles throughout the station
ARTIST: Mags Harries
AGENCY: Cambridge Arts Council; Metropolitan Boston Transit Authority (MBTA), Cambridge Seven Associates (Architects)
SIZE: Gloves are life-size
DATE: Conceived 1978, completion 1984
COST: Unknown
MATERIAL: Bronze castings of actual gloves
PHOTOGRAPHY: Renata von Tscharner

1977, including a bronze shopping bag, handbag, sweater, and set of luncheon items. These objects, fully life-size, are so realistic in texture and detail that they are occasionally mistaken for real.

Another of Harries' recent works is the "Glove Cycle" in Cambridge, Massachusetts, an arrangement of discarded gloves for the new Porter Square subway station, installed in 1984. Passengers encounter the bronze gloves throughout the station—first at the turnstile, next along the center of the escalator as it descends into the station, then scattered in the floor tiles of the subway platform, and finally in a pile near the elevator at the lower level. The gloves, in their various groupings, echo the movement pattern of the commuters in the station—forming a line along the escalator, and lying scattered on the subway platform. One art critic remarked in *Art New England*, "The hand is truly the most 'public' part of the body, the means by which we connect with others. Harries' gloves, of infinitely varied types and gestures, serve to relate the travellers imaginatively to their fellow passengers, and to create a genuine interaction between artwork and environment."[1]

YOUNGSTOWN, OHIO

The Steelmakers

Background

The future role of the steel industry in the daily life and economy of Youngstown, Ohio, is at best uncertain. One after another, the giant steel mills have closed, the victims of declining corporate profits. Virtually no steelmaking continues. Yet it was the raw power of that burgeoning industry which breathed life into the Mahoning Valley in the first half of the century, spurring the development of an all-embracing economy. George Segal's "The Steelmakers," which depicts two bronze figures working at an open hearth furnace, is a tribute to those who participated in that growth.

For the Youngstown Arts Council, its dedication on May 14, 1980, was the culmination of a four-year campaign to acquire a major work of sculpture for the city's new Federal Plaza pedestrian mall.

The predetermined plaza site was a considerable obstacle; the location was confined physically by a large, misplaced kiosk and the proximity of a heavily-used thoroughfare; and visually by a cacophony of storefronts, advertisements and traffic signs. Segal visited Youngstown to review the site within a week after he received the selection committee request, and was struck by the beauty of the region, which he saw as similar in environmental composition to his native New Brunswick, New Jersey. The steelworkers theme emerged through his subsequent visits to Youngstown and interactions with the community. In his letter of acceptance, Segal expanded on his impressions:

The open hearth scenes were spectacular—gloomy darkness, hissing steam and smoke, urgent foghorns . . . railway cars moving fluidly in all directions—the awesome pour, light you can't look into, heat sparks hugely bigger than we are and dangerous unless you move exactly right. This reality is more fantastic than the most fevered imaginings . . . I found the look of the furnaces and the people of Youngstown to be staggeringly impressive.

Almost every facet of the process of design and construction required community involvement. One of the large steel mills donated a 46-ton hearth, the local labor unions offered manpower and expertise for disassembling the machine and rebuilding it at the site, and, at the suggestion of the artist, two members of the steelworkers' union were selected by their peers to be models for the figures. The two men, one black and one white, have a combined seniority of fifty years with the steel mills. While they were being subjected to the standard Segal method of casting from life using plaster and burlap, one noted, "I feel as though I was representing every Youngstown worker of the past, present and future."

Funding for the sculpture came from individuals, local businesses, industry, foundations and arts organizations; larger sums were provided by the Ohio Arts Council and the National Endowment for the Arts. Segal said it was the first time in over twenty years that so many other people's attitudes and decisions had been involved in his work.

NAME: *The Steelmakers*, Youngstown, Ohio
PROJECT: Talbeau of two life-size bronze figures, depicting steelworkers, with tools and helmets, working in front of an open hearth furnace in Federal Plaza
ARTIST: George Segal
AGENCY: The Youngstown Arts Council
SIZE: 216 x 240 x 180 feet
DATE: Conceived 1976, completed 1980
COST: $70,000 plus donations of in-kind labor equalling approximately $70,000
MATERIAL: Bronze, with authentic props and furnace
PHOTOGRAPHY: Courtesy of Sidney Janis Gallery, New York

Description

The two steelworker figures are shown in one of the final stages of the steelmaking process, testing the carbon content of the molten steel by the mouth of an open hearth furnace. As with many of Segal's works, every effort was made to select and project a scene as natural as possible, without the use of intricate detail. Thus the poses are casual, as if captured offhandedly in a Polaroid snapshot, and the surface texture of the bronze is irregularly burnished. The faces are not markedly recognizable, and it is the slope of the bodies more than any other factor that defines the figures as individuals. Each man is equipped with actual tools—a bucket, poles, goggles, and helmets painted a bright industrial orange to offset the rusty black furnace and the dark muted patina of the bronze.

Dominating the scene is the furnace itself, a monolithic composition of scraped walls, chains, iron beams and concrete. Because of aesthetic considerations, the furnace is not entirely authentic; the brickwork that would enclose the structure was left out, to keep the space open and the view across the plaza unobstructed. The tableau is simultaneously intimate and dynamic, and rivets attention even in the fragmented and active cityscape around it. From the imposing monotonous office buildings rising abruptly from the pavement, through the mammoth five-part hearth, to the absorbed individual figures, stationed slightly apart from the furnace on the open plaza, the sculpture manipulates scale so as to directly involve the viewer with the statues. The sculpture's solidity brings a sense of stability to the overwhelming framework of the plaza. Viewed as a frozen moment of an evolving historical progression, the scene is charged with movement and energy.

Design Impact

Because no solution seems imminent for Youngstown's steel crisis, and the predicted mass layoffs have become a reality, the tableau is particularly poignant, inspiring deep emotion and pride among the workers that constitute the community. Not uncommonly, people will stop, point, and narrate their personal stories to their companions. It is a readily identifiable acknowledgment of these men's importance to the growth of the city around them.

That it is a non-political statement is stressed in the first sentence of the accompanying plaque: "This is a tribute, not a memorial." When a number of workers raised their objection to the project at the sculpture's dedication by occupying seats reserved for the city officials and dignitaries, the denunciation against trying to politicize the work came loudly from the ranks of the other workers who questioned the validity of spending money on art, at a time when the community's main source of economy was in danger. The timeliness of the building of the statue has earned it national visibility, including a television spot on "Good Morning, America." Significantly, the sculpture's success encouraged the state legislature to approve an arts subsidy of eight million dollars for 1980–1981, double the amount allotted for the previous two year period. The arts budget has continued to increase each year.

Unfortunately, vandals have damaged the sculpture; in one instance someone broke off a ladle which a steelworker holds.

For Segal, "The Steelmakers" continues a history that began in the 1950's, when he was first hailed as a Pop hero for assembling tableaux of solitudinous life-size plaster figures using barstools, subway seats, theater marquees, and other props from the grittier side of real life. He has since been labeled a "proletarian mythmaker" and the single artist who has done most to revive the human figure as an artistic subject. "The Steelmakers" marked a change for Segal in its concentration on community, as well as aesthetic, values. Segal has other public sculptures in Buffalo, New York; Greenwich, Connecticut; Philadelphia, Pennsylvania and Princeton, New Jersey.

In 1980 he completed a controversial work

entitled "Gay Liberation," depicting two pairs of homosexuals, one male, one female, which led to four years of "hurdle jumping" according to Joseph Bresnan, Director of Planning and Preservation of the New York City Department of Parks and Recreation. The proposed site for the sculpture is Christopher Park, a small triangular green designed as part of an early Victorian neighborhood now within the Greenwich Village Historic District. Run-down in recent years, it was scheduled for upgrading to accommodate the Segal sculpture. The site was chosen to commemorate the 1969 riot between police and homosexuals after a police raid on a bar frequented by homosexuals across the street from the park. The incident is considered a milestone in the homosexual rights movement.

The controversy developed when some members of a local neighborhood group, the Friends of Christopher Park, objected to the sculpture—calling it inappropriate because Segal's sculpture conflicted with the nineteenth century character of both the park and its architectural setting. In addition, they also protested the scale of the art work for the site. Proponents of the sculpture suggested that it was also the gay theme which caused opposition.

There is mixed response from the gay community concerning the choice of the artist and the portrayal of the gay couples. Bruce Voeller, president of the Mariposa Foundation, said he chose George Segal, because of his prominence as a figurative sculptor. "To have selected a sculptor because he was gay would be discrimination on the basis of sex" he said, "and opposition

Castings of the 'Gay Liberation' sculpture by George Segal are situated in Christopher Park, New York City, and on the Stanford University Campus, Palo Alto, California.

to that kind of discrimination is what our movement is all about." Other gay members of the community disliked the stereotypical figures and pointed out that community opinion was not solicited.

Besides the controversy over the placement of the sculpture, the City's intricate approval process further delayed implementation. The community board approved the sculpture in 1980, and voted again in 1982 to approve the preliminary nineteenth century park design. Then, the Landmarks Preservation Commission, the City Department of Parks and Recreation, and the Arts Commission each gave their necessary approval during 1983–1984, completing design plans, which integrated Segal's white bronze sculpture with Victorian elements—cast iron fencing and landscaping. Each city group based its approval on the design quality, finding the sculpture an appropriate addition to the site. The neighborhood controversy has died down.

One last hurdle must be met before Segal's sculpture is installed. The donors want the city to return the sculpture if it is re-moved from the site within the next twenty years. The city is negotiating, and one alternative is to call the sculpture a long-term loan, as they are unaccustomed to a 'strings attached' gift. The city is also reluctant to promise that the piece will remain on one particular site. In the event that it is repeatedly vandalized, the city wants the right to move it to a safer location. They do not want the financial responsibility of having to make frequent repairs because of a prescribed location. The sculpture which was on exhibit in the Brooklyn Museum was installed in spring, 1985.

The Mariposa Foundation requested that Segal make two castings of "Gay Liberation," one for each coast. The western site at Stanford University, Palo Alto, received the sculpture in February, 1984. It stands on a grassy area near benches, next to the main administration bulding. The sculpture was badly vandalized a month after installation. Sent back to Segal's studio in New Jersey, repaired, and re-installed on the same site in June, 1984, it has suffered no further damage at this writing.

Tree Sculpture

Summary

The giant Elm, perhaps 200 years old, used to shade the whole quiet corner of Gorham and Lincoln Roads in Brookline. When it was affected by Dutch Elm Disease, the Parks Department of the town tried hard to save it but without success. The neighborhood was very saddened to see the massive elm cut down to a stark stump about 11 feet high which dominated the corner. Some months later, after looking at it repeatedly, local artist Douglas Smith, a commercial illustrator
with a few small carvings to his credit, was drawn to the door of 21 Gorham Ave, almost against his will, to ask the homeowners Mr. and Mrs. J. F. Louis what they planned to do with the dead tree. He showed them photos of Fred Faller's tree sculptures in Cambridge, which had been a delightful revelation to Smith years earlier.

I had always thought what a great new form of American Folk Art they were, and had filed the notion away in my brain that I would

Douglas Smith working on dead elm in Brookline, Massachusetts

Dragon and Child Tree Carving

love to give that kind of gift of public art to *my* community someday. Eight years later or so, the impulse emerged when I saw this unusually large, unusually shaped stump in an ideal sculptural setting: a quiet, straight street, corner location, framed by bushes and picket fence, lovely Victorian house behind. . . . Though I'd never carved *anything* of this scale before, and wasn't certain I was capable of it, I couldn't resist.

The owners of the dead tree, the Louises, were enthusiastic. The artist assured them that he would not carve anything lewd, political, grotesque, or abstract; that probably the sculpture would be some bird or animal form, something both the neighbors and their children could enjoy. Smith also obtained the approval of the Parks Department, as the elm was considered a "Public Shade Tree," and within their jurisdiction.

As Smith sat across from the stump sketching possible subjects that would fit the odd shape, neighborhood adults and children stopped to overlook and comment on the sketches. When Smith first tried a dragon, the children almost universally declared it to be their choice. One in particular, Sasha Wizansky, 9, was enthusiastic about it. Smith started to focus on dragons,

and when faced with an excess of wood where the creature's tail would fall, hit on the notion of a sort of 'built-in' community involvement; the extra wood could become that small girl lifted in the benevolent dragon's swing-like forked tail!

The rough-carving began in June '83, after Smith had modeled some small clay mockups of the piece. Working solely with hand tools passed on by once tree-carver Faller, whom Smith had consulted on the project, the artist roughed out the sculpture by the fall. Over the next two summers, working whenever possible and having obtained a $500 grant from the Brookline Council for the Arts and Humanities which paid for supplies, Smith finally completed the carving in August 1985. The sculpture has become a landmark, as hundreds of people have

Open Hand Free Sculpture by Fred Faller, Cambridge, Massachusetts

Playground sculpture by Richard Beyer in Buries Park, Seattle, Washington.

stopped by to enjoy the much-lamented old elm's new life as public art.

Smith says:

> I hope to find time, and the means, to do more public sculpture, because the *obvious* excitement and enjoyment that lights people's faces when they come by the tree is a tremendous reward for an artist. While I worked, school groups would come up with their teachers to talk to me; older kids would want to try the mallet and chisel, and I'd give little demonstrations. They'd climb the dragon and chat with me while I worked. The corner almost became a social meeting place. It was wonderful—I don't believe I could give this up now!

The Cambridge tree sculpture that inspired Douglas Smith is still standing on Putnam Avenue. Fred Faller's "Open Hand" was funded by the Cambridge Arts Council's annual River Festival. Al Gowen, the Council's first administrator, described the tree sculpture in *Nuts and Bolts*, a casebook on public design projects, written in 1980. He expressed the hope that one day the City Parks Department would emply an artist-in-residence to carve all the dead trees that the department usually removes.

Artists in other parts of the country are also transforming dead trees into sculptural landmarks. In a suburb of Seattle, Richard Beyer sculpted a cedar stump as part of a playground in Buries Park, designed by landscape architects Jones and Jones. Entitled "Dancing Around the Tree to Make it Green Again," it is designed so that children can climb onto the carved fairy tale figures that encircle the tree stump.

A seventeen foot tall oak trunk on a busy corner near a Silver Springs, Maryland metro station is no longer an eyesore but a modern day totem pole, sculpted by Michael Higgs, a self-proclaimed "third generation whittler." Entitled "A Tribute to Man's Endurance Over Time," the sculpture combines figures of the seven sages of time and an anonymous trio of man, woman, and child, symbolizing the family unit. The faces are composites of passersby, who spontaneously posed for him. Because carving 'in situ' is a necessity for dead tree sculptures, the process often causes more of a stir in the community than the finished carving. Passersby can witness firsthand an artisan at work.

Kent City Hall Reliefs

Background

When the city of Kent, Washington, allocated $1,500,000 for the construction of a new City Hall in 1969, architect Fred Bassetti decided that artwork of some sort should be incorporated into the building's brick design. Setting aside a sum of $1,000, he contacted Seattle sculptor Richard Beyer. Beyer, who had never used the medium before, was unsure of the brick's malleability, hoping that it could be used for complete reliefs rather than merely as individual ornamentation. After experimenting with brick carving and finding it to his liking, Beyer agreed to prepare a panel for the lobby. The initial sketch, consisting of a large television set with the words, "VOTE NO!" across the center, indicated the artist's personal disdain for government. The Kent Art Council

NAME: *Kent City Hall Reliefs*, Kent, Washington
PROJECT: Over twenty pictorial reliefs, carved in brick, located throughout Kent's new City Hall; among the subjects depicted are local history and poetic pictorial narratives
ARTIST: Richard Beyer
AGENCY: The City of Kent; Architect Fred Bassetti
SIZE: Each varies from approximately 1 foot to 12 feet across
DATE: Started 1970, completed 1971
COST: $1000
MATERIAL: Green Brick
PHOTOGRAPHY: Kent Photography, Kent, Washington

approved the submission anyway, but the mayor intervened, expressing a desire for a more historical theme. The series of reliefs finally chosen stretched the $1,000 fee to its limit. Beyer became engrossed in the process, and before he was finished created over twenty separate carvings. Besides the main panel in the lobby, works were created for the building exterior, the stairwells, and the jail cells.

Description

The panel in the lobby is the largest and most intricate of the works scattered throughout the building, and the only one directly addressing historical themes. In three dozen representative scenes, it depicts the history of the valley as it might have occurred: Chief Seattle speaking at the 1855 signing of an Indian treaty; the pioneer, Ezra Meeks, as an old man, with birds nesting in his beard; a collection of stills from the Prohibition era; a family of Japanese-Americans departing in trucks for "resettlement camps" during WWII. Deep relief in the surface of the brick heightens the drama of each scene. The smaller panels protrude from the walls, and they usually consist of fewer than a dozen bricks. Most notable of these are a series of poetic pictorial narratives, which use modern citizens and animals to illustrate the theme of relationships between people and community. In a booklet displaying some of the carvings, Beyer accompanies each with a descriptive poem; one example concludes:

> Labor breathing dirty air
> Old people left to die in cold rooms
> Men walk on the moon
> And recall our innocent enthusiasm for
>   innovations

With Beyer's verses, the pictorial narratives become strong evocations of frustration and melancholy as reactions to modern life. Unaccompanied by any other explanation on the walls, they are left open to individual interpretation. The jail cell reliefs are light-hearted reflections on incarceration. Inspired by the fable of Jonah, each separate cell carving depicts a man inside the belly of a different animal. A fierce pair of carved dogs, one atop the other, guards the police car entranceway.

The City Hall, an unadorned four-story structure of red brick and glass, expresses the architect's personal philosophy of government, which he feels "should not harm people." Thus, the edges of the building are blunted, so that no one could possibly get hurt on a sharp corner. With both artist and architect working from a shared humanistic ideal, the artwork fits into the building as a part of a unified whole.

Design Impact

The City Hall carvings, Beyer's own anti-governmental views notwithstanding, have been praised and welcomed by city officials and town residents alike. While ostensibly simple, they work on many levels. Most obviously, the carvings make local history and topics of concern accessible to the public in an imaginative style. Architecturally, they ornament such generally sterile institutional spaces as stairwells and corridors, and, located at eye-level, reinforce the human scale of the building. There is an additive effect in their being spread out; the same amount of work seems to achieve more in dispersal than it would as one solid display. To be experienced fully, the carvings not only require personal interpretation, but a tour of the City Hall. Thus they reach out to the individual, and to a degree imply the same concern for the individual on the part of the city government housed within. The personal scale and folkart style in fact seem in keeping with the scale of the small city. In 1975 a similar project was attempted in downtown Seattle. Fred Bassetti, who was the architect, engaged Richard Beyer again to ornament the building and surrounding plaza with a series of dispersed brick carvings. In that case, the would-be sponsors at GSA rejected the proposal, in favor of several large-scale pieces.

Steaming Kettle

Summary

The steaming copper tea kettle above the old Oriental Tea Company storefront is a noticeable landmark, emphasizing the juxtaposition of modern and 19th century elements in Boston's Government Center area. At the time of its installation in 1873, it was the focus of city-wide fascination. Constructed on commission by Hicks & Badger, the largest coppersmiths in Boston, the kettle was in the heart of the downtown district. It naturally drew attention to itself, with its imposing size, placement fifteen feet above the storefront façade, and steaming spout—connected by a pipe to a boiler behind the store. Describing the object's significance to Boston, a *Boston Times* article

of 1875 noted: "We all ought to take pride in our big tea kettle. We have long had the biggest organ, the biggest monument, and the biggest bass drum, and now we have the biggest tea kettle in the country."

Since the vessel had been sold by weight, its capacity was unknown and became the subject of intense speculation. Deciding to capitalize on public curiosity, the tea company announced a contest, awarding a chest (40 lbs.) of tea to whoever most closely estimated the volume in gallons, and 25 pounds of coffee as second prize. The measurement would be performed by the City Sealer of Weights and Measures in a public ceremony at noon, on the first of January, 1875. By the day of reckoning, over twelve thousand guesses had been registered, estimates ranging from under ten to over three thousand gallons. The same *Boston Times* article of that month described the enthusiasm directed towards the contest:

> The tea kettle excitement has run nearly as high as the tea excitement of old, and is almost an historical incident in the career of our noble city . . . It has been talked about everywhere except in prayer meetings, and we doubt not that some of the guessing professors of religion have had hard work to keep their minds free of the problem even on those sol-

NAME: *Steaming Kettle*, Boston, Massachusetts
PROJECT: Large copper kettle, with steaming spout, hanging above storefront of tea company in City Hall Plaza
ARTIST: Hicks & Badger, Coppersmiths
AGENCY: Oriental Tea Company
SIZE: "Eight boys and a six-footer"
DATE: 1873
COST: Unknown
MATERIAL: Copper
PHOTOGRAPHY: Renata von Tscharner

emn occasions. Schoolgirls and bootblacks, clergymen, laborers, college professors, keno-players, duck-shooters, wealthy merchants, strong minded women, politicians, lawyers, editors, hotel keepers, dignified judges, city and state officials—all, and more, have, without regard to sex or previous condition, had their minds chained to this problem.

The ceremony attracted between 10,000 and 15,000 people. At the very beginning the crowd was roused to applause, when eight boys and then a six-foot man emerged from the container as the measuring commenced. After an hour of suspense, the final result was announced: the kettle held 227 gallons, 2 quarts, 1 pint and 3 gills. The first prize was divided between eight people who had guessed to the pint, the second prize was divided between seven people, and for a generation the incident remained in the public memory.

When a large-scale urban renewal program created Government Center in the 1960s, a great many square blocks of old buildings were destroyed, and only the Sears Crescent block including the tea store was left standing. Today, silhouetted against the monolithic structures of the Center, the kettle, still steaming, hangs above the tea company's storefront, a symbol of Victorian Boston. The company, in fact, has thrived. Converted into a coffee-shop, it has opened two new branches, each with a miniature kettle of its own. Modern sign ordinances, attempting to control visual excess, would not permit similarly sized replicas of the kettle to be hung.

Pioneer Murals

Background

Experiencing the walls of downtown Chemainus gives the sensation of moving through the pages of an illustrated history book. Larger than life-sized figures ride by in a horse-drawn cart. Further down the street, loggers hang out in front of their 1902 bunkhouse, operate a steam donkey to pull logs from the forest, or fell gigantic trees with axes. Around the corner a herd of oxen parade through town, lugging lumber as they did in 1898. These are not mirages but some of the subjects for the sixteen historically accurate murals that cover building facades and walls of Chemainus, British Columbia. The murals have literally caused a renaissance in this small logging town of 5000 located on Vancouver Island, fifty miles from Victoria, and forty-two miles (or a one and a half hour ferry ride) to Vancouver. In a brilliant strategy combining art, history and tourism, Chemainus conceived and implemented a unique economic and physical revitalization plan.

Like so many other towns whose destiny has been determined by the rise and fall of a single industry, only a few years ago Chemainus was close to becoming a ghost town. In 1862 a small, water-powered sawmill was built here, and four generations of mills succeeded it, representing the longest continuous lumber production on one site in Western North America. By the 1970s the mill's business diminished, causing downtown commercial activity to decline. This economic recession was augmented by the construction of new shopping malls in the region, which drained sales from the small businesses in the area.

As local shopowners in Chemainus pondered their dilemma, an event occurred which unwittingly became the catalyst for revitalization. In 1980 a Vancouver Island tourist map was published and inadvertently placed Chemainus in the wrong location. It did not seem terribly important, as few visitors came to Chemainus. However, this minor mishap was the straw that broke the camel's back, or perhaps in this case the last blow of the axe to fell the tree. Community members refused to view the mistake as a bad omen. Instead they decided to find a way to bring *more* tourists to Chemainus as a solution to their economic problem and to show the city officials in Vancouver that their mistake would have serious repercussions. The local Chamber of Commerce asked Chemainus resident Karl Schutz, then a semi-retired businessman, to produce a tourist map for local promotion. Schutz in turn enlisted W. H. Olsen to write an accompanying text. Olsen, author and local historian, agreed if Schutz would help him publish the second edition of *Water over the Wheel*, a history of Chemainus' pioneering days. In a stroke of intuition, Schutz decided that the book, which included many old photos of Chemainus, could become the catalyst for attracting tourists to the town. He foresaw that the town's history could be visually displayed and integrated with other physical improvements to stimulate commercial investment.

In 1981 the Mayor instigated the creation of a Downtown Revitalization Committee, at a public meeting, with Schutz as the full-time coordinator and seven other members. The committee's plans included traditional streetscape design elements—widening sidewalks, re-routing traffic, adding canopies, arcades, new benches and lighting. When someone suggested painting roses on the building facades, Schutz recalled a visit he had made fifteen years ago to a monastic town in Romania, which was decorated with sixteenth-century frescos depicting the town's history. Schutz suggested a similar series of historic murals for Chemainus. Photos and tales from *Water over the Wheel*

would be the subject matter for the murals and become a promotional tool. He believed this scheme for making Chemainus a new attraction recognized for its public art would put the town on the map forever, and this time in the right location.

NAME: *Chemainus 1891*
PROJECT: One of the first murals which greets visitors near the entrance to the shopping district and Heritage Square; it is the only mural in the ensemble which includes a bird's eye view of the natural and built environment of Chemainus, British Columbia
ARTIST: David Maclagan
SIZE: 54 x 12 feet
DATE: 1983
COST: $15,000
MATERIAL: Acrylic paint
PHOTOGRAPHY: Chemainus Festival of Murals

Schutz had yet to convince the town that the scheme would work. While street revitalization plans were underway in 1981, Schutz searched for an artist and found Frank Lewis, who created the first mural under the critical eyes of the townspeople. In April, a two-day Pioneer Celebration inaugurated the revitalization effort begun just four months earlier. Instead of the standard ribbon-cutting event, the Mayor cut a log with a cross-cut saw, announcing the opening of the new downtown shopping district, and a month later the first mural was completed. Said Schutz, now full-time director of Chemainus' Festival of Murals, "People were skeptical at first because they did not know what to expect, but after they could see the amenities in place, they wholeheartedly approved," and supported the art plan which specified more murals.

Having read about the Festival in regional newspapers, tourists soon began to arrive. The physical revitalization was accompanied by a psychological one, and so even when the saw mill soon closed down, spirits managed to remain positive, especially with the anticipation of increased tourism. The community's mood was reflected in the following statement by the Mayor, "We intend to let the whole world know Chemainus is still alive and kicking."[1] Five murals were painted by the end of the summer of 1982. Businesses began to see their investments returned. Funding for the revitalization projects came from a $300,000 long-term low interest loan and a grant supplied by the Ministry of Municipal Affairs. Private donations of materials and labor help support a yearly Festival of Murals, which has become an institution, as each summer more murals are added to enhance the town.

The initial five murals and the ensuing street facade renovations of 1982 nurtured the annual Festival of Murals, fostered more commercial activity, new businesses, an increase in population (mostly retirees) and a general resurgence in downtown activity. A full-time year-round Festival of Murals Office opened to plan the future summer events and coordinate new murals. Seven murals were painted during the 1983 Festival of Murals. The artists' progress became a public attraction, rivaling the finished results. The artists coordinated their work schedules so there would always be at least one mural in progress each day of the festival. At the July 2 kick-off celebration hundreds of townspeople and visitors were treated to parades, concerts, barbecues, and the Miss Chemainus Valley Pageant. This Festival of Murals hosted tens of thousands of visitors.

The 1984 Festival of Murals drew even larger crowds, with the organizers selling over $25,000 of mural-related souvenirs. While four new murals were being painted, townspeople and visitors also watched the progress of a 68-foot brigantine vessel under construction, with boatwrights using traditional methods. Named "Spirit of Chemainus," daily trips carried tourists from the 1986 Expo Fair in Vancouver to Chemainus.

A six-month mural symposium took place in 1986. Major Canadian artists have been invited to paint murals and hold seminars on the art of mural making. This symposium is an example of the new cultural opportunities now available to the region's residents. In addition to the three new art galleries, the influx of artists who have moved to Chemainus has helped expose "those who had never thought of art before," says Schultz, to both the visual and performing arts. A new theatre group is forming, and children in area schools have taken a greater interest in drawing and painting.

Description

Each of the sixteen murals scattered throughout the town depicts a historic vignette—portraying the logging industry, legendary individuals, memorable structures, and often the presence of the ocean, the forests, and the mountains. Each scene is an accurate depiction derived from historic photos. Many of the murals are by well-known Canadian artists such as Harry Heine, Harold Lyon, Paul Ygartua, David White and David Maclagan. There is no sequential connection amongst the murals, but a dramatic visual experience unfolds as one walks through the small downtown district. Although each mural was executed as an individual project, the cumulative effect is the attraction.

While other communities have used mural projects and facade renovations to create a Disney-world atmosphere, attracting tourists, Chemainus' murals offer authentic his-

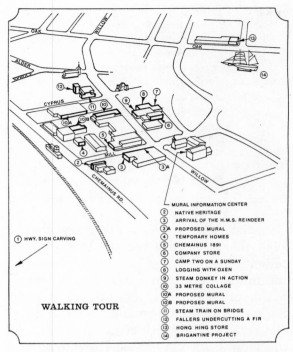

A map showing the location of the murals in Chemainus.

The following list appears within the map:

MURAL INFORMATION CENTER
② NATIVE HERITAGE
③ ARRIVAL OF THE H.M.S. REINDEER
③A PROPOSED MURAL
④ TEMPORARY HOMES
⑤ CHEMAINUS 1891
⑥ COMPANY STORE
⑦ CAMP TWO ON A SUNDAY
⑧ LOGGING WITH OXEN
⑨ STEAM DONKEY IN ACTION
⑩ 33 METRE COLLAGE
⑩A PROPOSED MURAL
⑩B PROPOSED MURAL
⑪ STEAM TRAIN ON BRIDGE
⑫ FALLERS UNDERCUTTING A FIR
⑬ HONG HING STORE
⑭ BRIGANTINE PROJECT

① HWY. SIGN CARVING

WALKING TOUR

toric documentation of local people, places and events, interpreted by reputable artists. The Revitalization Committee selected well-known artists based on their expertise in wildlife, pioneer history or maritime themes. Other less known artists came to visit Chemainus and offered their services. Despite the thematic unity, the murals display variations of representational styles of painting, from super-realist to naive. Both brushstroke and air brush techniques were employed.

Chemainus 1891

"Chemainus 1891" by David Maclagan portrays the Esquimalt and Nanaimo Railway running along the center of town as it looked in 1891 with the ocean and mountains as familiar background; in the foreground a horse-drawn cart brings a family back home from a visit in town. Like many of the other murals, it covers an entire side wall of a low-rise building. The surface is completely painted, and because these modern structures do not have cornices or exposed rooflines, the murals seem to pop out, without architectural border or contain-

ment. Bold additions to the town, the murals' impact upon the streetscape is mitigated by their shared color palette—mostly natural hues of browns, terra cottas, greys and greens. Real trees rise above the murals, and the painted sky fades into the real one.

Fallers Undercutting a Fir Tree

"Fallers Undercutting a Fir Tree" is painted on the firehouse tower by a visiting artist from Scotland, Thomas Johnston Robertson. Unlike the horizontal orientation of the other Chemainus murals, this four-story, twelve-foot-wide tower facade is a perfect foil for illustrating the felling of an enormous cedar tree. Two men work on the tree in the traditional manner with double-edged felling axes and a thin bladed, two-man crosscut saw. The dark branchless trunk rises from the earth and reaches up to the top edge of the painting. One imagines the trunk continuing upward invisibly, lost in the thick forest glimpsed behind the firehouse.

Besides representing some of Canada's most prominent artists, what makes Chemainus' murals special is their close spatial proximity, which affords the opportunity of discovering the series on foot. A pedestrian pace offers ever-changing views as one approaches each successive mural, like the sensation of viewing a motion picture.

The art is effective *because* of its setting, not in spite of it. Compared to a larger physical area or more populated town, the intensity and number of visual cues are minimized in a small place like Chemainus. Therefore the addition of sixteen large-scale murals to this kind of setting has a much grander visual impact than if these same sixteen murals were similarly spaced in a city like Boston.

Design Impact

In 1983, during the second annual Festival of Murals, a Canadian film crew—Petra Film Productions, in cooperation with the National Film Board of Canada, began a seven-week filming project, documenting the story behind the rejuvenation of Che-

NAME: *Fallers Undercutting a Fir Tree*
PROJECT: This mural, depicting an early method for cutting down trees, is painted on one of the most prominent locations in town—the four-story fire tower, which rises above most other structure
ARTIST: Thomas Johnston Robertson
DATE: August, 1982
SIZE: 12x33 feet
COST: $10,000
MATERIAL: Acrylic paint
PHOTOGRAPHY: Chemainus Festival of Murals

Canadian Artists in Vancouver, says that in 1984 they created a special Award of Excellence expressly for Chemainus "because the murals represent an enormous contribution of high artistic merit to public art in the Northwest." Chemainus also won top distinction along with eight other cities in the New York City-based Downtown Revitalization Awards in April, 1983.

Elmar Schultes, a renowned Canadian sculptor/carver, was commissioned in 1983 to carve a three-dimensional monumental sculpture based on the mural of the same name, "Steam Donkey at Work." Located on the Trans-Canada Highway one mile from the town center, the 18x10 foot wood sculpture greets passersby on the highways traveling north. It marks the turnoff for those visiting Chemainus, and acts as a gateway to the city. It displays the words, "Chemainus—Municipality of North Cowichan" and "The Little Town That Did," the motto which sums up Chemainus' revival.

In addition to the murals, local artists contribute their skills during the summertime Festival of Murals "beautifying" trash bins and selling their crafts at sidewalk sales. The Festival of Murals Office sells souvenirs, including pins, mural books, posters and T-shirts. The annual proceeds for the most part make the summer-long Festival a self-supporting venture, though the government has continued to help defray the costs of the festivities.

A new kiosk now supplies mural information. It was designed to be dismantled

mainus. They produced a thirty-minute documentary film which was shown across Canada, in which the murals were called "one of the most dynamic displays of color, history and art in North America."[2] Bunty Hales, gallery manager of the Federation of for winter storage and re-assembled each summer. A summer staff of students paid by a government program helps run the festival and gives group tours of the murals.

Business in the downtown not only has stabilized but is growing. Merchants estimate a 30–40 percent increase in sales since 1982, compared to the period preceding the revitalization project. Fourteen new businesses have opened since 1982—including an ice cream parlor, a tea house, an arts supply store and the three art galleries—a significant figure for a town located in a rural region. Facade renovations are an ongoing process along Willow and Mill Streets, the main shopping area, reviving the "heritage" style—with rusticated timber logs or fish-scale shingles. Both renovated structures and new buildings are given a historic flavor with boardwalks, planters, and lanterns. In some instances, the addition of covered arcades have unified blocks of store fronts.

Recently there have been three new commercial developments, all entailing expansion or renovation of existing buildings. Christy Lapi, a staffwriter for the local newspaper, calls this development "a direct spinoff of the Chemainus revitalization and the Festival of Murals tourist-attracting power."[3] Two of the projects convert existing single-unit structures into multiple retail units. One of the restoration projects on Willow Street, called Willow Street Place, allotted space for two murals, an example of how this town's established precedent for art planning has propagated.

Tourists, at the rate of roughly twenty a day, continue to seek out Chemainus in the off-season and swell to tens of thousands a day in summer, adding to the commercial activity. Beginning in May, 1985, touring companies are sending thirteen buses a day throughout the summer. The tour offers a showing of the film "The Little Town That Could," lunch and a guided tour of the murals.

Schutz says the economic impact "goes above any expectations originally conceived by the Revitalization Committee. What was achieved in three years was more than was envisioned in their five year plan." But the other new market group is the people from the region who now make special trips to shop in the pleasant atmosphere of Chemainus.

The latest addition to Chemainus is Heritage Square—a people-gathering spot at the intersection of the main shopping streets. Framed on two sides by murals, the small open space serves as a meeting place and rest stop. The Revitalization Committee, which also reviews all mural proposals, commissioned a fountain in the center entitled "In Search of Snipes" that is based on a folk tradition of legendary snipes existing in the area. Gullible people were given lights and sacks at night and told to hunt the ever-elusive mythical beasts. Phase One of the fountain incorporates falling water and landscaping; Phase Two will be a life-size bronze of the "snipe searchers". The North Cowichan Council donated $20,000 for the site preparation, and additional money is being sought for Phase Two.

In January 1985 the MacMillan Bloedel sawmill reopened after three years and the "revitalization indeed became a revivification". But Chemainus is no longer a one industry town. Tourism has joined the lumber trade. In addition to the economic prosperity and the visual enhancement of the town, the people of Chemainus have gained a sense of community pride. Their collective energy was the driving force behind this merging of art, history and economic growth. Not only did they achieve all this without the aid of private developers from outside Chemainus who would have taken much of the profits out of the community, but they implemented their plan in a record time of less than two years. The townspeople have given Chemainus a self-sufficiency that marks a new chapter in the town's history and is a rare enough occurrence in small towns today; the art work that has ensued is a nationally recognized tribute to Chemainus' history and to the craft of mural making.

Bojangles

Background

Bill "Bojangles" Robinson, in a sense, is a perfect subject for a monument. He is the epitome of the local boy who made good; he tapped his way to wealth, international acclaim, and a place in history; but he never forgot his hometown. Richmond returned the compliment in 1973, more than a generation after Robinson's death in 1949, with the dedication of the Bojangles statue. The statute represented tribute from the community to its progeny who became the greatest tap dancer of his time.

Robinson was as extraordinary a person as a performer, and at the height of his fame, during the Depression, he was probably the most famous black man in the United States, a celebrity of almost mythical proportions. Orphaned at an early age, Robinson spent most of his youth in the streets of Richmond, working as a peasheller, and dancing on the sidewalks for pennies from passersby. He began performing in minstrel shows at the age of nine, and for the next three decades worked steadily in vaudeville and nightclubs, charming audiences while expanding and perfecting his technique.

With the Broadway musical "Blackbirds of 1928" Robinson achieved overnight fame. In the next decade, he became the first black man to star in films, including four immensely popular musicals with child star Shirley Temple. He also starred in several Broadway shows, and played the lead in "The Hot Mikado" at the 1931 World's Fair. He always highlighted his acts with incomparable dance routines, and would often sing and joke while dancing, generating an ease and charm that endeared him to critics, peers and audiences alike. Off stage, his fiery temper, penchant for vanilla ice cream, and record-breaking times for running backwards

added to the larger-than-life image of Bojangles as a personality.

In the course of his career, he earned over four million dollars, gambled much of it away, and donated almost all the rest to charities.

Robinson never forgot his birthplace. In 1933 he presented the city with a set of traffic lights, then a rarity in Richmond, which were to be installed at the site of a dangerous school crossing. Later, at the peak of his fame, he wrote:

I love my home town of Richmond . . . like people love the town they were born in and where they played when they were little . . . Those people in Richmond loved me and gave me a lot of things I can never pay for, no matter how hard I try.

Throughout his life, Bojangles regarded Richmond as his home, visiting local friends often, and contributing to city institutions, both black and white.

In 1972, the Richmond City Council renamed the small triangle of land in his former neighborhood where the dancer had donated the traffic lights as Bojangles Robinson Square. The Astoria Beneficial Club, a men's civic organization, felt that something more representative of the man was in order. A proposal to bronze a pair of the famous dancing shoes was discussed and rejected, and a fund-raising campaign was initiated for a larger-than-life statue. After consulting with Reynolds Aluminum Company, which offered financial and technical assistance, the club decided that the medium should be aluminum alloy.

Chosen to sculpt the work was John Temple Witt, a Richmond native and teacher at Randolph-Macon College, one of two men recommended as experienced in the medium. The project was delayed at first, when the clay support for the model collapsed and had to be replaced with styrofoam. A protest by some members of the black community, who felt that it was inappropriate to commission a white sculptor for the work, also hindered the campaign. The $20,000 required for construction was at last achieved through contributions from Reynolds, banks, tobacco companies, businesses, civic groups, a local theater, and many community residents; an independent drive launched by the Peony Garden Club went towards landscaping the park. A life-long childhood friend of Robinson dedicated the statue in 1973.

Description

While selecting a pose for the figure, Witt repeatedly viewed films of Robinson dancing, particularly one scene from "The Little Rebel" and a five-second newsreel. He chose the famous backwards stairstep, an intricate move which Robinson reputedly learned as a child on the entrance to the Sixth Street Police Station.

The finished statue depicts Bojangles in the middle of the step, one leg behind the other, arms poised deftly at his sides, and a characteristically broad, gleaming smile. The figure is roughly textured, giving the overall work a muted sheen. Disappointingly, the features are not perfectly descriptive of Robinson, who had broader shoulders and less angular face than his monument portrays. But the spirit is his: a kinetic pose that captures the natural ease and charm that defined the performer. The figure of Bojangles is nine feet high, rising sixteen feet above the small park on a black granite pedestal. A cobblestone base underneath represents the streets of Richmond, where Robinson started it all.

Design Impact

Some blacks questioned the selection of a white sculptor. Clarence Hagins, the black

NAME: *Bojangles Statue*, Richmond, Virginia
PROJECT: Larger-than-life statue of famed tap-dancer Bill "Bojangles" Robinson located in the neighborhood of his youth on a triangle now called Bojangles Robinson Square
ARTIST: John Temple Witt
AGENCY: The Astoria Beneficial Club
SIZE: Statue is 9 feet tall; the base rises 16 feet above street
DATE: Started 1972, completed 1973
COST: Monument—$20,000; Landscaping—$12,000
MATERIAL: Statue—cast aluminum; Pedestal—black granite; Base—cobblestones
PHOTOGRAPHY: Richmond Newspapers

New York artist who led the protest, argued that only a black man could fully understand the black man's culture, and therefore "do his subject justice." The sponsoring Richmond club maintained that the choice should be made on the basis of merit alone, regardless of race. (Similarly a proposed George Segal work depicting two pairs of homosexuals has broached related questions in New York's gay community, amidst a wider and more heated controversy.)

Among the scores of public monuments in Richmond, so many of which honor Confederate heroes, the Bojangles statue is the only sculpture honoring a black man.

The mutual affection between Robinson and Richmond was an ongoing event. Probably the greatest expressions of gratitude the city gave its son occurred during Bojangles' lifetime: a theater was named after him, newspaper editorials lauded the man regularly—at least annually, on his birthday—

and crowds went "steadily gaga" at each of his frequent appearances. The statue commemorates an inspirational individual at the place he considered his home, among people he considered his neighbors.

In 1976, after the installation of the statue, the neighborhood was designated as a district on the National Register of Historic Places, and has since undergone considerable revitalization.

Brickworker and Ballplayer

Background

The Midas of Greek mythology possessed the ability to turn everyday objects—including people—into gold. The citizens of blue-collar North Cambridge, Massachusetts, have seen a similar transformation of two familiar figures, converted this time to solid brick. The brick-maker and ball player of the Rindge Field playground link the neighborhood's past to its present. Golden memories have been transformed into a tangible contemporary tribute.

Brickworks, the kilns and sheds where bricks are molded and fired, once dotted the landscape of North Cambridge. Long after their disappearance, their residue remains—small ponds formed from used clay pits, and a city carpeted in brick sidewalk. The brickworks operated from 1844 until 1952, providing jobs for first generation Irish and French Canadian immigrants, who settled in North Cambridge in a neighborhood soon to be called Dublin. The neighborhood has retained its character; descendants of many original families still live in this district of densely packed wooden triple-deckers.

The brick sculpture grew out of a neigh-

NAME: *Brickworker and Ballplayer*, Cambridge, Massachusetts
PROJECT: A solid brick and mortar life-size depiction of a brickworker and ball player taking a rest, located on edge of Rindge Field
ARTIST: David Judelson
AGENCY: Cambridge Arts Council
SIZE: 6½ feet high, 12 x 6 feet
DATE: July 1983
COST: $15,000 initial commission, $10,000 additional before completion
MATERIAL: Brick
PHOTOGRAPHY: The Townscape Institute

borhood improvement project for Rindge Field, the major playground in the area. The neighborhood was first concerned with the safety of the intersection behind the backstop of the playground's baseball field. Under the Community Development Block grant process, local residents held a number of neighborhood meetings to discuss enriching an expanded corner crossing area. Residents wanted brick surfacing for the crossing, rather than concrete, as well as protective bollards and plantings. One neighborhood activist, Conn Nugent, also headed a foundation which channeled some of the philanthropic interests of a distinguished and traditionally affluent family on Boston's North Shore. Nugent saw a way of combining the foundation's interest in neighborhood projects with the Community Development Block grant proposal for streetscape improvements: the Rindge Field crossing would include public art that would evoke some of the neighborhood's historical associations. To this end, Nugent arranged a grant to the Cambridge Arts Council for North Cambridge, which then secured matching funds from the Community Development budget for the beautification of the intersection.

The One Percent for Public Art Commission, which administers the Arts Council's public art projects, designed a process that involved both the neighborhood and the Community Development Department in decision-making for the project. Three neighborhood residents, including a ceramic artist, a Planning Department officer, and Conn Nugent, met with the Arts Council staff and one member of the One Percent Commission, forming a Rindge Field art committee. Since an open competition would have required considerable staff energy, eroded funds, and possibly produced highly visible proposals for art that the community might subsequently have rejected, this committee chose to hold a limited competition and define the key metaphors of the project. It gave much more guidance than most public art competitions because the committee

felt that, if they had clear criteria for evaluating proposals from selected artists, they would reduce the risk of public disappointment. John Chandler, director of the Public Arts Commission, and Ronald Lee Fleming, chairman, with the assistance of the Cambridge Historical Commission staff, discovered old photographs of the brickworks, and with the neighborhood committee gathered information about the families that lived there. With this material, they compiled an "Environmental Brief" defining the site and its design contraints and surveying how people used the space and their concern for practical utility. The brief also included some photographs of the kilns and information about the history of brick making in Cambridge and Somerville. Finally, after reviewing all this information on history, design and behavior, the committee was ready to suggest themes and metaphors which the artists might consider. The metaphor of brick as a bond between the community and its past seemed the strongest idea.

Six artists, selected for their skill in ceramics, received copies of an "Environmental Profile" that combined the information in the brief with the thematic suggestions. Their submissions included two proposals for brick sculptures recalling the shapes of the large round kilns that used to stand nearby. David Judelson suggested a carved brick figure of a brick worker. The art committee considered these proposals in light of the available budget, quality of design, and capacity to evoke neighborhood associations. The neighborhood advisory board involved in the Community Development Block Grant also reviewed the projects. Both favored the brickmaker sculpture. Community representatives from the two committees suggested that the proposal include a ball player since the piece was to be located on the edge of a ball field, and since the ball field had been a traditional vehicle for upward mobility in the neighborhood. The young sons of brick workers who excelled on the Rindge sandlot received athletic scholarships to college. Judelson, an architect and ceramicist, expanded this proposal to include a drinking fountain. This served the community's interest in meeting a utilitarian as well as an artistic function behind the backstop.

Description

Two life-size figures—one a brickworker sitting on a bench, the other a ball player leaning against a drinking fountain—face each other across a two-foot span of paved brick. The figures are made of standard-sized brick and mortar set in Flemish bond, which imposes a certain level of abstraction and compactness to their demeanor. However, the blockiness of the material is softened by the sculptural treatment of the hands, feet and faces, which give the shapes a certain stolid personality.

The artist produced his bricks in the Stiles and Hart Brick Company, in Bridgewater,

House Speaker 'Tip' O'Neill, grandson of a brickmaker, points at the names of brickmaking families at the dedication ceremonies for the Brickworker and Ballplayer sculpture, located in the Cambridge, Massachusetts, neighborhood where he grew up and continues to live.

Massachusetts, working alongside professional brickworkers. First, the pieces were constructed of green, or unhardened, bricks. They were then carved, and next, dismantled, so each brick could be numbered and then fired. Last, Judelson reassembled the work for the final installation on site. As an integral part of the art work, a veritable directory of neighborhood names is carved into the brick. On the bench are inscribed the brick companies and the dates of their operations in North Cambridge. The surface around the drinking fountain contains names of actual brickworkers—families like Sullivan, O'Connor and Desrosiers. A local youth, stopping for a drink after a ballgame might find his own history at his finger tips. A short historic account of North Cambridge compiled by Eve Sullivan, a local resident and school teacher, has been impressed with lead type in the brick pavement between the figures.

Design Impact

Celebration of the sculpture's completion took place in July, 1983, with House Speaker "Tip" O'Neill, who grew up in this neighborhood, acting as guest of honor. On a platform lined with red, white and blue bunting, Tip O'Neill, the grandson of a brickmaker, was presented with a brick stamped with his family name, like those set around the drinking fountain. O'Neill's speech rose above the usual political sophistries expected on such occasions, as it wove the history of the place, his own childhood, and the childhoods of many in the audience of three hundred. "Place connections," said the speaker, "create a sense of community and proprietorship in neighborhoods." The Chairman of the One Percent Commission, in response to this talk, asked the Speaker of the House to encourage national public art funding which could have an impact on neighborhoods like North Cambridge, and which would acknowledge the legitimacy of having works that are both commemorative and responsive to neighborhood concerns.

The Environmental Profile concept utilized in this project is now being employed for some of the other projects of the One Percent for Public Art Commission, and also by the Arts-on-the-Line Program, which commissions art for new and renovated stations on the subway lines run by the Metropolitan Boston Transit Authority.

The artist, David Judelson, found O'Neill's remarks "a gratifying validation of my work." The neighborhood seemed to like the work because it acknowledged them, not only in the process of gaining consent, but also in the way the product was crafted—involving two skilled bricklayers utilizing neighborhood names around the drinking fountain, and serving a utilitarian function that supports their athletic facilities.

A Drop in the Bucket

Background

Today, Foley Square in lower Manhattan is a cityscape of concrete and steel. But until about 1810, the area just north of the square was the site of Manhattan's largest body of fresh water known then as Collect Pond. The lost memory of that pond and the degradation it suffered offer a metaphor about the American experience which artist and lawyer, Jane Greengold, recalls with a wooden sculpture of a late eighteenth century water filter. She creates a fictional character, Charles Cooper, who cares enough about the pond to invent a filter designed to save it, and thus reminds us, with this temporary exhibition, of both the fragility of our resources and promise of redemption.

Now, the visitor can find it easy to believe that under the concrete sidewalks of Foley Square, there is only more concrete and the rubble of early buildings. But, when this area was a body of fresh water, some fifty feet deep, clear and filled with fish and fresh water oysters, it was surrounded by rolling hills and blackberry brambles. The pond was a locale of natural beauty, the sort of place that people now would drive miles to see.

By the 1730s, distilleries, ceramic potteries and tanneries were constructed around the pond. Slaughter houses, rope walks, and furnaces followed: the filthy nuisance industries all dumped their waste products into the pond. In 1778, during the British occupation of the city, a British officer published a notice forbidding people "to wash clothing of any kind in the fresh water pond, or have garbage and dirt in or near the same." However, by that time people doing their laundry were far from the worst offenders. The industries were making the water stink. In 1785, the pond was referred to as a very common sewer.

By 1789, private developers tried to create a real estate development that would have saved the pond by surrounding it with a park. The plan failed because local industrial land owners would not join in or sell their land, and property buyers could not believe that land so far north would become valuable.

The pollution was allowed to continue until the pond smelled so foul it could no longer be tolerated. By then the city had grown northward to the pond, and the land had become so valuable that the city decided to do away with the pond. Over a period of eight years, from 1803–11, cartloads filled with earth that once formed the surrounding hills were dumped into the pond,

NAME: *A Drop in the Bucket*, New York City
PROJECT: Re-creation of a fictional water filter, and written journals of its inventor, in memory of a pond which actually existed on the site
ARTIST: Jane Greengold
AGENCY: Sponsored by Creative Time, a not-for-profit arts organization that assists visual and performing artists in realization of work designed for public spaces in New York City, in cooperation with city Dept. of Parks and Recreation.
SIZE: 10½ feet high, platform 12 x 24 feet
DATE: Completed 1985
COST: $7500 for materials (All time and labor donated by artist.)
MATERIAL: Wood, copper, sea sponges, and text
PHOTOGRAPHY: Jane Greengold

completely obliterating it as a natural feature.

Intrigued by this history, Jane Greengold invented a person named Charles Cooper as a way to bring the story of the pond to life. Through his eyes she hopes her audience will be able to see the pond and the process by which it was destroyed, as a theme in American life.

Description

The sculpture in Foley Square depicts an early 18th century water filter invented by the fictional character, Charles Cooper, to clean the fresh water pond. Ms. Greengold invented the 18th century environmental activist, Mr. Cooper, to add narrative to her sculptural piece. Accompanying the water filter, she drafted a pamphlet purportedly by Charles Cooper, dated Sept. 5, 1786, which asks New York citizens for the necessary funds to wage a campaign against the spoliation of the fresh water pond. He seeks money to continue his research on the filtering of polluted water and invites subscribers to sign up at the taverns in Bowery Lane and at the coffee house. Those who have tickets will be allowed to sample the filtered water first!

Ms. Greengold once before used the technique of creating an imaginary character to personalize and make vivid the environmental history of a site. In 1984, she designed a piece inside the Brooklyn anchorage of the Brooklyn Bridge celebrating the centennial of this structure. She created Agatha Muldoon, an old woman whose life paralleled the life of the bridge. Agatha's family home was torn down to make room for the bridge, and her brother, a diver, was invalided by a case of the bends after working on the pilings. As personal history, the account was clearly exaggerated and fictionalized, but the underlining history of the bridge and its content was a matter of record. Ms. Muldoon's life was dominated by the bridge. She was obsessed by it—coming every day to the anchorage to mark off the days of its existence with lines on the wall. Eventually, she literally moved into the anchorage reclaiming her family's property. The artist says,

> I knew that I would draw Agatha's 36,500+ lines on the wall. But that alone was stark, simplistic and boring. I wanted to make her character and history visible. So, I decided to recreate her home under the bridge. I assembled her clothing, personal affects, her pots and pans . . . everything she needed to live. I found the furniture and clothing in antique stores in New York City and Upstate New York. Agatha's home was not systematically furnished at any one particular moment. She had accumulated items throughout her life so I did not try to recreate one moment in the hundred years. Instead, I included pieces from throughout the period, to develop a sense of the passage of time. The objects were presented not for their own sake, but to create a composite portrait of their eccentric owner. The long underwear on the clothesline and Irish lace shawls over the chairs, strongly suggested the old lady in the eerie semi-public place under the bridge.
>
> The anchorage is a private part of a public place. I also made hundreds of drawings of the bridge's towers allegedly made by Agatha. Just adding the visual presence of the upper-bridge to the work, and adding to the sense of Agatha's obsession with the bridge. Then, in order to include details about Agatha, and about the history of the bridge, I wrote about forty pages of excerpts from her diaries which were published and available at the site.

The work was extensively reviewed and praised by the press. People were drawn into the fictional story of the old lady. They wanted to believe in her. They were even willing to suspend their disbelief about the fact that she was said to be 106 years old. The mythical character provided eyes through which to see the past. She awakened memories of the neighborhood's past and old timers talked about the neighborhood in various stages of Agatha's life. She treated thoughts about individual's relationships to physical spaces. Viewers marvelled at the idea that an old lady could live in such a space, and it seemed to give them a new perspective and ability to see the space in relation to themselves. The historical resonance of the site itself provided a powerful emotional, as well as intellectual context.

It was the positive reaction and success of the Brooklyn Bridge work that made Jane Greengold want to create more historically based urban myths. She read various histories of New York City searching for enticing material. Struck by the story of the Collect Pond, she dug deeper. The circumstances in the lower Manhattan project are entirely different from those presented by the bridge. Very few people know about the pond. There are no affectionate memories on which to build. Indeed, part of her goal in the project was to create nostalgia for the pond and an awareness of the process in which it was destroyed, because she considers this process as important as the pond itself.

She did not want simply to present the image of the pond, so she created the fictional character of Charles Cooper (1747–1820). As the keeper of a tavern in the neighborhood of the pond, he lived near the pond all of his life, swam in it as a child, ice skated on it, and picnicked beside it. He loved it and could not bear to watch it and smell it being destroyed, so he launched a personal crusade to stop the surrounding industries from dumping their waste into the water. When that failed and he had to admit that he could not prevent the ruin of the water, he turned to tinkering and tried to cure it.

In his own time Cooper might have been considered a crackpot. His love for the natural landscape led him to an activism that would become a visible movement only years later.

The visual element of the work is a re-creation of Cooper's water filtering device. It is not presented as the original device, but as a model reconstruction made from Cooper's notes and drawings. All the visible parts are made of material in the style appropriate to New York City in 1787.

Design Impact

The artist says

I hope work will enable viewers to share in the sense of possessiveness. I believe we all have a greater sense of belonging in a space and even a proprietory sense of power over it when we know about its past. The process can work in two ways: Not only can a public art work about the history of a site give people a more profound connection with the site, but also people's initial familiarity with the site can make them more receptive to the art work.

I do want to have viewers experience the work first and only afterwards learn about its fictional aspects. The moment of confusion about whether something is real or imaginary is a moment that if successfully orchestrated can loosen the viewers' imaginations and allow them to think more freely about what did happen, what did not happen and what might have happened. Once started on that path, it is easier to see that many different things might have happened and that the configuration of the present was not inevitable but the result of myriad decisions great and small, any one of which could have changed the outcome.

The more we understand then the more we are apt to believe that we can affect the present and even the future by exerting control over some of the many decisions that shape our environment.

I would like to encourage in my audience that sense of control, but I don't want my art to simply have a pedagogical or ideological function. I wanted ideally to inspire a frisson, a shiver of excitement, 'Oh, look!'—a visual and intellectual excitement at both what is there before the viewer's eye and what it reveals about what was there in the past. One of the functions of art for me is to nudge and prod the imagination to create or simply to recognize insights into how things are and how they might have been and how they might be.

Chris Archer, writer for the *Villager Downtown*, a guide to arts and entertainment, writes, "By personalizing the history, as it were, and the issue of environmental protection, she hopes the exhibit will help people to see how important it is to fight for whatever we believe is worth keeping." He writes further,

There is just one drawback; it has no water. Greengold had originally planned to exhibit a circular fountain using a mere 50 gallons of recyclable water. And up until the week of opening, the city had given her permission to use the water. But with the advent of stricter drought enforcement, she was denied. Commenting on the apparent irony, she said it was 'simply current events catching up with history.'

CHELSEA, MASSACHUSETTS

Streetscape Art

Introduction

Known as the 'junk capital' of New England because of numerous paper, cloth, and rubber recycling centers, Chelsea, Massachusetts, lost that title in 1973 when a catastrophic fire destroyed 300 acres of the commercial district. This blue-collar city on the Mystic River just north of Boston was described in the late 19th century as the "most desirable location in the metropolitan area." Founded in 1624, Chelsea has been the entry point for successive waves of immigrants during the past one hundred years, and now boasts a population of 25,000. A former mayor initiated a townscape plan to recognize the value of the city's lively culture, intimate scale, and handsome public spaces. Funds from the Economic Development Administration (EDA) supported the cost of lavish landscaping for the deteriorating Broadway area and the two squares marking the ends of the main shopping district. Brick sidewalks edged with granite, five-inch diameter trees whose handsome wrought iron guards match the design of adjacent trash receptacles, and Victorian street lamps give the area a turn-of-the-century flavor. The upgraded Chelsea is reminiscent of the city before the Great Fire of 1908 which destroyed its considerable grace and many mature trees.

The main street project also included a public art strategy which attempted to re-address the larger problem of "cultural amnesia." The idea was to strengthen the city's link with its own past. City officials adopted this art policy after viewing an exhibit of proposals solicited by the Cambridge Arts Council to enrich their cityscape. Chelsea originally determined to allocate two percent of the EDA budget for public art only to discover that the federal directives did not specify art as an allowable budget item. Undaunted, the city's Community Development Office called the project "Pedestrian Orientation," which is perhaps an accurate description. The $60,000 (approximately 2% of the total three million dollar budget) was probably the highest art budget in the nation using EDA funds at that time.

Background

The resurrection of Chelsea Square was

one item in the largest group of projects in that city's sweeping revitalization effort in 1977–78. The intersection had fallen into visible disrepair and misuse; much of it served as a municipal parking lot. The centrally located Art Deco fountain had begun to deteriorate after twenty years of not functioning. Distinctive features of many surrounding storefronts had been obscured by garish signs. The townscape and landscape effort reinstated the fountain, gave facelifts to some of the stores fronting the area, and brought in trees, shrubs, grass, benches and brick paving to create a compact urban green. The final element in the year-and-a-half-long project was the installation of a new sculpture on the pedestrian plaza.

Ronald Lee Fleming, the planner responsible for the townscaping program, had initially viewed one proposed sculptor's abstract work which consisted mostly of smooth, red, curving metal forms, and felt the need for greater reference to the site. A "Quality of Life" competition sponsored by the Cambridge Arts Council provided the inspiration—a proposal by MIT faculty members Dolores Hayden and Peter Marris for "Cambridge Conversation." Designed to enliven a small Cambridge park, the work presented a group of life-size statues of historical Cambridge figures, to be located on the sidewalk seemingly engaged in casual conversation. Fleming, the founding chairman of the Cambridge Arts Council, brought in Patrick Moscaritolo, Chelsea's Community Development Director, and several members of the mayor's staff to see the Cambridge exhibit. Moscaritolo agreed that such a work would be appropriate in the renovated Chelsea Square. Later, with the full support of the landscape architects recommended by Fleming, Carol Johnson and Associates, Chelsea was able to use a small percentage of the EDA grant for landscaping the square to cover the cost of the sculpture. A Boston artist, Penelope Jencks, known for her representational work, was invited to formulate a conversation statue for Chelsea. Her concept, unlike that of the Cambridge proposal, was to use living, recognizable Chelsea residents as models.

Description

The three bronze figures stand alongside one of the new Victorian wood and iron-work benches, in a clearly visible open plaza next to the green. Two of the figures are known personalities: a retired science teacher of Polish descent, beloved as a source of guidance to college-bound students, and a black high-school track star. The third character is a little girl, modeled after artist Jencks's daughter, leaning against a bench in a stance reminiscent of one of Degas' dancers, apparently listening to the conversation.

The stylization of the figures, and the accentuation of their postures, make all three believable. The teacher adjusts his glasses while holding a book under his arm; the high school student stands comfortably at ease, with loosely hanging bell-bottoms; the girl arches her head forward to hear better, leaning comfortably against the arm of the bench. The everyday scene does not cele-

brate the banality of modern life, but rather emphasizes the individuality and inadvertent humor of each character. The likenesses, according to one editor of the *Chelsea Record*, "couldn't be better."

Design Impact

The statue group is extremely popular among residents of Chelsea, and expectably,

NAME: *Chelsea Conversation*, Chelsea, Massachusetts

PROJECT: Three life-size bronze figures, representing locally known community members, standing on recently redesigned Chelsea Square

ARTIST: Penelope Jencks

AGENCY: City of Chelsea, Office of Community Development; Ronald Lee Fleming, planner in charge of townscape project; Tom Kirvan, vice president, Carol Johnson and Associates, Landscape Architects

DATE: Started 1977, completed 1978

COST: $19,000 (Material—$12,000; services—$3000; artist—$3000)

MATERIAL: Bronze

PHOTOGRAPHY: Renata von Tscharner

provokes all sorts of interaction on the part of children and amused visitors. It has been featured in several national magazines and was used for the official New Year's announcements of the city. Arts administrators, architects, and artists from abroad visited the street on a special tour organized by the State Department. They were interested in finding public art which supported neighborhood identity.

Chelsea Walk

Description

The "Chelsea Walk," formerly a fenced-off, refuse-laden vacant lot, is now a brick footpath linking Broadway, Chelsea's main street, and a new parking lot. The "Memory Wall," along one side of this new pedestrian link, consists of porcelain panels portraying the history and changing conditions of Chelsea. The photo panels record Chelsea-born or raised celebrities, including Barbara Stanwyck, Chick Corea, and George M. Cohan. They also depict less well-known personalities who have become community legends such as Harry Siegel, a veteran pho-

Chelsea Walk was an abandoned alley before renovation.

NAME: *Crab Bricks*, Chelsea, Massachusetts
PROJECT: 65 bronze crabs, embedded in brick sidewalk and crosswalk pavement, twenty yards from the 'Chelsea Conversation', commemorating the fresh crabs and fish that had been sold in the outdoor market in Chelsea Square a hundred years ago
ARTIST: David Phillips
AGENCY: City of Chelsea, Office of Community Development; Tom Kirvan of Carol Johnson and Associates, Landscape Architects; Ronald Lee Fleming, principal townscape planner
SIZE: Approximately 8 inches across
DATE: Started 1977, completed 1978
COST: $3000
MATERIAL: Bronze
PHOTOGRAPHY: Ronald Lee Fleming

NAME: *Chelsea Walk*, Chelsea, Massachusetts
PROJECT: Memory Wall, off Broadway, depicts changing conditions and residents of Chelsea on ten 4x6 foot panels.
ARTISTS: Ronald Lee Fleming, project director; Susan Roberts, Peter Johnson, designers; Thomas Kirvan of Carol Johnson and Associates, Landscape Architects
AGENCY: City of Chelsea, Office of Community Development; Patrick Moscaritolo, Director
DATE: Started May, 1977; completed May, 1979
COST: $18,000 ($10,000, brick wall; $8,000, fabrication and installation of panels; research and design research worker covered by CETA contract, $6–$10,000)
MATERIAL: Silk-screened enamel panels covered in epoxy
PHOTOGRAPHY: Renata von Tscharner

tographer who has taken instant portraits with a box camera on Broadway for nearly 50 years. The panels also describe such recent events as the Blizzard of 1978.

Because most city records did not survive the 1908 fire and Chelsea has no historical society, the designers solicited information by distributing a poster with an old photograph. They also organized a photo competition for 'best looking baby' which gave Harry Siegel some new business and allowed the designers to record the presence of the newest citizens of Chelsea, many of whom are Hispanics, adding another chapter to Chelsea's social history.

Design Impact

The Memory Wall has become a family album for the city, illustrating that each place has events worth commemorating, its own heroes and eccentrics. One panel depicts Laura Lee, an early feminist who designed and wore the first bloomers in America. Her remark reflects the boldness of this almost-forgotten Chelsea citizen:

I was looking on the world with a fresh eye, and saw so many things that need to be changed . . . there was too much secrecy then, it was not a good thing, for the secrecy was combined with ignorance.

Immediately after the installation of the Memory Wall, the city hired a guard to protect it from vandals. After a short period, the guard was let go, and the panels remained untouched for years. Unfortunately, vandals have now completely defaced the wall with graffiti, after tentative squiggles were not immediately removed. Fran Nugent, an engineer with the City Department of Public Works said, "The community con-

sidered the wall a fitting tribute to local heroes, historic and contemporary," and was saddened by the vandalism.

The Memory Wall, together with the other pieces of small art that were incorporated into the revitalization project, received extensive coverage in the local newspaper, appeared on television, and was the subject of articles in *Historic Preservation* and *Landscape Architecture*. In *Nuts and Bolts*, a book on public design projects, Al Gowan said that thanks to the Memory Wall, "the town has become a place again."

The idea has since been applied to commemorating the jazz culture of particular neighborhoods in New Orleans.

The Chelsea project because of its innovative public art component has received several design awards. (ASLA, DOT, and BSA).

In 1984, the new mayor removed most of the benches in Bellingham Square, and plans to remove the gazebo as well, to discourage gangs who sometimes use this area as their hangout. Unfortunately, this drastic measure is a disservice to the rest of the community, especially to the many elderly citizens who also use this spot to congregate and kibitz. The remaining bronze pieces in the square—a handbag on a bench, a shopping bag, a cup, and orange peels lose some of their impact without the context of the benches.

NAME: *Bellingham Square*, Chelsea, Massachusetts
PROJECT: Cast bronze shopping bag, cup, orange peels and sweater, rendered realistically and dispersed around the area of Bellingham Square
ARTIST: Mags Harries
AGENCY: City of Chelsea, Office of Community Development
SIZE: Life-size
DATE: 1978
COST: $6000 for five pieces
MATERIAL: Bronze
PHOTOGRAPHY: Greg Heins, Renata von Tscharner

Delacorte Animal Clock

Background

Since its construction in 1965, the Delacorte Clock at the entrance to the Central Park Zoo has been one of New York's most entertaining public ornaments, as much a part of the zoo as the electric billboard is a part of Times Square. With its duo of bell-striking monkeys, six dancing animals, and repertoire of thirty-two nursery songs, the clock is primarily a children's attraction; but it refers, in concept, to a European tradition, centuries old, of placing mechanical clocks in public spaces.

The clock was the idea of publisher George Delacorte and just one of many gifts he has presented to the park through his philanthropic foundation. Delacorte initially submitted his proposal to the Parks Department, and after receiving grateful consent commissioned a different artisan for each aspect of the design.

The most praised element of the design is the graceful, compact clock tower and kiosk above the animal figures, constructed by architect Edward Coe Embury in a style harmonious with the other zoo buildings. The six dancing animals and monkey figures were crafted and cast by Andrea Spandini in Rome, and shipped to America. The clock was fashionably dedicated on June 24, 1965, in a ceremony including Mayor Robert Wagner, the Parks Commissioner Newbold Morris, the Manhattan borough president, and other dignitaries. Delacorte's granddaughter, Cassandra, unveiled the structure.

Description

Each of the animal figures is four feet tall, and is postured in an act of celebration with a different musical instrument. The ensemble includes: a bear playing a tambourine, a hippopotamus holding a violin, an elephant rhapsodizing on an accordion, a goat playing the fifes and dancing a jig, a kangaroo and baby holding a horn, and a penguin counting time on a snare drum. The figures are each located on separate discs, and rotate in place as they circle the tower. Carillons, installed in 1969, create the bell peal, and play from a repertoire of thirty-two children's songs, including "Baa! Baa! Black Sheep," "Hickory, Dickory, Dock," and other nursery favorites. The clock is synchronized so that when the bells sound on the half hour, the monkeys strike, the music plays, and the animals dance around the tower. The performances last for about two minutes.

Design Impact

The Delacorte Clock is one of the few animated timepieces in American urban design. In Europe, such combinations of whimsical design and sophisticated mechanics are much more familiar, and numerous animated clocks were created for public squares. Many of these, most notably the Zytglogge in Bern, Switzerland, and the astronomical clock on the old Town Hall in Prague, Czechoslovakia, still function and attract crowds each hour. The clocks celebrate the passing of time: a meditation on this event seems less a part of the hurried lifestyle of the average American.

In its delicacy and compact scale, the Delacorte Clock would have been lost in the expanse of New York's concrete jungle; instead, it graces Central Park and the small Manhattan zoo. The location, at the gate between the main zoo and its affiliated Children's Zoo, is central enough to attract crowds of visitors, and, usually, balloon vendors. With towering offices, apartment complexes, and luxury hotels surging sky-

NAME: *Delacorte Animal Clock*, New York City
PROJECT: Clock tower above gate to Children's Zoo in Central Park, featuring six animals with instruments which circle the tower
ARTIST: Concept—George Delacorte; Designer—Fernando Texidor; Architect—Edward C. Embury; Sculptor—Andrea Spadini
AGENCY: George T. Delacorte Foundation; New York City Department of Parks and Recreation
SIZE: Tower—approximately 25 feet tall; Figures—each 4 feet tall
DATE: 1965
COST: $125,000
MATERIAL: Figures are bronze
PHOTOGRAPHY: Courtesy of City of New York Parks and Recreation

ward on three sides, the zoos with their animal inhabitants seem truly unreal worlds unto themselves; the clock is a playful reinforcement of that image.

The area directly surrounding the zoos in Central Park is rich in "lovable" sculpture, especially statues designed for children. The Alice-in-Wonderland statue, designed by Jose de Creeft, is an earlier donation of George Delacorte: located several blocks away near a boating pond, it attracts numerous climbing toddlers. Also close by are a statue of Hans Christian Andersen reading on a bench, and a popular statue of Balto, a heroic husky dog. Within the zoo area are two notable fountain sculptures, of a Dancing Bear and Dancing Goat, sculpted by Frederick F.G. Roth.

Minor repairs are occasionally necessary in the cold weather to ensure the animal's rotation in the Delacorte Clock.

BOSTON, MASSACHUSETTS

Milk Bottle

Background

For nearly half a century, a forty-foot Milk Bottle served as a family ice cream stand on Route 44 outside the city of Taunton, Massachusetts, an unacclaimed roadside oddity. Today the bottle announces the entrance to the Children's Museum and the Computer Museum on Boston's new Museum Wharf. Not only is the Bottle a landmark directing automobiles and pedestrians towards the wharf from blocks around, it is also a snack bar, serving salads, sandwiches and ice cream to museum visitors. Embodying kitsch and kitchen, the Milk Bottle has become a useful and recognizable addition to Boston's cityscape.

Built in the early 1930s by Arthur Gagner of Taunton, the Bottle has the distinction

NAME: *Milk Bottle*, Boston, Massachusetts
PROJECT: Giant milk bottle serving as a sandwich kiosk outside the Children's Museum and the Computer Museum on Museum Wharf
ARTIST: Arthur Gagner; Reconstruction by Ken Eckstein of H.P. Hood Company
AGENCY: (for reconstruction) Children's Museum; H.P. Hood Co.
SIZE: Height: 40 feet; circumference at base: 58 feet
DATE: 1934; Reconstruction and relocation 1977
COST: Original: Unknown; Reconstruction and relocation: $100,000
MATERIAL: Spruce, fir, pine, plywood and plaster
PHOTOGRAPHY: Renata von Tscharner

of being one of the first drive-in restaurants in the country. It changed ownership, but continued to operate in that capacity until 1967, when the business closed. A private citizen purchased the Bottle in order to preserve it. Architectural critic for the *Boston Globe*, Robert Campbell, wrote several articles praising it as an outstanding artifact of what was then just being recognized as "commercial archaeology," roadside buildings of the early auto age. The Boston Redevelopment Authority suggested that the Milk Bottle be mounted on the plaza front of the Boston City Hall, but this was stoutly resisted by the City Hall architects.

However, the Museum of Transportation and Children's Museum, which were moving back into the city, recognized its potential as a beacon marking their new location, a converted warehouse on the Fort Point channel. The H.P. Hood Company, which had been supplying ice cream to the stand for the last few years of its operation, offered assistance in refurbishing and relocating it. The entire structure was rebuilt and repainted, and the interior remodeled. When the near-finished Bottle was transported by barge through Boston harbor to its new site in 1977, it was accompanied by a small flotilla including spraying fireboats.

Description

Like any smaller milk bottle, this one is white, with a red cap on top, a wide neck, and a slightly brownish layer of cream toward the brim. "H.P. Hood, Inc." was stamped across the surface in block letters. This was repainted in a lettering reminiscent of the 1930s. "200,000 Quarts" was painted on the other side of the bottle in the same typeface, signifying the quantity of milk the bottle could contain.

The base of the structure has windows facing in all directions, each framed by a red aluminum awning. Inside seven employees can work comfortably at one time.

Design Impact

The Children's Museum opened at its new

Museum Wharf site on July 1, 1979, near the Museum of Transportation and the Boston Tea Party ship.

The Museum of Transportation has since moved, and in November, 1984, the Computer Museum officially opened in its place. Located amidst blocks of 19th century brick and timber warehouses, the Milk Bottle serves to define the revived Fort Point Chanel district being converted into offices, and condominiums, giving it a memorable emblem. The image has become a logo used by the two museums, which display it on jewelry, miniatures, and other items sold in the museum store. As an extension of the museums' displays, the Bottle is an amusing complement to some popular exhibits inside: an enormous coffee cup, telephone and pencil.

Like a giant frankfurter over a hot dog stand, the Milk Bottle is an authentic example of "Coney Island Architecture," defined by architect Norman Bel Geddes as "bizarre, overblown and eye-catching." Modernized, refitted and relocated to an appropriate spot, the Milk Bottle has attained new status. Architect Richard S. Gutman, an authority on roadside diners, justifies the

expensive relocation as an act of historic preservation, calling the piece "yesterday's eyesore . . . tomorrow's antique and the future's archaeological find." Ironically, while it is preserved as a symbol of the early highway architecture, the bottle no longer means milk to the museums' principle users, children brought up on milk in cartons.

Riverwalk

Background

An island peninsula has appeared on maps of Memphis as far back as 1790. Since then the island has shrunk and expanded with the floods and fortunes of the river. Today the ebb and flow of the river cannot alter the configuration of the concrete 'riverbed,' an interpretive three-dimensional model which runs along the shore of the Mud Island Recreation Park.

Sometime around 1912, the river gradually formed a sand bar which created an obstacle for people who relied on water transportation. This sand bar continued to grow into an island, becoming a threat to the commerce of the Port of Memphis. The Island still flooded sporadically and remained unusable. Appropriately, it was named Mud Island. In 1923, former Mayor "Boss" E. H. Crump stated, "Well, if we can't get rid of this thing, we'd better make a park out of

it."[1] However, it was fifty years before the city took action, when they hired a consortium of nine firms in 1973, overseen by Roy Harrover and Associates, architects, to develop Mud Island into a recreational urban park. Since the Island evolved as a result of the river, Harrover Associates decided to document the Mississippi's character and to devote the fifty acres of park to the story of "Ol' Man River."

The newly transformed Mud Island opened in July 1982, celebrating the Mississippi River in several ways: a river-themed children's playground, a museum commemorating the history of the river, souvenir and gift shops, open recreational areas, restaurants for different dining experiences, and a 5,000 seat outdoor amphitheater. It also featured the "Riverwalk," an exact scale model of the lower Mississippi River, including all the major towns and cities, streets, and indigenous vegetation found along its banks.

Description

The Riverwalk is a 2,000 foot or five city-block-long concrete replica of the lower Mississippi River from Cairo, Illinois, to the Gulf of Mexico, located along the edge of the real "Big Muddy." It channels through a series of courtyards, meanders past the amphitheater, and terminates near the southern tip of the Island in a four foot deep wading pond which is a one-acre version of the Gulf of Mexico.

The riverbed and the surrounding cities are constructed of pre-cast concrete panels. Mary Wilkinson, Senior Interpreter of Mud Island's Mississippi River Museum, says, "The model is built of 4 x 8-foot concrete slabs, like a jigsaw puzzle. While under construction, each slab was surveyed by the crew and tilted by means of leveling screws in each corner of the slab to the exact angle required to provide the proper rate of flow." Thus, Riverwalk's gradient is 3.5' in drop, scaled to the gradient of the terrain over which the real Lower Mississippi flows. To dramatize the change in the river's level, a scale of one inch to eight feet illustrates the subtle variation.

Inlaid in the concrete panels are detailed mosaics in the actual shape and proportion of the twenty major cities along the river's banks at the scale of thirty inches to the mile. Grey slate is used to depict the towns and cities. Streets, bridges, and highways are shown in stainless steel. Green slate indicates parks and open undeveloped natural areas. Prominent buildings such as city halls and universities are engraved in bronze. Riverwalk is designed to be a self-guided tour, with sixty-eight signs placed on pedestals providing historic interpretation. In addition, large wall signs inform visitors about the model's design and the tributary systems, and these coordinate with illustrative watershed panels, which depict the drainage basins of the major tributaries of the Mississippi.

Design Impact

The Riverwalk invites visitors to actively participate in learning about the Mississippi River's history, geography, vegetation and the physics of its flow. Visitors actually step

onto the cities and wade through the model river. Both children and adults enjoy the different tactile surfaces offered by the changing contours of the river and the smooth slate material of the cities. By reducing the form of the river to a manageable pedestrian scale, people can both catch a bird's eye view and pause to examine particular details. The perceptual effect is an intriguing one—viewing the terrain of a region from a distant height, but also exploring it tactually at close range. The Riverwalk's meandering course forces visitors to assume a more leisurely pace, perhaps metaphorically expressing the more languid style of Southern living. The descriptive panels encourage lingering, but do not obstruct those who want to continue walking. Though primarily a self-directed walk, free guided tours are offered several times daily in the warm seasons. Other than water treatment and scrubbing of the concrete to prevent algal growth, maintenance is minimal.

Mud Island and Riverwalk, attracting both tourists and residents for a convenient lunch break from downtown or a full day outing, give Memphis the distinction of having a fifty-acre recreational park within its city limits. The annual visitor rate for the first two years has been 900,760 visitors.

NAME: *Riverwalk*, Memphis, Tennessee
PROJECT: An authentic scaled model of the lower Mississippi River Valley depicting the configuration of the river from Cairo, Illinois, to the Gulf of Mexico and surrounding cities; located at Mud Island Recreation Park, Memphis, Tennessee
ARTIST: Roy Harrover and Associates, Inc.
AGENCY: City of Memphis, Mud Island Division
SIZE: Model is 2000 feet or five city blocks long
DATE: Design began 1973, construction commenced 1974; park opened July 1982
COST: $8 million (for Riverwalk)
MATERIAL: Pre-cast concrete panels support model made of blue and green slate, bronze and stainless steel.
PHOTOGRAPHY: Courtesy of Mississippi River Museum/Mud Island, Memphis, Tennessee

Cat and Dog Fountain

Summary

The lighthearted and historic "Cat and Dog Fountain" stands on a grassy triangle in the center of picturesque Stockbridge, Massachusetts, near the Red Lion Inn. The fountain depicts a cat and dog snarling at each other "in the traditional attitude of belligerence,"[1] the cat hissing a jet of water into the dog's face. Below is a pedestal with intricate carvings of corals, seaweeds, birds and dragonheaded serpents, which contributes a Beaux Arts richness to the overall design. The water streams down into a basin of Italian marble.

The basin was conceived first; town planners designed it in 1862, with the development of the town's water supply. The *Vil-*

lage Gleaner of August 1862, published in nearby Lee, congratulated "our friends in Stockbridge on securing this great addition to the attractions of that most lovely village." The cat and dog statue and pedestal were added in 1885, as a donation to the town from John Gourlie, a wealthy summer resident of Stockbridge and a New York City man of letters who wanted to leave a mark of gratitude. A local social club described it at the time as a "generous expression of sympathy and interest in our little village" and continued, "The proofs of . . . its blessings are the daily groups of younger and older that we may see all through the summer days around its cooling air." The statue remained in place for almost a century, gradually eroding under the harsh New England winters. During the Bicentenniel, it became "a symbol of the concerned townspeople's battle over progress vs. preservation."[2]

Faced with the possible disintegration of the rock, town residents gathered $3,900 to reconstruct it and commissioned Otello Guarducci, a sculptor in nearby Great Barrington, to recast the original in stone. The reproduction now stands on the same site as the original, operating during the warm months, and covered during the winter. The weather-worn original is in a storage closet at the Stockbridge Town Hall.

NAME: *Cat and Dog Fountain*, Stockbridge, Massachusetts
PROJECT: Stone fountain in village center with life-size statue of a cat and a dog atop a pedestal
ARTIST: Unknown
AGENCY: Private Donation
DATE: Basin 1862, Sculpture 1885
COST: 1976 replacement: $3600
MATERIAL: Stone
PHOTOGRAPHY: Stockbridge Library Association

Forest Building

Background

In basic design, the BEST merchandise showroom in Richmond, Virginia, is an ordinary suburban department store, with wide, empty walls and plain glass and brick facade. What makes the building exceptional is that it is penetrated by a thick, towering grove of trees, which pushes through the front of the building and physically separates the entrance from the body of the store. At the base of the trunks the soil, leaves and roots of a forest floor are visible through the shop windows. What seems like nature wreaking revenge, however, was actually the conscious design of SITE architects: one in a series of bold, visually arresting catalogue showrooms constructed in collaboration with BEST Products Company.

SITE—which stands for Sculpture-in-the-Environment—is a New York based architecture and environmental arts firm headed by four principals: Alison Sky, Michelle Stone, Emilio Sousa and James Wines. Chartered in 1970, the group has since established a reputation for its daring constructions, which feature dislocated walls, misplaced facades and other large-scale manipulation of building elements. The purpose of this approach, which SITE labels "dearchitecture," is an effort to question the most standard assumptions in architecture, and expose the potential tensions within architectural structures. To the unexpecting shopper, the effect is often very jarring and somewhat humorous. The first BEST project displayed a brick skin peeling off an exposed concrete wall. Later projects include a showroom with a crumbling facade, one with the front portion of the building wrenched out and placed several yards away, and one with the entire roof facade lifted up on one side to a precarious diagonal.

The "Forest Building," conceived in 1979, draws its inspiration from its surroundings: a thick, deciduous forest, with oaks and maples rising up to sixty feet. Although located in a suburban neighborhood, the site is slightly isolated from traffic, and set off from the nearby highway and shopping mall. Construction of a standard showroom on the site would have required the destruction of six and a half acres of this woodland. Emilio Sousa of SITE instead chose to preserve part of the forest and integrate it into the overall mall design. The result was what Sousa called "probably the most difficult project we've done." During the construction process, drainage had to be provided for ground water, space reserved for tree roots and adjustments made to work around the 35-foot incline over the area. Cranes and other vehicles had to actively avoid the isolated groves and at one point every tree had to be wrapped in burlap as protection from

NAME: *Forest Building*, Richmond, Virginia
PROJECT: Suburban merchandise showroom is penetrated and surrounded by dense forest, giving the appearance of struggle between man and nature
ARTIST: SITE (Sculpture-in-the-Environment)
AGENCY: BEST Products Company, Inc.
SIZE: 6½ acres, showroom building 6500 square feet
DATE: started in 1979, completed 1980
COST: $4 million (Building construction—$2.3 million; landscaping—$1.7 million)
MATERIAL: Showroom: concrete, brick, steel, glass; Forest: oaks, maples, other deciduous trees
PHOTOGRAPHY: Courtesy of SITE, New York

sprayed concrete. By the time the development opened in mid-October 1980, it had become molded to match specifically the contours and features of its natural site.

Description

The contrast between the stark, conventional building and the unleashed force of nature permeates the entire site. Trees envelope two sides of the showroom, surround the parking lot, and at times break through the asphalt plain in groups of three or four. (see p. 19 for model) Most dramatically, the

147

man, it has the additional power, shared with other organic works, of changing with the seasons and over the years. The different layers of forest soil, as well as the roots of the plants, are visible through the display windows approaching the building from the parking lot.

Design Impact

Because the SITE philosophy views architecture as art, rather than mere design, SITE-designed buildings are a statement in themselves, usually ignoring the specific function of the building. Whether it is in response to SITE's approach, or simply because the buildings are unusual, business is better than ever at each of the SITE-designed showrooms. According to principal James Wines, the "Forest Building" is the most locally popular SITE work to date.

Each of SITE's showrooms for BEST is a unique environmental artwork. Another of SITE's designs, inspired by the American car-oriented culture, is Ghost Parking Lot, in the Hamden Plaza Shopping Center (p. 74). Twenty automobile frames covered with asphalt and submerged at various levels, are 'parked' in the lot, facing a main road. The ghostly silhouettes cause passersby to look twice at what they thought was a typical roadside facility.

front is riven from the body of the building, and full size trees and a rich collection of shrubs rise from a forest strip in between. A walkway across this wooded bed provides the entrance to the showroom. While the structure represents the simultaneous invasion of man into nature and nature into

CAMBRIDGE, MASSACHUSETTS

Harvard Square Theatre Mural

Background

A new facade only a paint layer thick has been added to the architectural melange of Harvard Square in Cambridge, MA. The imposing *fin de siècle* classicism of a trompe l'oeil theatre facade joins Georgian merchants' houses, and brick, concrete, and glass

office buildings, as the setting for the vibrant street culture of the Square. Street performers, shoppers, hawkers and Harvard students all cross paths in this historic but also very contemporary district that has evolved from a seventeenth-century village.

When a local theatre shifted its portal from the traditional entry on the Square to the featureless side wall along Church Street, the owner applied to the City Council for a special permit to extend his movie marquee over the sidewalk. Overhanging signs must be approved by a special permit process because the signs can disrupt the streetscape more than wall signs. The Council issues special permits for overhanging signs based on size requirements, not on aesthetic merit or architectural compatibility. The theater owner's request came to the attention of a City Council member affiliated with the First Church, an 1833 Gothic Revival Unitarian church across the street from the new theatre entrance, where the marquee would hang. As an unofficial representative for the Church, he was concerned that the overhanging, lighted movie marquee would detract from the view of the historic church. Since no *legal* means existed, such as a mandatory design review, to regulate any adverse effects from the internally lit modern marquee on the streetscape, the City Councilman suggested that if the theatre owner wanted the permit for the overhanging sign, he should first meet with Charles Sullivan, the executive director of the Historical Commission, with members of the church, and with other representatives of Church Street businesses to discuss ways of mitigating the impact of the marquee. Sullivan proposed the following two-fold solution: "Reduce the illuminated area of the marquee, and incorporate it into a new facade treatment for the entire 135-foot wall, which was a poster-covered eyesore."

The owner, having purchased the nonconforming sign before receiving the special permit, readily agreed to cooperate. Renata von Tscharner and Ronald Reed of The Townscape Institute conceived the preliminary design for a trompe l'oeil wall painting combining a traditional movie house facade with typical Harvard Square architectural elements, which could be integrated with the marquee. Once the Commission and the church had approved the facade design, the City Council released the permit, thus exercising a kind of "backdoor control."

Description

This "trick of the eye" mural, in shades of Pompeii pink and copper green is painted in an ebullient *belle-époque* style based loosely on 19th century theatre facades.

NAME: *Harvard Square Theatre Mural*, Cambridge, Massachusetts
PROJECT: Trompe l'oeil mural painted on the side wall of a theatre, converted into the entrance facade.
ARTISTS: Joshua Winer, Campari Knoepffler, with Renata von Tscharner, Ronald Reed, The Townscape Institute
AGENCY: Anthony T. Mauriello, President, Harvard Square Theatre; The Townscape Institute
SIZE: 50x27 feet
DATE: 1983
COST: $15,000
MATERIAL: Keim—a mineral-based paint that adheres permanently to brick
PHOTOGRAPHY: Renata von Tscharner

Joshua Winer and Campari Knoepffler, graduate students in architecture at Harvard, refined the preliminary design of von Tscharner and Reed. The final mural was designed in collaboration with the artists who painted it on the wall over a six-week period in the summer of 1983 using a special mineral-based paint that adheres permanently to brick.[1] They sealed it with an epoxy anti-graffiti glaze.[2] Classical columns frame the standard glass entrance doors, and an elaborate arched window flanked by rondels portraying the masks of "comedy" and "tragedy"—which look suspiciously like the artists who painted them—surmounts the marquee. Pigeons roost along an upper story window ledge, made of elegant (painted) copper grillwork in a green tone. At street level, Winer and Knoepffler brushed in the figure of a man intently regarding the movie schedule posted outside. They had observed this same man every day stopping to check on their progress before going inside to see a movie, and found out later that he has visited the theatre daily for over thirty years.

Design Impact

Pleased that the mural provides a strong identity for his property and has reduced graffiti, and in conformity with the original agreement for issuing the special permit, the theatre's owner then asked The Townscape Institute to extend facade treatment along the remaining portion of the wall. Awnings with a new theatre logo and lighted from within, which have been designed by Klaus Roesch, will be integrated with movie poster display cases on street level to break up the formidable scale of the wall. These plans will be coordinated with other improvements for the theatre, including repair of the sidewalk, changes in the entrance (which unfortunately resulted in removing the image of the moviegoer described above), and alteration of the marquee to accommodate an additional movie title. These changes have been reviewed by the Cambridge Historical Commission.

The Harvard Square Theatre Mural complements other recent efforts to conserve the Square's character and reinforce the pedestrian milieu. Renovation and extension of the subway line which travels through the Square included funds for widening brick sidewalks, extending adjacent spaces for street performers, planting generously-calipered trees, and adding Victorian style benches and street lamps. Meanwhile, Joshua Winer continues working in this trompe l'oeil genre. Sponsored by the Cambridge Arts Council, he recently covered a Cambridge newsdealer's stand in Central Square with classical motifs of Grecian temple architecture.

Nieuw Amsterdam Shoreline

Background

Meandering a mile and a half through the canyons of lower Manhattan, the "Nieuw Amsterdam Shoreline" is one artist's unique attempt at historic interpretation and a vivid reminder to New Yorkers of the city's early history, when it was a village instead of the metropolis it is today. The shoreline is represented by a painted blue and green traffic line—representing water and land, respectively—which stretches through streets, sidewalks and even across a plot of grass at one point to re-create as faithfully as possible the contours of Manhattan Island at the time of the Nieuw Amsterdam colony. The artist responsible for the work is Eric Arctander, a graduate of the Chicago Art Institute. As an environmental artist and "non-representational painter," Arctander had previously worked on "border" pieces confronting the issues of locality, history and identity: his first project entitled "Burning Water, Smoking Mirror" traced directional tracks around four Mexican mythological sites. A later work called "My Block," consisted of a chalk line drawn around the block on which he had grown up. The inspiration for "Shoreline" came largely through the historical plaques marking sites around the lower New York area. "I was just walking through the streets around where I live, and I could visualize the whole thing . . . I would tell people 'You are standing on what used to be an old Dutch canal. What do you think of that?' " When he saw their eyes light with interest, said the artist, "I knew this could be shared with the whole city."

Arctander approached two institutions, the Public Art Fund and the Lower Manhattan Cultural Council, for capital. Both sponsored the project, with corporate assistance from ITT World Communications, Standard & Poor, and Consolidated Edison. An archeologist, Jill Moser, specified and verified the location of historic landmarks. The NYC Department of Transportation was especially helpful, volunteering one of the city's line-painting machines accompanied by a crew of seven for one day, and sixty gallons of specially prepared paint. Arctander spent several evenings tracing the route in spray-paint, and with the crew completed the execution of "Shoreline" in one day, June 21, 1980.

Description

The two parallel lines are the standard size for traffic lines—each four inches wide with a four inch gap between—winding for 7,000 feet through the monumental and neoclassical buildings that compose the center of New York's financial district. They begin at the intersection of Wall Street and Pearl Street, named for the shells that had been common there on the site of the blockhouse and gate that terminated the famous Wall Street wall. The shoreline curves southward along Pearl to Broad Street, where the Dutch West India Company's two-story tavern once stood, converted in 1653 to become the *Stadt Huys*, City Hall. In front of the site the first wharf was constructed, Shreyer's Hook—circa 1648—which was reinforced in 1654, commencing the landfill process that would so expand the island. The path turns inward for several blocks along Broad Street, towards the Stock Exchange, following a channel that had jutted into the colony. Shored by timber and crossed by at least two footbridges, the inlet became pestilent and was filled in 1675. Continuing to State Street along the pathway of the oldest Dutch settlement, the lines curve around the northern tip of Battery Park, around the site of Old Fort Amsterdam and the protective earthworks that faced the harbor. Cutting matter-of-factly through a gate, and across a plot of grass, the shoreline winds north past the Customs House, along Greenwich Street, to stop behind Trinity Church.

As an aid in appreciating the project, Arctander prepared a brochure with a map and guide to the shoreline, available at no cost from the Public Art Fund and Lower Manhattan Arts Council. To keep a permanent record of the artwork, and make it potentially available to the rest of the country, the artist had a video tape made of the process of laying the lines. Exposed to weather and traffic, the lines are expected to fade with time—as did the original shoreline. Indeed, by the summer of 1981 several stretches were disappearing.

Design Impact

The "Nieuw Amsterdam Shoreline" is spare in its actual technique, but requires viewer participation in a way unique to itself. Visually it is unlike paintings, displays

NAME: *Nieuw Amsterdam Shoreline*, New York City
PROJECT: An on-site painting of parallel blue and green traffic lines along the streets of Manhattan, tracing the shoreline of the island as it was in its early days as a Dutch settlement.
ARTIST: A. Eric Arctander
AGENCY: Public Art Fund; Lower Manhattan Cultural Council, New York City Department of Transportation
SIZE: Lines are 4 inches wide × 7000 feet long
DATE: 1980
COST: $3800
MATERIAL: Westchester green and Oswego blue exterior paint
PHOTOGRAPHY: Map: courtesy of Eric Arctander; Photo: Donna Svennevik

or dioramas, because it evokes history without providing a picture for the viewer. Instead, it invites that person to visualize that scene for himself as the artist did, and compare in his own mind the differences between the landscape as it was then and as it is now. It communicates the change of scale in the city in a directly involving way. It makes itself accessible to potentially thousands of people at once. It is also singularly open on many levels, asking the participant to draw his own conclusions from what he seeks.

Artist Alan Sonfist initiated a similarly compelling interpretative project in the Wall Street area just a few years before: the re-creation on one square block of Manhattan soil of the vegetation of the island as it was in the 1600s. While such projects are not comparable to vast efforts such as Colonial Williamsburg for scale or accuracy, they require viewer imagination using fractured demarcations to merely imply a historical setting. Their incongruity with their modern surroundings itself comments on the change of the city.

To those unaware of the significance of the lines, they lose much of their value. For this reason, when the work was completed a large effort was made to inform the public: every 1,000 feet along the painting route had a sign reading: THIS LINE DEMARKS THE ORIGINAL CONTOUR OF MANHATTAN WHEN SETTLED BY THE DUTCH IN THE 17TH CENTURY. In addition, an explanatory exhibit of drawings for the proposal and documentary photographs occupied an historic bank on the shoreline route for two months. The artist, however, believes that other interpretations can also be valid:

> . . . the accessibility of the work as an historic 'painting' . . . is most significant, certainly, but there is also the sheer joy of seeing people bring their imagination to what I also saw. Watching people follow the line, children in hand, jogging, bicycling, and even roller-skating, demonstrated that the line has a life of its own.

The municipal transportation authority greeted the project with understandable enthusiasm. Traffic lines are an ever-present form in the modern city, and it took the artist to invest layers of meaning and beauty into such a common element. Planned as a temporary artwork, the lines have faded. Portions remain visible and the explanatory signs have been left in place. The artist believes both remnants serve as visual cues which continue to stimulate the viewer's imagination, even though the entire work is no longer present. Despite the artist's intentions, these leftover images puzzle some passersby. The artist is planning to redo the shoreline in a permanent material and has received permission from the City to install a permanent outdoor artwork.

Arctander researched various kinds of tile and glazed brick and eventually chose an appropriate material made by a Dutch ceramics factory, which has been operating since the seventeenth century. The artist calls the tile, "a high technology material in a traditional form." It is a round, delft-blue tile, 4 inches in diameter; which, when embedded in the pavement for a test run, withstood impact from traffic. The tiles will be inset into the surface like upside down waterglasses. Arctander chose individual tiles instead of a continuous strip of material because he can more flexibly space them ac-

NIEUW AMSTERDAM SHORELINE

1. OLD WALL
2. WATERPORT
3. STADT HUYS
4. SCHREYER'S HOOK
5. HEERE GRACHT
6. FIRST SETTLEMENT
7. FORT AMSTERDAM
8. CEMETERY
9. COMPANY GARDENS

cording to the variations in surface texture and level change of the city terrain. The Lower Manhattan Cultural Council will again sponsor Arctander's project. As of 1985 plans are now underway to find funding.

Community Murals

Background

There are now residents of Oakland walking around in T-shirts boasting "Yes, I am a Model." Probably some were tired of explaining that they were subjects for a community portrait in an alley near City Hall. It is certainly easy to be recognized on the 15th St. Alley mural, since the faces are three times larger than life size. The models as well as the artists are local celebrities in the Bay area, where outdoor wall art has a long-standing tradition. First influenced by the Mexican mural movement begun in 1922 and subsequent murals painted by Diego Rivera for the Bay area in the 1930s and

1940s, such as the San Francisco Stock Exchange mural and the San Francisco Art Institute's mural, many artists have continued this regional tradition.

In 1979 Daniel Galvez, a young artist working for the Alemeda County Neighborhood Arts Program on a CETA contract, wanted to paint an outdoor mural as part of this ongoing community arts project. His concern was to depict ordinary Oakland citizens. He found an under-utilized alley in the middle of downtown, a block from City Hall. After an entire year battling red tape, he received permission to use the wall of the Liberty House Department Store facing the 15th St. Alley. At the beginning of the project the artist supported the work with his CETA salary, but by July the CETA monies had run out. Instead of giving up, Galvez and the other artists involved decided to go ahead with the project, hoping to earn money elsewhere to pay for the mural. In several months' time they had collected $2000 in donations deposited in a bucket placed on the worksite while they were painting. They garnered other funds by selling blueprints of the line drawings for the mural as well as collecting donations from downtown merchants. To support their work, local restaurants provided free lunches for the artists. The impetus to continue the project in the face of financial uncertainties came from the community and the artists themselves.

Later, funding became available from the city, which paid for the paint, and from the L.J. and Mary Skaggs Foundation of Oakland, which gave $1,500. After ten months of work, the artists completed the mural, entitled "Oakland's Portrait" and the community held a party at City Hall Plaza, with local groups providing music and dance performances. As a result of the successful precedent, the artists received funds at the outset for a second Oakland mural. Sponsors for "Street Tattoo" included the California Arts Council Grant, Pro Arts (a nonprofit organization dedicated to promoting arts activities in Alemeda County), L.J. and Mary Skaggs Foundation, the Foremost McKesson Foundation, the Zellerbach Family Fund, the City of Oakland through its Community Development Grant Program, and the National Endowment for the Arts.

NAME: *Oakland's Portrait*, Oakland, California
PROJECT: Larger than life-size portrait of twenty-five Oakland residents painted on wall of downtown alley.
ARTIST: Daniel Galvez, Juan Karlos, Keith Sklar
AGENCY: Alemeda County Neighborhood Arts Program (CETA funded), donations from artists and community, City of Oakland, L.J. and Mary Skaggs Foundation
SIZE4: 23' × 187"
DATE: 1981
COST: $12,500
MATERIAL: Oil enamel, "Plastic Shield"
PHOTOGRAPHY: Daniel Galvez

Description—Oakland Portrait

A parade of jubilant figures painted in vivid colors and photorealistic clarity appear along the wall of the once dingy alley, as if pausing for an impromptu family portrait. Spanning 23 feet by 187 feet, the mural depicts twenty-five Oakland residents. The largest figure stands nineteen feet tall. Galvez chose subjects randomly by photographing people from all over the city. He first transferred the photos into simplified line drawings and projected slides of these onto the wall. The artists used enamel paint followed by a layer of graffiti-resistant sealer.[1] Each artist has his individual work methods, but the result is one integral style. All agree that the activity generated by their work has been a great incentive to persevere even when funding was dubious. Says Sklar, "People never see artworks before they're done, so we have people who come by every day to watch it grow."[2]

Description—Street Tattoo

Daniel Galvez headed the second mural project as well, which followed on the brush strokes of the 15th St. Alley project and took the process of community involvement a step further. The artists ran weekly open workshops, where the public could contribute black and white photos and help with the selection process. Twenty-two Oakland residents are painted on this mural, which is located on a freeway underpass near the Greyhound Station. Like the 15th St. Alley location, this site was also both under-utilized and without amenities, a sort of no-man's land in the inner city. Galvez chose these sites to prove that public art can become a vehicle to help a community reclaim its physical environment. Galvez and team now included fifteen volunteers of varied experience; some were professional, others were holding their first brush. They transformed the site with a mural in a similar photorealist style with a larger than life-size cross-section of everyday Oaklanders.

It is a livelier mural; characters are play-

NAME: *Street Tattoo*, Oakland, California
PROJECT: A mural of twenty-two Oaklanders taken from random photos painted on a freeway underpass near the Greyhound Station in downtown Oakland
ARTISTS: Daniel Galvez, Jamie Morgan, Dan Fontes, Keith Sklar
AGENCY: California Arts Council, Oakland's Pro Arts
SIZE: 15' × 220'
DATE: Begun February 1982; completed September 1982
COST: $25,000
MATERIAL: Oil enamel, "Plastic Shield"
PHOTOGRAPHY: Daniel Galvez

ing, making music, working and dancing, and it has the same high-spirited energy which is now a trademark of Galvez's work. Because each project involved separate fundraising procedures, and owing to their size—2000 square feet or more—it took a year between the painting of the two murals.

Design Impact

The most immediate effect of the murals was to demonstrate how moral and financial support can grow proportionately as the work progresses. It was a case where community enthusiasm helped generate the financial support to complete the project. But

TITLE: *The Carnival Mural*, San Francisco, California

PROJECT: A mural reflecting the pride and spirit of the Latino community in the San Francisco Mission District

ARTIST: Project Director, Daniel Galvez; Assistants: Jamie Morgan, Keith Sklar, Dan Fontes and Jan Shield

SPONSORS: San Francisco Office of Community Development as administered by the Mural Resource Center

SIZE: 24×76 feet

DATE: 1983

COST: $13,000

MEDIUM: Oil enamel

PHOTOGRAPHY: Daniel Galvez

this is a risky way to take care of business. The trade-off is that if the artists are willing to continue working after the initial resources run out, the momentum of the project itself is often enough to elicit addtional funds that might not have been available at the onset. Only after the public watched the daily progress of the mural coming to life did they contribute money and other supplies. Because the murals are so visible and successful, they helped finance subsequent projects in an area with rich artistic resources. Galvez has finished two additional community murals, one in the Mission District of San Francisco, entitled "The Carnival Mural," commemorating an annual Mardi Gras celebration held each spring in this Latino community; and another, "Grand Performance," in downtown Oakland. Here, Galvez and Sklar teamed up once again to paint a 3300 square foot tribute to local performing artists. Galvez's work will be included in a documentation project of Chicano murals that will be on record at the Smithsonian Institution's Archives of American Art, Southern California Branch, and the Social and Public Art Resource Center in Venice, California.

Galvez comments on the kind of impact for which he strives.

My involvement as a painter and image-maker is built upon the traditions of mural painting in part, but I am concerned in taking it beyond the political, religious, and socio-economic barriers that have confined it in the past. I see murals as a means for people to reclaim their environment, to express what is important to them, and to focus on the life energies in the community. Murals are an attempt to create a vital art connected again to the deepest needs of the people.

Creature Pond

Background

Some passersby have been so enchanted with the Creature Pond in Post Office Square, Boston, that they have thrown real bread crumbs to the bronze ducklings that rest on the metal surface of the pond. It is the major new sculptural feature of the triangular vest pocket park that includes bronze pavement inserts, new benches, and landscaping. Located in the heart of Boston's financial district, the square is aptly named after the site of the first post office in the American Colonies, established in 1639. It was the site of a Horse Fountain erected in 1912, to commemorate Dr. George Thorndike Angell, the founder of the Massachusetts Society for the Prevention of Cruelty to Animals. Once a popular drinking spot for the equine population of Boston, its use became obsolete, and the site was appropriated by the horses' successor—the automobile. It was later remodeled into a park, but by 1980 the site had fallen into disrepair—an island of concrete, dirt, and trees in a desert of asphalt and parked cars—without adequate amenities to attract visitors.

The new park redesign including the Creature Pond came from citizen advocacy. Sydney Roberts Rockefeller suggested this project to the Boston Redevelopment Authority (BRA) which had no implementation money but helped her raise funds from the Browne Fund, Boston's major source of public art support. This privately endowed fund "for the beautification of Boston" was established at the turn of the century, and in the 1980s generated annually about $400,000. The city-owned property is under the jurisdiction of the Parks and Recreation Department. The Boston Arts Commission's approval of the design and art component was necessary before support from the Browne Fund could be solicited. The project received a commitment for a maintenance program before construction from four corporate abuttors to the site who formed the Post Office Square Park Association. They are the Beacon Companies, Leggat, McCall and Werner, Hamlen and Collier, and F.M.R. Properties. The BRA supervised the project and coordinated the artists, designers, and public agencies involved. Flansburgh Associates provided design services, and City Life, a public interest group dedicated to enhancing the cityscape, recruited the artists who played a decisive role in the design process.

In this case, the collaboration which brought together artists, architects, landscape architects and the several city agencies was as significant a result of the seven-year-process as the park itself! A key factor in distinguishing this project from other park redesigns was that instead of the artists assuming the traditional role of contributing artwork to a finished design, City Life artists initiated the concept and sustained the project during the course of five BRA directors and three Park Commissioners. Though each successive administration approved the project, sufficient funds for the art elements remained a questionable issue. Rockefeller comments on the artists' motivation, "They were determined to have art be an important and *integral* part of the design."

The artists had to face two difficult obstacles inherent in collaborative projects—to expand the role of the artist to include skills outside the usual domain, and to combine artistic forces as a *team* of artists rather than a group of individuals. According to Rockefeller, new skills acquired included time lapse studies to determine pedestrian flow, sun/shadow studies, and user-needs interviewing. The artists collaborated on the conceptual designs for the art elements—the Creature Pond and pavement inserts—as well as seating, trash receptacle, and planting design. Commenting on the team approach for creating art elements such as the Creature Pond, Rockefeller said, "Each artist shed his or her individual style of working and conformed to an agreed-upon material. The result is a piece of sculpture that holds together like a single work."

Description

The Creature Pond is surrounded by recently installed park amenities. Handsome channel steel benches accommodate the crowds of office workers who find the park a welcome refuge, since it is the only public open space in the district. New plantings of trees, lawn, and annual flower beds and new surface materials of brick set in stone dust soften the barren ground of the 7500 square foot park.

The City Life artists based their design on information gathered from site analyses and from informal interviews with people using the existing park. They wanted to make the site especially "lovable" because there was no residential community nearby that would act as unofficial caretaker. Thus, to encourage the transient "community" of office workers to become attached to the park, they appealed for an emotive, whimsical human response. In an article in *Landscape* written by BRA designers Shirley Muirhead and Roger Erikson, the authors praised the park which "is made memorable with artwork at a personal scale."[1]

NAME: *Creature Pond*, Boston, Massachusetts
PROJECT: The renovation of Angell Memorial Park located in Post Office Square, Boston, includes a bronze pond with sculptured flora and fauna indigenous to New England, pavement inserts, and other amenities.
ARTISTS: D. Lowry Burgess, Donald Burgy, John Cataldo, Carlos Dorrien, Robert Guillemin, David Phillips, Sydney Roberts Rockefeller, Clara Wainwright, William Wainwright
AGENCY: Boston Redevelopment Authority with City Life: Boston, Inc., and Earl R. Flansburgh Associates, Inc., the Browne Fund
SIZE: Angell Memorial Park—7500 square feet; Creature Pond—14 feet in diameter (including granite edge)
DATE: Conceived—Spring 1975; Rededicated—June 29, 1982
COST: $35,000
MATERIAL: Bronze, granite
PHOTOGRAPHY: Renata von Tscharner

The artists from City Life wanted to reinforce the animal theme of the original fountain honoring Dr. Angell. They also wanted to use creatures indigenous to New England and to find a simple and inexpensive solution that was vandal-resistant. They decided upon a bronze pond fourteen feet in diameter, whose shape and scale would echo the circular form of the Angell Fountain. The pond is two feet above ground level and and is encircled by a granite seating ledge. Ducks and other birds 'swim' among the pond's lily pads; salamanders, frogs, and turtles emerge from under the water; and dragonflies skim the surface etched with delicate eddies. The granite border of the pond is interrupted by an outcropping of bronze rock, where a turtle suns himself, and by a frog whose head peeps out from the water. Two chipmunks perch atop the granite ledge next to office workers sitting and eating their lunches on warm days.

On the ground surface of brick pavement nearby are fifteen bronze inserts, including crabs, butterflies, fish, insects, lizards, lobsters, and frogs. Both real objects and modelled plasticine sculptures were cast in bronze, using the lost wax process. David Phillips, one of the artists on the team who also runs a foundry, did the castings. Silicon bronze, often used in the marine industry, and not a traditional sculpting material, was chosen because it welds easily and has a durable finish for outdoor use. The other artists of the group included Lowry Burgess and Sidewalk Sam.

Design Impact

Robert Campbell, architectural critic for the *Boston Globe*, cites "the marvelously restored park in Post Office Square" as one of the few sensitive additions to Boston's urban landscape in recent years, which retains a human scale and offers a pleasant setting for pedestrian interaction, reminiscent of our cities of the past.[2]

Since its completion in 1981 there has been no vandalism, probably because of the heavy use of the site and the quality of the maintenance program. Rockefeller felt one positive outcome of the project was that it set a precedent for further important collaborative efforts among artists, architects, city agencies, developers, and private contributors, to enrich public places. Since the completion of the project, the site of a city-owned garage adjacent to Angell Park will become the second park in the area. The Post Office Square, a large consortium of abuttors including the Post Office Square Park Association, the corporate abuttors who maintain Angell Park, hope to buy the property after the current lease expires, demolish the ugly garage, and build a multi-level underground parking facility topped by a park. Plans include the coordination of the design to be compatible with benches, lighting and trash receptacles in Angell Park.

Hyatt Fountain

Background

In contrast to the cool white marble and glass exterior at the entrance to the elegant Hyatt Hotel in Union Square, Ruth Asawa's bronze relief fountain is an exuberant medley of images and details. Depicting dozens of scenes and landmarks from all over San Francisco, the fountain is an unusual piece of public folk art, the result of a concerted effort involving over 200 people.

In its earliest stages, the fountain was very

simply a cylindrical concrete drum, with its water spigots facing inward, designed to counteract San Francisco's powerful winds and prevent the spray from dampening passersby. In 1971, architect Chuck Bassett decided that relief work of some kind would enhance the fountain. He had seen local artist Ruth Asawa's landmark mermaid fountain in Ghirardelli Square and admired its flowing, lively contours and its success in attracting visitors. Hoping she would be equally adept with decorative reliefs, he engaged her to prepare a trial panel for the fountain; she was awarded the commission to decorate the entire 14-foot diameter fountain shortly thereafter.

For the molding material, Asawa chose "baker's clay," an inedible dough used for centuries as a household sculpting medium, especially to occupy children. Unlike other molding substances, the dough has a natural spring that makes the figures look as if they will bounce to life, if touched. A San Francisco panorama seemed a logical choice with this process and material.

Description

The frieze consists of forty-one individual plaques depicting city scenes, organized geographically. At the rim of the fountain is the ocean; the bay defines the bottom. Between the two borders are several dozen of San Francisco's most famous sites, and typical San Francisco scenes: Coit Tower,

the Golden Gate Bridge, the Palace of Fine Arts, Fisherman's Wharf, New Year's festival in Chinatown, winding Lombard Street, even Asawa's own Mermaid Statue in Ghirardelli Square. At the front center is a large HH (Hyatt Hotel) and a banner reading "you are here." Protruding from the top of the fountain is a model of City Hall, draped with two large eagle-like wings.

Along with the recognizable landmarks, there are local figures and even fictional characters. The Grateful Dead are shown in concert, Seiji Ozawa is revealed conducting "The Nutcracker" with a symphony orchestra and ballet troupe at the Opera House. Babar the elephant, Superman and Snoopy are among the fictional participants. Some scenes depict surreal events like the tableau of a wedding where the bridal party is confronted by an enormous cake. Although only reliefs, with simple, playful stylization, each image is rendered in careful perspective.

Over two hundred volunteers—friends, family, neighbors—contributed to the design and sculpting of the massive artwork. All ages were involved, from preschool children to the 81-year-old San Francisco photographer Imogen Cunningham. "Like the Gothic cathedral," said Asawa, "this fountain is the product of many hands working together."

Design Impact

Located in Union square, in the midst of

NAME: *Hyatt Fountain*, San Francisco, California
PROJECT: Cylindrical bronze fountain at entrance to Hyatt Hotel in Union Square, depicting city scenes in bas-relief frieze
ARTIST: Ruth Asawa, many volunteers
AGENCY: The Hyatt Corporation; Chuck Bassett of Skidmore, Owings, and Merrill
SIZE: 14 feet in diameter, 1 foot to 10 feet high
DATE: Started 1971, completed 1972
COST: $94,300 (Plumbing—$22,000; casting—$48,000; artist—$18,000)
MATERIAL: "Baker's clay" used to model figures; cast in bronze
PHOTOGRAPHY: Peter Epstein

luxury hotels, expensive shops, and San Francisco's theater district, on steps that are a prime people-watching site, the fountain is a conspicuous new landmark. Standing out as the only intricate surface against a background of modern architecture, the fountain is especially alluring. Part of its attraction, also, is that it can be touched as well as viewed, and, because of its complexity, it always has new details to be discovered. For a tourist unfamiliar with San Francisco, it is an entertaining introductory guide to the city's highlights. One unintended use of the fountain: it has become the repository for donations to the City of Hope, a national medical center and research institute, which specializes in catastrophic diseases.

Dancer's Series: Steps

Background

The Capitol Hill area, just east of downtown Seattle, was once among the city's busiest small business districts: like many older sections in the country's urban centers, it deteriorated slowly while newer shopping centers sprang up around the city. In the mid-1970s, the city government, in cooperation with property owners along Broadway, undertook a streetscape revitalization program. Nine blocks along the avenue were substantially improved with repaving, landscaping, new lighting, and grounding of overhead wires.

Through Seattle's "One Percent for the Arts" Ordinance, which requires one percent of the city's capital expenditure to be used for art, Jack Mackie was selected to participate in the planning and to create an artwork compatible with the new street de-

sign. Both the artist and design team felt strongly that the transformation should encourage and accentuate the architectural qualities of the strip. For Mackie, this meant questioning the traditional forms of street art:

The scale and shape of Broadway . . . suggested muraling. But any additional information on these surfaces would have masked over and hidden the localized architecture, something that the design team felt should be emphasized. Any large scale sculpture would have likewise served only to block and interfere with pedestrian movement. . . . Here, the constant motion of the streetscape became the catalyst for my thinking. As I considered the 'hows' of this motion, I realized that one result of the project would be that we would define how people move within the area. . . . That idea of defining people's movement, when combined with the existing motion of Broad-

NAME: *Dancer's Series: Steps*, Seattle, Washington
PROJECT: Eight panels of bronze shoe soles arranged into dancing diagrams, with arrows explaining patterns, inlaid in cement sidewalk as part of urban improvement program
ARTIST: Jack Mackie in collaboration with MAKERS architectural firm
AGENCY: Seattle Arts commission; property owners in Broadway Local Improvement District
SIZE: Each panel covers from 6 to 12 square feet
DATE: Started in 1978, completed in 1982
COST: $25,000 (Materials—$20,000; artist—$5,000)
MATERIAL: Bronze with iron support frame underneath
PHOTOGRAPHY: Mark Ukelson, Renata von Tscharner
DRAWING: Jack Mackie

way, led me to consider 'street activity' and dance in a similar state of mind, as a similar language of motion.

Description

That concept was translated by Mackie into a collection of bronze panels representing dance diagrams, entitled "DANCER'S SERIES: Steps," set into the cement sidewalk at various points along Broadway. Using numbered men's and ladies' soles and arrows as guides to the motion, the patterns display different dance steps. There are eight separate dances, some traditional ballroom types, others invented to correspond to specific locations, such as a bus stop step. In addition, each panel is supplemented by a plaque suggesting an appropriate rhythm to accompany the steps. The installation of the panels was planned for 1980, but a moratorium on federal funds for the street improvements slowed the project. They were finally installed in 1982. Part of the opening ceremonies for the panels included a 2000

foot conga line organized by the Arthur Murray Dance Studios.

Design Impact

Because they are inlaid in the sidewalk, the panels will act as a surprise element to viewers—an unexpected visual discovery. Each series of dancers' steps traces the process of human motion, from some viewers an irresistable urge to pause and mentally reenact the dance combinations, and from others a spontaneous spurt of dance fever! Those congregating around the steps or actually dancing attract other passersby, creating a chain reaction of participation and shared amusement.

Since 1983, a local teacher named Mark Ukelson has run 'On Broadway Tours—A Street Theatre,' private tour billed "for those who know how to enjoy ourselves." The two-hour tour runs daily between May and September and makes stops at all eight dance steps. Music mime, and theatre performed by tour leaders accompany the dancing along with an historic commentary about the dance steps, music, background of the community, and improvisational street theatre. Participants are encouraged to try out the steps and enlist the help of unsuspecting passersby; tour tickets include discount coupons to restaurants and other businesses along the street—thus linking art and commerce. In 1984, Carol Channing danced her way across Seattle, via the Dancer's Steps.

While modern design usually stresses functionalism and bold, large scale geometry, the Dancer's Steps represent a contrasting movement—the reemergence of ornament to emphasize the human scale of an environment.

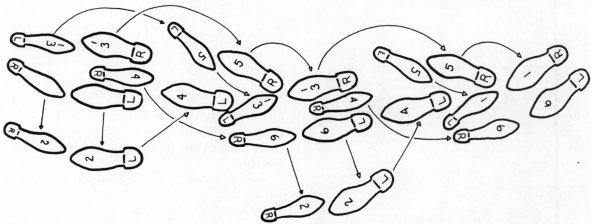

Flower Stand

Summary

The cast iron flower stand in Cincinnati's Fountain Square—a decorative anomaly of Victoriana against a backdrop of glass and steel—is the single reminder of an outdoor market which existed on the site over a century ago. Although small in size, the kiosk holds the city's legal claim to the entire plaza surrounding Fountain Square: under the 1831 deed, the plaza had to be maintained as a market place or else would revert to its original owners.

The Cincinnati Horticultural Society proposed the flower stand in 1864 because

the genteel residents of the surrounding neighborhood wanted an elegant alternative to the boisterous open woodframe markethouse where meat, produce and flowers were sold.

The Horticultual Society demonstrated an awareness of the connection between public amenity and commerce, while protecting the city's claim to the land as a market place:

A place furnished in a tasteful manner, with the necessary appurtenances for the display of cut and pot flowers, and choice conservatory plants, on sale by our enterprising gardeners, would speedily be occupied at a remunerative permanent rental and afford elegant resort for the citizens, as well as be an attractive place to strangers visiting here. It is to be admitted that our city has but few or no public institutions aside from our noble schools, of which we may be proud. It is by fostering innocent entertainments and promoting the general comfort of the citizens,

that a city may be made attractive to a large population, and good citizenship promoted, so that considerations of sound public policy would alone be sufficient argument in favor of all such projects as we hereby recommend. *They always pay.*

This proposal planted a seed, which the city eventually cultivated. Six years later in 1870, a bitter legal battle ensued, between the marketsellers, primarily butchers, who wanted compensation for the loss of their businesses, and the city which planned to destroy the unsightly markethouse. The butchers lost the battle: the old block-long building was destroyed in one evening by ninety "shock troops" from the city street cleaning department, and the site was cleared. Later that year, the city widened the plaza to accommodate the elaborate Tyler-Dickenson Fountain, donated by a wealthy citizen.

It was then that the diehard merchants "slipped into their deeds the provision that their ground was to be forever a marketplace."[1] The single flower stand presumably was installed at this time to ensure the city's legal right to maintain the plaza and fountain as they wished. Ironically, the fountain would later play a role in preserving the flower stand. The fountain stands forty-three feet high, and is topped by a nine foot woman of matronly proportions, representing the Genius of Water.

In order to maintain the legal fiction that the square was still a market place, the mayor made it a practice to purchase a flower once a year at the only remaining flower stand. This custom continued as Fountain Square became the most prominent civic space in the city and hosted many important celebrations, including some elaborate flower and produce festivals!

Over the years the sheet metal canopy of the little iron flower stand rusted, and the stand was shifted around the esplanade. In 1931 the City Traffic Department sought to remove both the fountain and the flower stand in order to expedite the flow of automobile traffic. This plan met with wide-

NAME: *Flower Stand*, Cincinnati, Ohio
PROJECT: Cast iron flower stand located in Fountain Square, maintained for many years to symbolically comply with an early deed requiring that the site remain a marketplace
ARTIST: Unknown
AGENCY: Cincinnati Horticultural Society; City of Cincinnati
SIZE: 10 feet × 4 feet 10 inches
DATE: 1864, used symbolically since 1870
COST: Unknown
MATERIAL: Cast iron painted dark green
PHOTOGRAPHY: Ronald Lee Fleming

spread oposition, and the square was modified to accommodate more traffic, allowing the fountain to remain. The flower stand, however, was put into storage. For a short time it staged a comeback, but by the 1960's the stand was again in storage as the esplanade was modernized to suit the new development taking place on several sides.

In 1969, the City Properties Director discovered the stand in a warehouse. He had it welded, bolted, repainted in dark green and reinstalled in the square. Since then, local garden clubs have unofficially adopted the stand, and during the summer months it serves its original function. Though the city has now assumed title to the square and the legal need for the symbolic annual flower sale ceremony has ceased, the tradition has survived. The flower stall is now sited only a few feet from the old fountain. They stand, two ornate survivors of another era, surrounded by somber black pavement and modern highrise buildings. Since there is no explanatory plaque, passersby are left to invent their own stories as to why the flower stand is there and to ponder any relationship between these two nineteenth century relics. Only insiders know the umbilical connection between them and how they nurtured each other to survive in this space. Initially the installation of the fountain depended upon institutionalizing the flowerstand as a remnant of the public market. In turn, the public's attachment to the fountain became the instrumental factor in retaining the site as a major public amenity and thus aided in the resurrection of the flower stand on its original site.

In recent years, Fountain Square has hosted numerous public events. The Downtown Council, an affiliate of the Chamber of Commerce, sponsors concerts two nights a week, weather permitting, and daily lunchtime events, such as dance performances and lectures. The latest addition to the square is a permanent performing arts pavillion, with an open air proscenium, completed in spring, 1985. Every spring the flower stand dons its red and white awning to host the annual flower sale.

Embroidered Bollards

Summary

Among the artworks installed at the new Porter Square subway station in Cambridge, Massachusetts, are six carved granite blocks. Designed at a height comfortable for sitting, these bollards will protect the new subway station with its pedestrian plaza from automobiles. However, they are more than merely street furniture: each stone is carved in relief with an embroidery pattern distinct to one of the area ethnic groups. Merging traditional folk art with modern urban design, the bollards are a small part of the "Arts-on-the-Line" project, which has allocated $695,000 to environmental artworks in Cambridge and Somerville's four new subway stations.

The bollards are the idea of Cambridge sculptor William Reimann, who had long been fascinated by the craftsmanship and richness of Portuguese bedspreads. Pursuing this interest in textile traditions, he discovered weaving and embroidery patterns unique to different ethnic groups and still cultivated and cherished today. He conceptualized the project as a way "to translate the weaving into stone without compromising

NAME: *Embroidered Bollards*, Cambridge, Massachusetts
PROJECT: Six granite blocks, with carvings representing ethnic embroidery, tile, and jewelry patterns; located at new Porter Square subway station
ARTIST: William Reimann
AGENCY: Cambridge Arts Council; Cambridge Seven Associates (Architects); Massachusetts Bay Transit Authority (MBTA)
SIZE: Bollards are each 27 inches high, 12 inches wide
DATE: Conceived 1978; inaugurated December, 1984
COST: $25,000
MATERIAL: Granite
PHOTOGRAPHY AND DRAWING: William Reimann

the ethnic integrity." Reimann researched and found patterns representing all the major ethnic groups of the Porter Square area—Portuguese, Spanish, Irish, Polish, Slavs, Russians, French-Canadians, Asians, Africans, and Penobscot Indians (who were the original inhabitants).

Transferring these motifs—designed for the delicacy of jewelry and fabrics—into hard stone required special treatment. The artist chose a method used frequently by tombstone cutters, in which a rubber sheet with the pattern cut out is glued to granite, and the exposed areas are carved out by sandblasting. Details and texturing are added with hand tools.

Because the artist's intention was "not to make a sculptural statement, but to serve as interlocutor" for the ethnic neighborhood groups, the designs achieve their effect subtly. The relief is not deep, and similar granite is used frequently throughout the station. Only on close inspection will the bollards reveal their richness. This subtlety, though intentional, might be lost in this bustling intersection. The visual impact of the carvings depends very much on the shadows cast on the reliefs. Some bollards carry two patterns providing different images in morning and evening light. The artist intended the carved patterns to be most noticable during commuter rush hours—in the early morning and late afternoon sunlight—owing to their orientation when shadows are most prominent. Reimann sees no need to have these patterns labelled or interpreted; he wants people to have something to discover, something to wonder about. "If they really want to know, they can find out, but deciphering is part of the fun."

Seattle Substations

"A wonderland of color, humor and harmony . . . a high tech Oz"[1] is how one Seattle reporter described a local electrical substation. Electrical utility substations are not exactly the first thing that comes to mind when hearing such a description, or when searching for a pleasant urban setting for a family outing. However, for people in Seattle, electrical substations have been transformed from sites of utilitarian drabness to whimsical respite.

Substations, like manholes covers, and telephone poles are familiar elements in a city landscape; but usually we view them as eyesores, or prefer not to 'see' them at all. Indeed most substations are not likely to be visible, much less open to the public.

The city-owned utility company, Seattle City Light, and the Seattle Arts Commission have changed all that. They have discovered that substations are an untapped source of visual interest, and an uncharted territory in which to commission public art. Since the 1950s, Seattle City Light has been visually upgrading its 100 neighborhood electrical substations. The station treatment has expanded from modest landscaping in the earlier projects, to architectural design in later projects, and is now resulting in the intergration of public art in the preliminary design phase.

Using the City's One Percent for Arts requirement, the Commission integrated public art into two substations: first in 1979, and then, based on the success of their first experiment, in 1982. There are plans to extend the program to more stations. Substations are now being considered as living museums of technical and artistic achievement, fusing references to visual imagery, the technical process and the historic evolution of electricity. Design teams transformed a traditional public utility into an unconventional public amenity.

Viewlands/Hoffman Substation

Background

Seattle Light constructed the Viewlands/Hoffman substation in 1979, replacing a block-long area of housing in a blue collar district. Chosen, due to the architect's strong encouragement, as the first collaborative effort for one percent for Arts projects, it brought together artists, architects, engineers, city officials, and community members to plan how the art elements would relate to the site design.

Richard Hobbs, project architect of Hobbs, Fukui, Davidson Associates, said,

When we were selected by the City Light we were told that artists will be involved in the project at some point, because the project qualified for one percent for Arts funds. I mentioned to Bob Bishop, City Light architect, that the way we work is, that if you're

NAME: *Viewlands/Hoffman Substation*, Seattle, Washington
PROJECT: A Windmill Park, illustrative warning signs, concrete wall mural, color-coded equipment, furniture and paths incorporated into the design of an electrical power station.
ARTIST: Art Team: Andrew Keating, Sherry Markovitz, Lewis "Buster" Simpson
AGENCY: Seattle City Light Co.; Richard Hobbs, Project Architect, Hobbs, Fukui, Davidson Associates; Seattle Arts Commission
SIZE: Approximately 1 square acre
DATE: 1975–1979
COST: $62,700
MATERIAL: Variety—including machine parts, wire mesh, paving brick, household items, colored exterior paint, concrete
PHOTOGRAPHY: Air view and warning sign: Charles Adler, Courtesy of Seattle Arts Commission and Seattle City Light; Other photos: Ronald Lee Fleming

going to work with somebody on a project, you bring them in at the beginning, before anything is there, and before anybody has pre-conceived ideas.[2]

The jury consisted of Hobbs, project architect; three Northwest artists—Norie Sato, Lee Kelly, and Miro Fitzgerald; G.R. Bishop, City Light architect; and Tom Berger, project landscape architect. They selected Andrew Keating, Buster Simpson, and Sherry Markovitz from among eighty applicants. All three are local artists. Keating is a painter, Simpson was trained as a ceramicist and a sculptor, and Markovitz is a printmaker and painter. The jury selected artists whom they believed had the flexibility to collaborate at the conceptual stage of the project. The design process lasted one and a half years, and articles in the *Seattle Arts Newsletter*, *Seattle Post*, and *Seattle Voice* testify to the difficult and time-consuming nature of the collaboration between architects and artists. Says Nancy Joseph, Art in Public Places Program assistant, in her *Seattle Arts Newsletter* article entitled "Artist on Design Teams":

> Artists on design teams have to learn a "new language" as well as learn how to focus on specific ideas earlier than they do in their private work. The learning process, and the necessity to be open to having other team members criticize one's ideas, can be difficult.[3]

Despite the arduous process, Nancy Joseph reported that artist Buster Simpson considered the lack of definition of the artists' role as an asset. "We're the random element . . . that's what they're hiring us for."[4] He also spoke of the Viewlands architects, saying they "turned us around on a lot of procedural things—the way to communicate . . . the way to present ideas. It was a learning experience."[5]

They found there was a major difference in how architects and artists thought about design problems. Artists tended to start a new concept when confronted with a critique rather than refine an existing design the way architects do. Another difference was that each group was used to expressing its ideas in a different medium, causing a communication gap. It was difficult for artists to decipher blueprints, and it was equally difficult for architects and engineers to cull meaning from schematic sketches.

Adjacent property owners and other neighborhood residents met with project architects, landscape architects, artists, and representatives from City Light and the Seattle Arts Commission in a series of three community awareness meetings. The designers outlined the direction the project would take, stressing their goal: to keep the site as open as possible—visually accessible to the public—and to integrate the industrial site with the least disruption to the neighborhood context. The designers took into account residents' comments, mainly concerning landscaping, public parking, and the inclusion of a play-area for children.

The art works were installed in 1979, at a cost of $62,700.

Description

Elves have not been at play at the Viewlands/Hoffman substation—artists have been the ones who enlivened the substation's functional character, painting transformers "pastel green, yellow and blue Easter egg colors," and "planting a forest of completely wacko little windmills."[6] The centerpiece is a halfmoon-shaped field of gravel planted with 30 whirligigs, circumscribed by the wire mesh boundaries of the substation, which is otherwise off-limits to visitors. The whirligigs are fanciful found-object sculptures which twirl and flutter in the wind. Each free-standing concoction, designed by two folk artists, Emil and Vera Gehrke, is a unique mix of wheels, spoons, tennis rackets and bits of household appliances. During the design stage, on a trip to Grand Coolee in the desert region of eastern Washington, artist Buster Simpson discovered an entire "plantation" of whirligigs in the Gehrkes' front yard. He had stumbled upon a perfect solution for attracting people's attention inside the substation. The whirligigs offered

unusual visual and auditory stimuli, and at the same time reinforced the theme of electricity, because some of the concoction's components were originally parts of household electrical appliances. Simpson bought a small cache of whirligigs, and as the elderly artists were unable to visit the site, he oversaw their incorporation into the overall design.

Viewers' only access into the substation yard is to enter a semi-circular tunnel of wire fencing which matches the boundary fencing, and follows the periphery of the arc-shaped whirligig field. This allows a better inspection of the windmill forest; a closer look at the electrical transformers nearby which have been painted bright hues of green, yellow and blue, corresponding to stages of the breakdown of electricity; and a sharper view of the concrete wall surrounding the

edge of the substation, where Keating painted a 400 foot mural. He placed colored shapes like flags or banners in an intermittent pattern corresponding to the grid made from the form lines and expansion joints of the concrete surface.

Another artistic enterprise was the enamel safety plaques designed by Keating and Markovitz which warn visitors of the serious repercussions of entering the fenced-off areas. These plaques communicate their message in a pictorial comic/tragic style, with caricatures of workmen being electrocuted.

Rae Tufts, architecture and art critic for the *Seattle Times*, commented on the "off the wall humor"[7] of the artwork, and a spokesman of the selection jury called the design "a good example of what interface of design disciplines with community input can achieve . . . It's a very humanistic approach."

Creston/Nelson Substation

Background

Following in the wake of the Viewlands/ Hoffman project, Creston/Nelson became the second substation to utilize the team approach for incorporating artists into the

process at the schematic design stage. The Commission announced the competition in *Seattle Arts*, the Commission's newsletter, and sent the press release to artists in the Registry of Northwest Artists. The Registry mailing did not prove a successful means of soliciting applicants, and has since been dropped from the selection process. City Light and the Seattle Arts Commission again co-sponsored the competition.

This time, four artists, including Markovitz and Keating, who were part of the artist team for Viewlands/Hoffman, joined the project architect and the chief of engineering from City Light to choose three Seattle artists. Those selected included Clair Colquitt, who specializes in 'vehicle' constructions which are drivable artworks; Merrily Thompkins, who works in wood, metal and other salvageable materials; and Ries Niemi who is an industrial artist and printmaker.

The artists for the Creston/Nelson project then met with the artists who did the Viewlands/Hoffman art work to discuss their experiences and approaches to incorporating art into substations. The Creston/Nelson crew opted to make their artwork more physically accessible to the community than the art work in Viewlands/Hoffman. Niemi says, "I like to put art in the streets. I like people to see the stuff." As part of the collaborative process, meetings were held with community members.

Description

Instead of electrical current, it is the people that flow from "plug," through "extension cord" to "wall outlet" on the Creston/Nelson substation site. The team devised this thematic idea to "transform" the new substation into an art park. When shut, the gates form an Art Deco-like motif of zigzagged lightening bolts, pulsating from a stylized "electric plug." The pathway, set in an open hillside setting, is the "extension cord" winding towards the sub-station. Along the way, three light bulb-shaped concrete pads each host a sculpture expressing the leitmotif of electricity. The path ends, appropriately enough, "plugged into" the wall of the substation which houses three transformers. Clair Colquitt's monument to "Electrical Abuse" is a tinted pastel cast concrete sculpture of "how *not* to" overload

sockets. Reaching eight feet high, the totem-like stack of multiple plugs is labeled simply, "NO." A solitary plug, also concrete, sits on an outlet nearby. It is labeled "YES."

A four-foot high mustachioed head of Nikola Tesla, a Seattle engineer and inventor of the formula for alternating current, leans into the hillside. Grass and flowers grow wildly out of the top of his head, a visual conceit acknowledging Tesla's hair-raising experiments with alternating current electricity and his reputed later years of insanity. Merrily Thompkins designed the head of wire and concrete covered with bright fragments of mosaic tiles, planting vegetation in the head so it would blend with the grassy incline where it rests.

Ries Niemi's cast concrete and aluminum sculpture has been called an "altar-like tribute" to the light bulb and the switch-plate and is thought to resemble "a church organ."[8] It sits at the summit of the pathway, a fitting location since it also serves as a bench. The three-tiered piece schematically represents the substation's function—

NAME: *Creston/Nelson Substation*, Seattle, Washington

PROJECT: A cast concrete sculpture depicting electrical abuse, a gigantic mosaic head of inventor Nikola Tesla, and a cast concrete and aluminum sculpture dedicated to the switchplate and light bulb are main attractions set in a park-like context; other designs include aluminum gates, a birdbath, decorated chain-link fencing, and decorative warning signs

ARTIST: Art Team: Clair Colquitt, Ries Niemi

AGENCY: Seattle Arts Commission, Seattle City Light

SIZE: 2.7 Acres

DATE: Dedication Activities—1982

COST: $58,000

MATERIAL: Variety including aluminum panels, concrete, tinted cast concrete, wire mesh, mosaic tiles, grass, chain link fencing, plastic strips, epoxy-on-metal signs

PHOTOGRAPHY: Light bulb sculpture, electric plug gate, Tesla Head, electrical abuse, courtesy of Seattle City Light, by Charles Adler

transforming electricity from 230,000 volts down to household current. The highest tier has three large light bulbs and switchplates, symbolizing the substation's three transformers, which direct the current first into neighborhood branch circuits—represented by the second tier's fifteen pairs of bulbs and switchplates—and then into household current—expressed by the row of aluminum rods connecting the second tier to the third and lowest tier, which is the bench.

In addition to these three main attractions, other artistically designed amenities include a concrete and tile birdbath with inlaid inscriptions about Tesla; a patterned design of plastic strips woven into the standard chain link fence; and epoxy-on-metal danger signs. Even the gate stops are fashioned after electrical plugs. Seattle City Light and One Percent for the Arts funded everything except the fabrication of the main gate, for which Clair Colquitt bid and won. It cost less than a standard gate that was itemized in a line in the budget. Rae Tufts, art and architecture critic for the *Seattle Times*, called the art work, "avant garde, but without self-conscious pretense . . . they [the works] are enormous fun," and, she said, "the sheer joyousness of this public art for public enjoyment is, indeed, to be valued."[9]

Design Impact

The two substation projects differ in their effects, but share a common team-oriented process. Richard Andrews, coordinator of the Seattle Arts Commission, defined the objective of the process, "Ultimately, both sides moved towards each other; the artists found that ideas that did not work in sketches become more understandable to their colleagues in the language of blueprints; the building professionals recognized the contributions of the artist; and the artists' ideas became reflected in the overall design."

Nancy Joseph said as a result of the experience of these two projects, artists chosen for subsequent teams have been given, "a brief introduction to the restrictions and scheduling details of a design team process, before they join design teams."

Matthew Kangas, a freelance arts writer, said in the *Seattle Voice* that these projects have brought "new drama to publicly-financed architecture in the Seattle area . . . Viewlands (Hoffman) and Creston (Nelson) are great because artists left their stamp" and succeeded in fashioning "a more humane environment."[10]

The Viewlands/Hoffman project won four awards in 1979: a Washington Aggregates and Concrete Association Excellence in the Use of Concrete Award, an honor award from the Seattle chapter of the American Institute of Architects; a First Honor award from the 1978–1979 American Public Power Association; and the 1979 Awards Program for Utility Design. The Viewlands/Hoffman artwork remains in good condition since installation in 1978, but the whirligigs need constant maintenance, which is executed by artist Buster Simpson.

Weather conditions damaged some of the artwork at Creston/Nelson. As the site is partially hidden from the road, it is also particularly vulnerable to vandalism. One of the artists cites another reason for damage, the sculptures' "responsiveness—mosaics crack, aluminum bends." Learning from this experience, Ries Niemi, previously unfamiliar with the construction materials, is re-designing the concrete bench in his piece to withstand site conditions.

As a result of this integrated process, further collaborations are planned for two police precinct stations, and the expansion of two additional power substations. The Broad Street substation will incorporate fencing treatment, altering the shape, color, and patterning of standard chain link fencing.

The Canal Street substation will include symbols of human "power"—love and law being two examples depicted by silhouettes of a couple kissing, and a judge, painted on translucent plexiglass, with colored plexiglass backing, placed inside the windows. These figures will be lit at night.

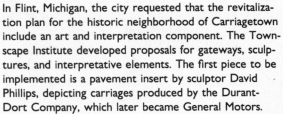

This iron gate in a Seattle alleyway, designed by Jean Paul Jones, recalls the basket patterns of the Northwest Indians. Even modest changes in standard building elements can build place reference.

In Flint, Michigan, the city requested that the revitalization plan for the historic neighborhood of Carriagetown include an art and interpretation component. The Townscape Institute developed proposals for gateways, sculptures, and interpretative elements. The first piece to be implemented is a pavement insert by sculptor David Phillips, depicting carriages produced by the Durant-Dort Company, which later became General Motors.

The travel agency Nouvelles Frontières on the Boulevard de Grenelle in Paris rebuilt a historically listed building from the 1930's. The architect Jean Jacques Ory integrated the original artwork into the new façade which was completed in 1986. Perhaps this comparatively rare effect can demonstrate how contemporary architects might further incorporate decorative and narrative elements to strengthen the alliance of art and architecture in new construction.

Public Art Planning: Encouraging Artists to Respond to Place

A CRITICAL LOOK AT NATIONAL PUBLIC ART POLICY

The Recent Evidence of Placemaking Art as an Argument for Policy Review

The works of public art and urban design chronicled in the preceding pages under the generic name of "placemakers" have for the most part been the subject of community accord rather than approbation. They have been accepted in their own time because they acknowledge some compact with their public and convey a discernible meaning to that public. Unlike much "plop" art—a name given to gallery art plopped in public places—placemakers do not foist themselves on the public for its own aesthetic good, in the conviction of appreciation in some future time. Invariably they support their context rather than remaining isolated from it or deliberately standing in contrast to it. Many of them sustain a narrative tradition, and some are unabashedly emotive. To some extent, this increasing presence of placemakers in the American cityscape implies a certain heresy about how public monies should be spent for public art. They threaten vested interests in the art world that have influenced the way federal money for public art has been spent. These interests accept the abstract tradition of public art in past decades as "progressive" and support the credo that if a work is not initially shocking to many viewers, it must be mundane and not worth supporting with public funds. Conversely, placemaking art does not usually shock; it often creates bonds between people and their spaces which nourish a sense of proprietorship.

As the debate over public arts policy grows in this country, the case studies examined here should fuel discussion about the "process" of selection and the kind of art that process fosters. This is a propitious time for such a discussion, because the growing visible presence of public art around the country—evidence of the increase in funding for public art—is encouraging some critical reevaluation. Both cities and states are adopting laws that require a percentage of their construction budgets to be devoted to public art. The largest purchasers of public art are the federal government's General Service Administration's (GSA) Art-in-Architecture program and the National Endowment for the Arts' (NEA) Art-in-Public-Places program. Both these agencies are critically evaluating their procedures for commissioning art, at least partly because of some of the antagonism individual pieces have encountered in the communities that the art was intended to enhance.

This final chapter addresses the impact of these government-sponsored programs and their changing guidelines, and then through the lens of one particular controversy—the hearings over the continued presence of the sculpture by Richard Serra on Federal Plaza in New York—questions some of the assumptions that have anchored recent commissioning procedures. Finally, it examines some trends in arts planning, as a basis for proposing a process for commissioning public art that the authors believe will strengthen the alliance between art and place.

Thoughts about NEA and GSA Funding Guidelines

When looking at governmental policy toward public art, we have argued for one goal which we think has been neglected—placemaking—the building of the sense of a community ethic—by activating constituencies that can then feel more responsive to their place. And this goal can only be achieved through a process that encourages a broader consensus. This leads directly to the question of how the largest of the sources of funding for public art—the NEA's Art-in-Public-Places program and the General Service Administration's Art-in-Architecture program—approach this issue of community choice.

Present policy in these agencies is directed toward supporting the creativity of the individual artist, rather than the particular community that wants to commission art or the context of a given site. Policy also appears biased against "commemorative art." Indeed guidelines discouraging this sort of art seem to reflect a distrust of the taste of the community and a fear that art that is focussed on conscious community support must lead ineluctably toward "socialist realism." The pariah of such didactic art has in the past been called forth to quash public art proposals that display a broadly accessible meaning to the general public or that actually commemorate some aspect of local culture or history.

Our own experience does not support such a view, and we are not even convinced that art with an accessible content must be didactic, predictable, or mundane. We note with interest that both GSA and NEA programs are reconsidering their guidelines, as public art controversies persuade them to be more responsive to local constituencies and the evident desire of communities for art that respects a sense of local identity.

Obviously, many of the works commissioned under these two programs fill the larger definition discussed in the Introduction as generic placemaking art. They do "mark" places, though to date only a few of them have been responsive to the particular culture of an environment in a way that appeals to laymen. Constructions like Alan Sonfist's forest block, a re-creation of vegetation from the time of Manhattan's first settlement on a block on the edge of SoHo; Luis Jimenez's "Vaquero," a sculpture of a Mexican-American cowboy that stands in a neighborhood park in Houston; and George Segal's Steelmakers in Youngstown (see p. 110) are examples of NEA funded pieces that express a link with specific places and their traditions or constituencies. But they are a precious minority.[1] NEA's Art-in-Public-

Places program appears to be a little more responsive to this direction than the GSA's program. This may be because NEA is less insulated from the public and requires matching funds from local sources, whereas GSA's art projects are set on federal turf and therefore may not stir as much argument unless they do violence to the image of a particular place or affect the use of a public space.

Perhaps the experience of working directly with communities will produce a greater sensitivity in the NEA program. The director of the program, appointed in 1985, Richard Andrews, is an artist already experienced in implementing public art on a municipal scale, and he understands the technical as well as the political ramifications. While the guidelines remain locked in place until 1987, there appears to be an increasing flexibility about examining their impact.[2] A serious flaw in past guidelines was the explicit provision against funding projects that were *solely* commemorative, for fear, one supposes, that the program would be reduced to commissioning war memorials, until now the most pervasive image in American public space. However, the actual impact of this provision has been to inhibit the commissioning of representational art that can more readily serve a commemorative purpose, even though it may not be solely commemorative. A growing national shift away from the Minimalism in the public art of the sixties and seventies and the critical reassessment of the abstractions of the International Style in architecture presage a change in this approach. Even an abstractly commemorative work like the Vietnam Memorial in Washington challenges this guideline. In the 1987 NEA guidelines, this provision against *solely* commemorative art was simply removed. However, this action still does not encourage commemorative work.

The argument is still a live one. Donald Thalacker, the director of the Art-in-Architecture program—while courageously documenting the full extent of the controversy

Luis Jimenez sculpted this super-realistic "Vaquero" in molded fiberglass—one of few NEA commissions in a representational mode. Paying homage to Mexican-American cowboys, it was installed in Moody Park in 1982 adjacent to a Chicano neighborhood near downtown Houston. Though not a requirement in the artist's commissioning process, the sculpture commemorates the Hispanic heritage.[1]

over many of the program's art works in his book, *The Place of Art in the World of Architecture*—continues to give voice to the "modern" view of the passing of commemorative art. In the preface to Thalacker's book, Professor Sam Hunter, a consultant to the program, argues that contemporary monuments "can no longer plausibly celebrate national heroes, patriotic or personal virtue, or great historic events. Both the mythologies and the sustaining artistic conventions for such themes have vanished."[3]

Hunter contends that this art does nevertheless affirm "communitas." Although conceding that "the deeper aesthetic levels of contemporary public sculpture may communicate to the man in the street imperfectly," Hunter surmises that there may be social meaning in art, "primarily through the act of commission and display in public places."[4]

Hunter's elevating the act of commissioning as the most meaningful transaction seems patronizing and ultimately self-deceiving. What regard does he have then for the *content* of the works or its relevence to the people who are going to experience the art? And indeed has all heroic action disappeared with men on horseback? There are still themes for public art that are in some larger sense commemorative and mark the heroism of individuals as well as the collective heroic action of communities.

LEARNING FROM EXPERIENCE: SOME MEDITATIONS ON CONTROVERSY

Cambridge and Hartford from Labyrinth and "Stone Field" to Stone Wall—the Public Art Impasse

As the profiles in this book suggest, even humble neighborhood experiences can serve as an important impetus to the commissioning of public art. For instance, after an advisory committee had suggested brick-

making as a theme for an art commission on a playground in North Cambridge, Massachusetts, community representatives at the hearing on the proposal requested the commemoration be extended to the ball-player sons and grandsons of the brickmakers who had used the playing field, and whose prowess had won them athletic scholarships and upward social mobility. The happy result of this joint decision to represent both brickmaking and ballplaying is in marked contrast to the earlier effort to achieve the non-commemorative labyrinth sculpture with NEA funds in the park adjacent to Cambridge's new public high school. (See page 128.)

For the high school project, the Cambridge Arts Council applied for and was promised a $50,000 grant from the NEA to match *city* monies set aside during the extensive renovation and reconstruction of the Cambridge public high school. A panel, operating under NEA's revised guidelines, which now included three *local* people interested in contemporary art as well as three panelists of regional prominence suggested by NEA's Art-in-Public-Places program, selected a well-respected New York artist to do his first public sculpture. The artist proposed an abstraction of a labyrinth-like form that continued in concrete the imagery of his life's work which is on paper—a progression of elegant drawings depicting imaginary, maze-like habitations.

The well organized neighborhood group, which had earlier presented its views against this proposal orally to the panel, vowed to cut off the city's share of the funding if the project went forward as proposed by the artist.

The community did not oppose the concept of public art; indeed their membership is characterized in city politics as enlightened and progressive, including many young professional people. But they did resist the idea of concrete walls and earth berms imposed on the green space adjacent to the new high school they had spent years fighting to preserve. They viewed the artist's proposed maze primarily as a potential crime and litter trap, and they effectively stalemated the work of art that was being foisted on them. Though the artist was made aware of their concerns, he stuck to the integrity of his original conception and showed no inclination to adapt his ideas to the community's different vision. At this point a cutback in city funds and uncertainty on how to pay the mounting costs of reviewing the next artist on the panel's list of nominees caused the project to be dropped and the city to forfeit the NEA money, which, under the terms of the grant, could not cover the front end expenses of the site visits, etc. . . .[5]

We tell this embarrassing little "tale out of school" so to speak, because it confirms our conviction that procedures for commissioning works of art through federal programs must come to grips with the community's concerns for both the *content* and the quality of the artistic ideas that will occupy their environs. It is not enough to improve the *quality* of the process by translating the artist's intentions more explicitly to the public. This is just an effort to make the so-called local philistines comfortable with the artist's predetermined proposal, and it reinforces the notion that the artist's integrity and creative energy would be impaired by collaboration with the community. Rather, we must accept the paradox that even a brilliant artist may design something that is wholly inappropriate for a particular site. Instead of coming to terms with this dilemma, a sort of cultural phenomenon of this age, many artists and their supporters are wrapped in the self-deluding prophesy that opposition to their work merely demonstrates that they are ahead of their time—a reflection of the primacy that the present-day art world gives to the notion of being avant-garde.

As it happened in Cambridge, the local arts administrators working for the Arts Council felt quite protective about the proposal for the high school, so that lessons or failures were not readily communicated back to the Council members or to the En-

dowment. The administrators held that, when a well recognized artist, chosen by a panel with good qualifications, executed a proposal in good faith, it should then go forward, and that it would be a violation of artistic *integrity* to modify the proposal. Consequently, the administrators were psychologically predisposed to hoist themselves on their own petards, proposing works with little or no relation, and hence little or no meaning, to the surrounding community. Such projects seem destined to incur public opposition, just as they engender among the arts groups that support them certain acts of self-destruction that rarely elicit the community's sympathy. This condition deprives the administrators of even the self-satisfaction of martyrdom. The community simply shrugs and goes on to other concerns, though perhaps a bit warier about public art.

When a project is imposed and actually implemented without community input and without agreed-upon content, sometimes the results can have a chilling effect on other art proposals. This could be the long-term consequence of the NEA-funded sculpture by Carl André, "Stone Field," a graduated series of thirty-six glacial boulders arranged in rows on a grassy triangle in downtown Hartford adjacent to an old church and colonial burial ground, across from the Wadsworth Athenaeum. In the artist's conception the piece would reach beyond the physical context of an eighteenth-century stone wall and church tower to a feeling of ecologic time that in the artist's words "extends the serenity of the graveyard."

Like the artist for the Cambridge High School site, the artist was selected on the basis of his prior work and without having submitted a proposal for the specific site, which is customary with NEA Art-in-Public Places, matching grants.

Unlike the proposed Cambridge maze, which exists only on paper, the Hartford stones lie at the site near the heart of the city. Did the decision-making process fail to embody in the selection enough content

Carl Andre's "Stone Field" sculpture, funded by NEA and private matching monies, occupies a grassy triangle in downtown Hartford, Connecticut. Abutted by clumsey street furniture and greeted by an unsympathetic press, its presence created a stumbling block for subsequent proposals for abstract works such as those by New Haven born Sol LeWitt.

to satisfy the citizenry? This is a key question, for an examination of the process reveals that the six panelists apparently spent about a year reviewing the slides of many different artists' work without ever defining ideas for the site. When the artist was selected, there was neither a broad set of community objectives nor carefully documented evidence that could set parameters for the artist's creative act or give the panelists (including one from the city administration) any future basis for evaluating it. And what of the content that emerged, which the artist said was inspired by a Japanese garden and Stonehenge, which he had recently visited?

As Tom Wolfe, both cultural critic and curmudgeon, wrote about the meaning of the piece in *Harpers Magazine*

André's Stone Field, for example, was created to illustrate three devout theories concerning the nature of sculpture. One, a sculpture should not be placed upon that bourgeois device, the pedestal, which seeks to elevate it above the people (therefore the rocks are on the ground). Two, sculpture should express gravity (and what expresses gravity better than rocks lying on the ground?) Three, a sculpture should not be that piece of bourgeois pretentiousness (such as statues of Lee . . .); it should force the viewer to confront its "objectness." (You want object-ness? Take a look at a plain rock. Take a look at thirty-six rocks.)[6]

As in Hartford, public bafflement and even widespread opposition are sometimes taken by both artists and art administrators as evidence of an object's spiritual worthiness. In the words of another Minimalist artist, the virtue of such art is that the public's "preconception of reality (has been) changed."[7] The question we ask is whether such an objective is worth the investment of considerable public funds. This may be a valid artistic concept, but does it justify so much time and expense and antagonism in a public environment? Of course, Andre's commission of $87,000 generated resentment, not only because of the avowedly Minimalist aesthetic content but also because, in the minds of many citizens, it represented a civic short changing as newspapers reported that the actual cost of the rocks and their transportation to the site was $6000.

A truism about controversial public art often advanced by its supporters is that the controversy will dissipate and the piece will gradually be accepted by a more educated and discerning public. But the fact that the "Stone Field" no longer inspires irate letters to the newspaper as it initially did, or that it may no longer be the object of protest does not necessarily mean that people accept it or have even become accustomed to it. In an intensive planning charrette organized by the Greater Hartford Arts Council and Partners for Livable Places (Washington, D.C.) in the summer of 1984, a number of cultural and business leaders were interviewed, many of whom asserted that the effect of "Stone Field" would be to lessen the likelihood of another large public art initiative (which the charrette hoped to encourage) despite Hartford's substantial tradition of corporate largess and support for the arts.[8]

Several alluded to the Hartford Civic Center Coliseum, where Hartford born artist Sol LeWitt, a pioneering conceptualist who had received a similar NEA grant to create panels on the interior walls, was rejected by the city council, source of the matching grant, and replaced by a black artist who worked in a more narrative tradition, and with whom LeWitt had originally generously offered to share his grant. The community leaders felt that this project suffered the backlash of public resentment created by André's "Stone Field," and that for these reasons no further large commissions were contemplated.

These vignettes in Cambridge and Hartford do not appear to be isolated incidents. Interviews with administrators and critics across the nation from Baltimore to San Francisco indicate that there is widespread concern about many federally funded public art projects. In their tightly reasoned (if whimsically malicious) article in the policy journal, *Public Interest*, Douglas Stalker and Clark Glymour argued that public art as currently constituted and promoted by a small network of critics offends the core of public sensibilities. They propose that public art should "realize, and celebrate, and exemplify a common tradition and shared political, cultural, and esthetic heritage."[9] Since most contemporary public sculptures do not meet such a standard, these academics asserted that the public should not have to pay for such work. Or if it is to be tolerated, it should be put into special districts—akin, one supposes, to red light districts—little storyvilles of loitering objects like the sculptural art parks around museums.

Obviously the authors of this book do not take so extreme a view. Rather than the dissolution of publicly sponsored art programs,

Aloofly viewing the André stones across the street, Nathan Hale, a Connecticut patriot, on traditional pedestal, stands in front of Hartford's Wadsworth Atheneum, surrounded by more recent arrivals—unrelated objects which typify the "museum grounds as art dump" approach of the 1970–80s.

as we argued in *Public Interest*, we would like to see a balance in which "public sculpture would both express the artist's personal vision and also, as the best public sculpture always has, strengthen a sense of place."[10] Consequently, we would propose that the process leading to the selection of art should express a more holistic and humane view of our common culture. To the extent that we are able to plan spaces and buildings to better accommodate these aims we may also take the care to commission public art that does not further exacerbate the alienation that many modern buildings express.

Revising Guidelines of Federal Programs Funding Public Art

Given this concern and the problems we have identified with the present policy, what recommendations can be made to the GSA and to the NEA for the revisions of their public art selection procedures? Here are some modest proposals that we believe these agencies might profitably examine:

1. Every application for a public art commission should require an effective planning process, and this process should be funded by the granting agency. In fact, NEA's Art-in-Public-Places grants increasingly include small planning stipends in advance. But unlike the agency's Design Arts program whose planning funds go to administrative organizations responsible for a space, NEA art planning funds now go only to artists. This perpetuates the difficulty of developing a process that includes the interests of other constituencies besides artists which might more thoroughly address issues of place meaning and content. These concerns grounded in the memory of experience with the site are often opposed to the more formalist conceptions of many artists who may wish to advance their own particular development or something they are currently interested in realizing.

2. There should be a greater emphasis on the content or meaning of the site or space—pulling together physical, cultural, and behavioral information about the space—as part of the planning process. Some specific procedures for developing what we call an "Environmental Profile" to discover and document this information are developed in the appendix at the end of this chapter.

3. There should be special incentives for collaborative projects between designers and artists as well as between different artists and artisans. The funds should thus support more than one artist in a collaborative work. The GSA guidelines give the responsibility to the architect to decide whether the Art-in-Architecture program should be involved. The name is really a misnomer, since only rarely has the program produced *art in architecture* in the broad sense of selecting the artists at the same time as the archi-

tects, and choosing the architects at least partly for their capacity to work with artists (and vice-versa) and to realize projects which are part of the architecture. Projects should be identified where an architect-artist team including artists can be awarded particular building commissions.

4. Collaborations formed around a specific theme or metaphor should be encouraged. This can be supported by the information in the "environmental profile" (see §2). In some recent collaborations, the results are described as the "new functionalism," where artists have not created their own separate monuments but rather have designed elements as part of the environmental design such as street furniture or building arches, stairways, or lighting that are more aesthetically pleasing. This kind of collaboration can be seen in Seattle's National Oceanic and Atmospheric Administration Building grounds, at the Jerome B. and Laya Wiesner Building at MIT, in Cambridge and at Battery Park City in New York City. Some recent collaborations touted in the architectural press are so minimal as to be insignificant in terms of their effect on the entire building project. Collaborations should sometimes go beyond functionalism to achieve greater enrichment or density of meaning. The art elements might advance beyond minimal poetic compatibility and instead create layers of metaphor or refractions of meaning that build relationships between one piece and another of some larger significance.

5. The role of the artisan or craftsman should be supported in public art projects because of their ability to create surfaces that have particular appeal for many parts of the population—children, the blind, the aged. Artisans have for the most part become divorced from the building arts and, as individuals, have no easy way to incorporate their work—stained glass windows, wood carving, metal work, ceramic tile—into contemporary structures. The NEA and

GSA might well fund some team approaches in which groups of artisans treat major surfaces of important new buildings and where the entire team is financially supported. Schools of crafts and artisanry might be given grants to assemble teams who compatibly could work together and who could then market their services through city and state one-percent-for-public-art staffs.

6. Prohibitions, implicit or explicit, against commemorative work should be removed from grant guidelines. As discussed earlier in the text, this does not have to mean a resurgence of war memorials in front of public buildings, but rather a recognition that in most communities today some aspect of their material culture and history, not necessarily the traditionally heroic aspects, have more meaning than the private aesthetic concerns of the individual artist, and that most communities, given a choice, would prefer art that made those connections to their identity.

7. Fund the community as well as the artist. The focus of the NEA program is on the individual artist, and the grants seek to support the creativity of the individual as opposed to the collectivity of the place where the art is to be commissioned. If the focus is difficult to shift, then it might be useful to combine Design Arts and Public Arts grants so that both the administrators and the artists are supported at the same time and place. In the GSA program, this proviso should mean greater attention to the planning process and more investment in proposals and in the community information that can inform these proposals.

A Matter of Sensibilities: Serra and Federal Plaza

In a recent introduction to an exhibition catalogue of public art at the University of Pennsylvania, Janet Kardon, director of the Institute of Contemporary Art at the University of Pennsylvania, wrote: "In the broadest sense public art is now the major area in which democratic ideas and esthetic elitism attempt to come to terms with each other. Why is it proving so difficult?"[11] In her analysis, Kardon noted that an overriding issue scarcely noticed in museum spaces was realism.

> In no other area of art activity does the public's "right to recognize" the subject, content and meaning of the art work apply with such force. . . . There is a basic incompatibility between the concepts of space generated by the modern movement and those invoked by traditional realism. . . . The space of abstraction is a different space. Its gravitational rules, its metaphors, its illusions, and purities are far from the everyday space in which the realist figure stands. . . . The huge abstract sculpture, which celebrates the fact of art before all else, is a threatening experience for a public who finds it without rationale, motive, or beauty. The way the abstract artwork relates to the space of the passer-by is one key to the negative reception that has become a kind of certificate of merit among modern artists; it redefines space in a way that is sensed rather than understood; it unsettles perceptions and does not reassure the viewer with an easily shared idea or subject. . . . Yet those responsible for creating, funding, and carrying through such projects often are astonished by such a basic human response.[12]

If we are to enlist the public's interest in public art, this "basic human response" must be accommodated. The providing of a more comprehensive planning process should challenge the artist to relate his work to concepts that attract meaning—"an idea that gives the pedestrian's imagination some access to the work" so that he does not feel insulted.[13]

"Modern" art's credo, expressed in the following words that accompanied the Count Panza exhibit at the Contemporary Museum of Art in Los Angeles in 1985, is often ill-equipped to make a pact with the community on a public space.

It is wholly indeterminant
It has no specific traits
It is entirely ineffable
It is never seen
It is not accessible

It can only be known as something else.[14]

Nowhere has the issue of site planning and the appropriateness of an arts commission been more vividly joined than in the recent tempest over the tenure of the GSA-funded sculpture "Tilted Arc" by Minimalist Richard Serra, a 12-foot high, 120-foot long 75-ton Cor-Ten inward-leaning slab of rusting steel that bisects Federal Plaza in

front of the Federal Building in lower Manhattan. As Calvin Tomkins has written, "The wall's height shuts off the view of Foley Square and its architectural monuments—McKim, Mead & White's soaring Municipal Building, Cass Gilbert's neoclassic United States courthouse, and other souvenirs of a bygone era."[15] It generated a sustained resentment among people who regularly used the space. On March 6–8, 1985, and as a result of a petition to move the Serra sculpture signed by 1300 employees from the adjacent Federal Building, the regional director of the GSA held a three-day hearing on this issue.

This disagreement over the Serra work was obviously a kind of landmark case for testing the parameters of public art. It brought into the light a range of issues including the sanctity of contract between artist and governmental agency, whether any governmental action to remove a piece of commis-

The "Tilted Arc" implacably bisects Federal Plaza, forcing governmental employees in adjacent buildings to confront it when attempting to cross the space to and from work. It is site specific and thus is designed to block their view of the fountain from the federal building lobby.

sioned art constituted censorship, the aesthetic choice of minimal art for the space, the relation between an object and its context, and the legitimacy of the public behavioral evaluation in the previous public art choice. The hearings were well attended, and the atmosphere was tense. Part of the "New York art world" made a sometimes eloquent defense of a sculpture that the artist claimed was site specific and would be destroyed if it were moved to another location.

While Richard Serra threatened suit if his piece was moved, workers employed in the Federal Building complained that the wall blocked their view of the fountain at one end of the plaza and created a sense of confinement that they resented after being indoors all day.

Almost all the testimony given in support of the work made *no* acknowledgement of the indignation it created among the people using the building, but defended it on art-historical terms as an important work for the city. Serra is an important artist—ergo a great city should have a Serra. Serra's fellow artists and defenders also raised the issue that removing the piece might create a precedent for destroying the GSA's Art-in-Architecture program. A music teacher and friend of the artist even claimed that the Cor-Ten wall had acoustical properties that would enhance the use of the remaining space for performances. The contest seemed to pit insiders against outsiders—with a few environmental behaviorists and a handful of more traditional artists siding with the office inhabitants—lawyers and judges and others opposed the work against the well-orchestrated opinion from the "art world"—artists, critics, arts organizations, and dealers in contemporary art. Those who defended it were also those who did not have to experience it on a daily basis.

The social effect of the Cor-Ten wall was a specific concern for Roberta Degnore, a doctoral candidate in Environmental Psychology, who opined at the hearing that the most important function the piece performed was to demonstrate the need for broadening the art selection process to include an evaluation of how a piece altered behavior in and use of space. Her conclusion, based on extensive interviews with people on this and other public art sites, had been conducted over the previous year—as part of her doctoral thesis. In her argument for the *public* in public art, she testified:

These questions have not been addressed in any nonemotional way . . . I understand the reluctance. The fear, especially of the art community, is real. We worry about the setting of a precedent, we worry about the political ramifications of this. Terrible consequences, we imagine. But the fear of setting a harmful precedent will be real only if we accept the falsehood that we can generalize from this situation . . . and what of the prior precedent that placed a piece with such a special, limited esthetic in a public space? . . . And the feared consequences could be real only if we ignore what we can learn, in a positive way, from this particular situation. The "public" is not the enemy. . . . To believe that most people cannot and should not understand, or appreciate, or make decisions about art works in *their* space is a view that is narrow and elitist and patently untrue. . . . There would be no shame in learning something here. And no shame in listening to the primary users of the space. . . .

In no other setting I have studied have people been so intense and clear about their feelings. And it is not the piece alone, but the interconnections, the way the piece acts in the environment. . . .

Indeed people here have testified that sometimes great art is not appreciated in its time. And given the tenor of these times, our times, perhaps the last thing people need is to feel, to experience yet another barrier to openness, in concept and in fact.

No matter how great a work it may be, for *these* people in this space, at *this* time, the piece simply does not seem to work.[16]

Or perhaps the piece works too well, if, as at least one defender asserted, one of the objectives of the design was to express hostility to this space.

At the time of the testimony, Donald Thalacker, director of the GSA program, acknowledged that the procedures for reviewing potential GSA commissions have been modified several times since the fall of 1981, as a result of the reaction to the Serra installation. Modifications include discussions with a cross-section of community members, building occupants, civic groups; local suggestions for nominations to serve on the selection panel of art professionals and citizen review of artists' proposals. In addition, more recent changes in the operating procedures utilize a descriptive analysis of site conditions, including drawings and photographs, and some user polling is now undertaken by GSA before site selection.

However, this experience illustrates perhaps more plainly than those previously recounted the need to make more changes in the guidelines for these federal programs because the GSA guidelines still do not address head-on the issue of community values and aspirations for a site as a basis for creating metaphors that might inspire (and constrain) the artist. As Donald Gray, an artist and critic, observed at the hearing:

> Tilted Arc is cold, brutal, sterile, depersonalized and dehumanized, a mannered, empty work academically following fashionable minimalist formulae.... The selection panel, the artist, and indeed, the art world, all share responsibility for perpetrating and perpetuating the horrors of such fads and fashionable aesthetic clichés. . . .
> The only healthy things connected with Tilted Arc have been the negative response of those daily forced to live with it, and this hearing resulted from that outcry.[17]

Gray called for the removal of the piece on the same grounds as museums use when they de-access a work even though it may have been at one time site specific like a church alterpiece.

Tilting the Arc: Is the Rationale for Keeping it in Federal Plaza as Formidable as Cor-Ten?

The "Tilted Arc" project is discussed here at length because we believe some of the basic assumptions behind the defense of the piece are askew. Of concern in a litigious society, there are legitimate legal issues of due process and the limits of contractual responsibility. Very likely the existing agreements for purchase of the work failed to define "ex post facto" review and evaluation, nor apparently did the GSA anticipate the prospect of removal, although in retrospect they should have that right as they own the work. Indeed, sculptor Louise Bourgeois's written testimony at the hearing suggested that contemporary art should be guaranteed only a temporary stay in public places. Certainly many critics of the Federal Plaza sculpture at the hearing acknowledged that they would not want the removal of the piece to be used as a precedent for censorship of the arts which the supporters of the piece strongly asserted would be the result. But let us examine some of the basic arguments of the defense in light of larger urban design objectives which we claim should rightfully measure the utility of public space. For we believe these assumptions are responsible for some of the conditions we have described earlier in the book.

Other arguments that were called on to defend the GSA's then-current guidelines at the time of commissioning bear some critical review. We first state the premise of the defense and then comment upon it. Both the arguments and short rebuttals follow:

● Argument 1:
"THE GENERATION OF CONTROVERSY IS A VALIDATION OF A PUBLIC ART COMMISSION"

This argument is used to defend a piece of public art that detractors find inappropriate for a particular locale even though the artist claims it is site specific. Taken to its logical conclusion, this position allows one to justify, even laud a work in exact proportion to the outrage it generates. However, impassioned dialogue does not guarantee a change of attitude or taste, or conviction; in fact, as an indicator of value, controversy is neutral, neither positive nor negative.

● Argument 2:
"PEOPLE DO NOT APPRECIATE GREAT ART IN THEIR OWN TIME"

This art historical argument is fortified, of course, by a view of the artistic triumph of once neglected art. Such movements as the eventual critical affirmation of the Impressionists over the academicians, led by the painter Bourgereau obviously demonstrate the point. It is a seductive argument to the college-educated traditional supporters of the arts who, no matter how dismayed they may be by an artist's work, fear being on the wrong side of history. However, one can also observe that there is a qualitative difference between the carefully wrought content of an earlier era—what Rilke called the "stored humanity"[18] of objects—and the industrial aesthetic of some sculptural materials today such as Cor-Ten steel elements which can be easily manufactured, assembled and reproduced somewhere else. This does not deny the artistic validity of using such materials in contemporary art.

Just as architectural historians have to learn to distinguish between the careful workmanship of even a modest nineteenth-century vernacular building and a vintage McDonald's, so the art historians must learn to distinguish between an object that has value because of particular craft and aesthetic content and something that is valued mainly as an expression of a particular era.

● Argument 3:
"IT IS TOO SOON TO JUDGE. LET THE WORK STAND AND PEOPLE WILL GROW TO LIKE IT"

This argument is related to the "great art not appreciated in its own time" arguments because it too pleads for long term perspective. Obviously, perspective is a useful condition. However, because art in public places is necessarily of a durable sort, that perspective gained over time on a particular piece is not necessarily sacrificed by moving the art. The public should have the right to de-access the art and reuse the space if the art is perceived as an impediment to that use. Letting the art stand in one space forever may conflict with the larger purposes of the public space for public enjoyment. The times and purposes change even when an art work is universally praised initially. Even when a piece is specifically designed for a space, as Mr. Serra says of "Tilted Arc," protesting its removal to another site—possibly in an art park—demonstrates an extraordinary conceit. Why should a particular piece have an advantage that most other sculptures have never enjoyed? Conversely, the history of art is replete with site-specific works like the Elgin Marbles or the Cincinnati murals—originally designed for Union Station now at the airport—that have been removed from their original locations to preserve them or to increase their accessibility to an appreciative public.

● Argument 4:
"THE EXPERTS HAVE SPOKEN; A PRESCRIBED BUREAUCRATIC PROCESS HAS BEEN FOLLOWED; WE CANNOT INTERFERE NOW"

This argument again assumes that there is some objective standard for setting value and particularly intimidates the educated classes, for though they may privately disagree, they have been trained to respect the opinions of experts! Most art experts have not had experience in designing spaces. The experts employed for public art juries—usually curators, art consultants, and gallery directors—often evaluate such art by the gallery criteria they use in their professions—having an exemplary or representative piece of a particular artist's work in the city instead of the gallery may well take precedence in their judgment over the public's concern about the livability or meaning of a given space. There is a particular vulnerability to many public spaces because only a few have organized constituencies that are activated to support a *general* public interest—as opposed to the promotion of special objectives—such as the siting of a particular artist's work. Processes should not preclude an evaluation of how an object commissioned for a space impairs its utility or livability which obviously have to take place after installation. Of course, this should be made explicit at the beginning of the planning process in the future.

● Argument 5:
"THE ARTISTS' INTEGRITY IS SANCROSANCT; WE SHOULD NOT INTERFERE WITH THE ARTISTIC PROCESS"

This defense assumes that the integrity of the artist's conception is the paramount value, once a certified jury has selected that artist. This argument fails to acknowledge the compact that the larger community should be able to make with a space in which there are a collection of values—utility, pleasure, discernible meaning. No amount of rhetoric from the artist about the integrity of his intention should justify a result in the space that deprives the community of these larger values. Ironically, the community's consciousness of a space and its value may not be activated until a source of irritation like an artwork appears in their midst. Conversely, the community may appreciate the value of what it already possesses only when the bulldozer arrives to destroy it. Ultimately, the collective value of an environment ought to prevail over the single-purpose thinking of one organized constituency which would impose its will upon it—whether this is a dedicated artist or a determined developer. This should not result in a banal neutralizing of all initiatives through the tedious act of gaining consensus on what might be accomplished, but it does illustrate the need for caution when *multiple* benefits of the public environment are threatened. Even the most intuitive artist who claims his work is specific to a given site may fail to discern the collective of values that a space can represent to its constituency—the people who use it—particularly when there is no process for discerning these values. And such a collection of values may legitimately be claimed as a public benefit that should not be diminished when scarce public funds are allocated to the space for art work. Of course, the artist can sometimes propose something that adds an entirely different dimension and gives the public a new perspective. This can be a valid reason for the artist's going off in a different direction.

A Modest Proposal: Life After Cor-Ten

Given these concerns about a collective value for public space, we need to define a higher meaning of the word *integrity* when evaluating art in public space. It should relate to the capacity of public space to realize multiple public benefits. The argument about the notion of the artist's integrity vis-à-vis this higher integrity that attaches to a space causes us to examine how consciously listing performance criteria for spaces can be used to clarify broad public benefits that any art proposal must then respect. Of course, communities would do well to *start* with such performance criteria as a part of their planning process when designing public space, rather than have to apply the criteria retroactively against a particular art proposal which seeks to be part of the space.

If we examine a vision of what the Federal Plaza at Foley Square might become as a result of utilizing such a planning process, it may help us to work backward and then determine what performance criteria we should apply to any art-and-amenity strategy proposed for such a prominent public space. One vision of Federal Plaza reveals teams of artists designing street furniture so that passersby can sit down and enjoy the fountain. (It is currently devoid of seating except on the rim of the fountain and flower pots, and on the stairs.) Carefully wrought benches commemorate the process of the law in the adjacent courts. The floor of the fountain is transformed by a mosaic that interprets the surrounding cityscape with its fine examples of Classical Revival architecture. Or perhaps given the recent Serra struggle, the fountain or the pavement around it depicts the seven muses bringing culture to man. Artisans using wood and iron are creating a special trellis to enclose the space and provide shelter for lunchtime use on hot summer days. A crystal pavillion that refracts the sun's light onto the pavement plays off the shape of the fountain and offers interpretive information about governmental agencies located nearby, a guide to Tribecca, neighborhood history, and a schedule of performances that are now regularly programmed in the plaza.

In conclusion, in our vision the plaza has exploited a new GSA commitment to public art in the space, following the removal of Richard Serra's "Tilted Arc," for the many people who work in the buildings adjacent to it or nearby, who are now organized into an active constituency for Federal Plaza. The GSA has affirmed its concern for commissioning teams of artists and the public, which met performance criteria that give the public what it clearly wanted—a more livable space. By the design that was created, we can see that these criteria included public comfort, cultural orientation, animation by both scheduled and impromptu entertainments, and physical definition of the space, which increases its potential for use. Fulfilling these criteria could employ a number of artists and artisans in a team approach,

which has not typified the Art-in-Architecture program in past years. Let such an innovation begin here where the positive publicity of such actions can transcend the stain of Serra's Cor-Ten on the pavement and support a new focus of public meaning and community involvement in the commissioning of public art.

A Brief Survey of Public Art Plans

From Houston to Seattle

After the rust settles, the Cor-Ten scar on the pavement of Federal Plaza in lower Manhattan where the Serra sculpture stood might serve the same exorcising function as did David Levine's cartoon of President Johnson showing his abdominal suture in the shape of Vietnam. The Serra controversy has helped us to reexamine how we plan for public art. Though Mr. Serra did not take credit for this particular accomplishment at the hearing, this new interest in planning may leave a more lasting impression than the sculpture's stain on the plaza pavement. Witness the change in GSA procedures in selecting public art implemented soon after the Serra installation in 1981. According to Donald Thalacker, the director of the GSA program, the agency now undertakes broader surveys of the public users who will regularly experience the proposed art; these procedural steps evidence an increased concern for planning that respects context.

Perhaps more significant, because of their potential integration with the cityscape, are the public art plans that cities and their art-commissioning bodies are beginning to publish as a way of establishing goals and objectives for public art projects, as well as implementation strategies for particular commissions.

These plans are sometimes extensive doc-

The artist Jeff Oberdorfer utilized this model to present his mural proposal and to elicit support in a neighborhood divided by other issues. The Cambridge Arts Council funded the Saginaw Avenue mural. Since murals can now have a life span of over 50 years, the planning process is crucial. For this mural the artist also enlisted nearby residents to repair the lower parts of the painting.

uments that include maps and photographs of sites where public sculpture, wall murals, light sculptures, and environmental pieces might be located. Of course, this sort of planning is not really that innovative; the City Beautiful plans of the late nineteenth and early twentieth century set a certain precedent in this country for documenting the potential of selected sites for artistic embellishment. But the *written art plan* as a policy instrument did not emerge during the early years of the GSA and NEA Art-In-Public-Places programs. This is at least partially the case because there were no guidelines from these principal funding sources that required developing written plans as the federal government did for other categories of grant programs.

Instead the presumption has been to begin with the artist, to center support around a constituency of artists and empower their particular vision, which in general during the 1970's and '80's have not been synthetic but individualistic expressions. Indeed some of the early art plans also took this approach. The city of Houston, for example,

which does not have a one-percent-for-public-art ordinance, simply provided a list of potential sites for which a work of art might be commissioned or more frequently donated.[19] However, no strategy was created to coordinate this plan with an established process for selecting art or facilitating the matching of selected sites and their constraints to the capability of particular artists.

The Houston Plan to "create a framework for assistance in the acceptance and placement of major artworks"[20] was prepared in 1976 by the city's planning staff, for the Municipal Art Commission, which advises it. The underlying assumption of the plan was

In Seattle's Occidental Square in the heart of an historic area undergoing rehabilitation, a long struggle over the appropriateness of a proposed Cor-Ten steel sculpture consumed part of the budget for it. Finally, the landscape designer Ilse Jones of the firm of Jones and Jones, broke the deadlock by transforming a functional object which the community agreed it needed. The bronze drinking fountain is designed to be polished by the hands that must stop up one of its spouts in order to drink. Its sensuous shape marks the site where an early spring once ran into the bay. Its water helped sluice the logs down the hill prompting the name skid road, which later found a place in the American lexicon as skid row.

that private philanthropy could be stimulated to give sculpture for downtown plazas, and indeed over the years this appears to have worked! Since that time a substantial number of sculptures have been situated in many of the new downtown corporate plazas. Though the city still has no one-percent ordinance, the arts plan is *one* of the most graphically developed documents for encouraging private-sector philanthropy that has come to our attention. It makes no effort to connect separate sites for public art into a more comprehensive framework, but it does recognize existing planning initiatives that encourage integrated approaches (such as the development of a linear bayou park or a publicly owned tunnel system).

Some art plans of recent years have followed a more activist mode of shaping public art commissioning, and as a consequence the public sector has become more involved in the commissioning process, whether the art is publicly or privately funded. The matrix that is shown on page 192 identifies characteristics of some of these new art plans.

The five plans in the matrix can be viewed as representing a chronology of art plan development, with the Cambridge, Massachusetts, art plan of 1982–83, posited between the older "inventory" plans of the 1970s, such as Houston's, and the later focused strategy within an analytic framework as expressed in the Phoenix and Seattle plans. These later plans demonstrate how art proposals can be linked to urban design work.

Cambridge's 1982–83 art plan inventories and locates on a city map more than fifty public art projects commissioned since 1975 through various funding sources.[21] These projects have been accomplished on both public and private sites. The Cambridge approach marks a stage of art planning that goes beyond the passive role of site assessment utilized in Houston and offers limited guidance to artists and art administrators. It was used to solicit proposals for nine different projects on various sites around the city. The owners or public agencies in charge of the sites were consulted on

each of these projects and their advice on proposals and budgets was elicited. Funding was made available through the one-percent-for-art ordinance established in 1979. The descriptions of these projects were brief and consisted mainly of limited analyses of context and such physical and behavioral observations as "this path is popular with joggers."

Underlying the Cambridge plan is the assumption of community involvement. Local artists are given preference in the selection process. A clear goal—the one comprehensive element linking these otherwise disparate and discrete projects—is that each artwork should enhance a neighborhood-scaled site. Artists are expected to respond to the information that the plan provides about the site, thus shifting the focus of the proposals from the artist's inner vision to a creation more related to site and community. Unlike other plans, where decision-making is centralized in the hands of the Arts Council staff, this plan experiments with a different process, in which site and artist selection is initiated by a central source, with the subsequent decision-making delegated to site owners including other government agencies and neighborhood representatives who are impaneled to serve with One-Percent-for-Public-Art committee members on a project-by-project basis.

In contrast, the Arlington County, Virginia,[22] and Phoenix, Arizona plans,[23] both formulated in 1984, are a refinement of the inventory-type plan but represent a new type of thinking. Oriented toward action rather than assessment, these plans begin with a set of objectives for integrating art into a particular section of the city. Site selection for proposed art projects is still the main focus, but now the criteria for *why* those sites were chosen and *what kind* of art might suit those sites are articulated more explicitly, giving both artists and administrators a common ground from which to plan.

The Arlington, Virginia, plan developed by the Community Arts Council, was initiated to encourage public art for new sites,

Arts Planning Matrix

PLACE/DATE	HOUSTON, TX 1976	CAMBRIDGE, MA 1982–83
TITLE	*Public Art in Public Spaces*	*ART PLAN 1982–1983*
SPONSOR	Municipal Art Commission/ City Planning Department	Cambridge Arts Council/ Cambridge Public Art Commission
FOCUS OF PLAN	Downtown Houston	City of Cambridge, emphasis on neighborhoods
OBJECTIVE	Inventories indoor and outdoor sites for potential public art in downtown and lists existing sculpture.	• Requests proposals for five planned art projects to enhance the city's neighborhoods. • Requests artists to submit slides of existing artwork for the "Art Bank"—a resource for public places when appropriate.
FORMAT	Glossy booklet with color photos.	Newspaper insert with black and white photos and map.
A. Background Information	Brief account of national history of public art	Defines 1% for Art Commission's commitment to the role of public art in the community—expressing a preference for "art which engages itself directly with the surrounding environment. It may create, enrich, or reveal a 'sense of place.'"

B. Inventory
  1. Existing public art locations
 	
  2. Potential public art locations
	• Lists existing city-owned and privately-owned public artworks in public spaces in the cityscape.
	• Selects potential locations for public art on previously developed sites.
		• Lists more than fifty public art projects implemented during the past seven years in Cambridge.
		• Selects five new specific locations for public art to enhance neighborhoods, including sites adjacent to existing buildings and sites on undeveloped land.

C. Site Analysis
 	
  1. Physical components
 	
  2. Social/behavioral characteristics
 	
  3. Historical content
	Limited site analysis.
	
	Specifies indoor vs. outdoor sites, includes dimensions of locations.
	
	Day vs. night use, vehicular vs. pedestrian use.
	
	No historical content.
		Limited site analysis.
		
		Brief description of natural and built features.
		
		Brief description of users—i.e. "path popular with joggers."
		
		No historical content.

1. Site selection
 	
  2. Artistic criteria/performance/ content
  3. Process for selecting artists
 	
  4. Planning/implementation linkage
	• Merely lists priority sites—awaits private sector initiative.
	
	• Offers limited performance guidelines for each site i.e.—"excellent potential for mural or wall graphic."
	• Contains no strategy for selecting artists—awaits private sector initiative.
	• Makes no link to art implementation procedure already developed by Houston Municipal Art Commission.
		• Lists specific five priority sites, based on appropriateness and available funding, to solicit artists' proposals.
		• Limited performance guidelines for each site—i.e., "artwork limited to recreational use."
		• Open to all, but prefers Cambridge and/or Massachusettts artists.
		• Defines no single procedure for art implementation; will be tailored to each project; however emphasizes community involvement.

ARLINGTON COUNTY, VA 1984	PHOENIX, AZ 1984	SEATTLE, WA 1984
Sited Toward the Future—Proposals for Public Sculpture in Arlington Country	*Artworks Program for the City of Phoenix (final report)*	*Artwork Network—A Planning Study for Seattle: Art in the Civic Context*
Community Arts Council of Arlington	Arizona Commission of Arts/Phoenix Redevelopment Office/consultant-artist Mark Lere.	Seattle Arts Commission/Art in Public Places Program
Arlington County, Virginia	Downtown redevelopment area of Phoenix	Downtown Seattle
Publicizes selected proposals created by collaboration of artists, designers, and developers, for seventeen sites of major new private development, civic spaces or highway-related spaces, which satisfy one or more of the stated goals: a) provide a gateway to the county b) mark vistas c) highlight metro stations	Incorporates public art planning into streetscape design for downtown Phoenix, and to be used as a potential promotional tool for the establishment of an arts commission.	Sets theoretical framework for evaluation and siting of public artwork, with emphasis on special characteristics of downtown districts.
Catalogue from exhibit includes text, artists' statements, and photos of models of proposed artworks.	Final draft of report with black and white photos.	Booklet with extensive graphic analysis—maps, diagrams, photos.
• Discusses past and present role of public art in public spaces. • Reviews Nancy Holts' Dark Star Park in nearby Rosslyn, VA, which set the precedent for organizing the art plan and exhibit to promote future collaborative artworks. • Describes Arlington County as a context for public art and mentions what each of the 17 selected artists contributed to this developing district.	• Identifies rationale for incorporating public art into the streetscape scheme for the redevelopment district in downtown Phoenix. • Promotes functional public art—artist-designed street furniture, architectural shade areas, gateways and water elements. • Discusses role of public art in civic areas, and benefits of temporary public art.	• Overviews last twenty years of public art in Seattle. • Analyzes civic urban spaces including models for physical and social analysis of urban settings (William H. Whyte and Kevin Lynch). • Presents typology of public art, including relationship of art to audience and to site.
• No existing public art inventory (except for review of Dark Star Park, see above).	• No inventory of existing public art work.	• Locates existing public artwork and existing public places by district for downtown Seattle.
• Presents each of the seventeen proposed art projects designed for sites which contain no prior development.	• Selects three sites within the downtown redevelopment area as prime locations for artist-designed street furniture, and other amenities.	• Proposes sites for public artwork including both developed sites and future development locations.
Varies by site—from limited to extensive analysis, depending on developer/designer's input.	Site analysis varies by location.	Extensive site analysis.
Brief description—i.e. "landscaped semi-circle . . . 2000 ft. wide, surrounded by streets, driveways and highways."	No description of physical components—relies on photos.	Brief description, i.e. "formed by intersection of two arterials" . . . "uninviting bus shelter."
Brief description—i.e. "rest area activated by pedestrian traffic."	Brief description for each proposed site "high density pedestrian interaction," with emphasis on specific physical amenities suited to Phoenix desert climate.	Brief description—i.e. "gathering place for people working in government center."
No historical content.	No historical content.	No historical content.
• Identifies 17 priority sites after a review of 47 proposed sites, based on their potential for fulfilling art plan goals.	• Identifies three priority sites and encourages Redevelopment Agency to incorporate public art in ongoing streetscape plan.	• Defines proposed sites in downtown Seattle into three categories: 1. priority sites 2. future sites 3. temporary sites
• Offers performance guidelines which are site specific—according to each collaborative team of artists, developers, and architects.	• Offers limited performance guidelines which are specific to each site; emphasis is on functional elements—benches, fountains and shade structures.	• Offers limited performance guidelines specific to each site—i.e. "artwork could mark entry points to Seattle."
• Invites only metropolitan Washington artists invited to participate. Devises procedure for matching artists' experience to particular sites.	• Does not solicit proposals but recommends using local artists.	• Makes no recommendations for artist selection.
• Increases awareness of public art potential in new development and encourages discussion through exhibit and catalogue, however makes no explicit link to implementation.	• Links no procedure for art implementation to plan.	• Discusses no procedure for art implementation; however, Seattle has a city ordinance for 1% for Art and has a well established and active Arts Commission that solicits art proposals.

particularly related to development projects now being constructed in this burgeoning commercial district across the Potomac from Washington, D.C., and adjacent to the highways that border it. Nancy Holt's Dark Star Park, constructed between 1979 and 1984 on the edge of this area, served as a precedent, showing how contemporary art could transform an otherwise mundane urban triangle against a background of standard commercial office towers into a place of some interterrestrial mystery. The new Arlington plan, really a catalogue of projects, now documents a procedure by which a jury made a two-stage selection of both sites and artists.

In the process that followed, seventeen potential public art sites were chosen from a pool of forty-seven, based on how well they satisfied the following goals: 1) to provide a gateway to the county; 2) to mark vistas; and 3) to highlight metro stations. In the hope of attracting developers and others who might commission public art, the Community Arts Council sponsored a competition for these sites. The Council selected artists according to how well their previous accomplishments and interests matched the requirements of the selected sites. Local artists were given preference to help promote talent in the area. The winners then received a stipend to work with design teams made up of developers, architects, and other professionals affiliated with the selected sites. They created maquettes of the proposed artwork. The projects produced a range of site-specific works—some were monumental sculptured walls or gateways, others pavement environments, amphitheaters, fountains, kiosks.

The proposed projects formed an exhibition mounted at the Arlington Arts Center in June and July, 1984, and also at the Georgetown Court Artists Space in August and September of the same year. Lynda Roscoe Hartigan, guest curator of the show, spoke of the ensemble of artists and their works:

Consistently, all have expressed and acted upon their interest in proposing sculpture that would relate to people, and many have carefully integrated visual pleasure and functional facilities in their designs. All too often in the past, communities, when presented with the activity of a commissioned sculpture, have expressed dismay and confusion, usually because the work has been perceived as foreign to their needs. . . .[24]

Photographs of the models and recorded artists' statements remain as an archive of this elaborate promotion of public art. Including the artists' statements within the written art plan encourages artists to articulate their intentions explicitly, thereby providing a basis for discussion. The community as well as team members for the selected sites and other artists can compare the particular artists' intentions with the quality of the art idea presented in their drawings or maquettes.

It is noteworthy that *both* the exhibition and the accompanying catalogue become the art plan, thus enabling the audience to more fully envision various public art concepts. Producing such an accessible visual display of what could be rather than only what is, and combining it with a list of potential sites for new art result in a significant art planning document. For turning ideas into visions at least opens the possibility of creating a common vocabulary for discussing public art options over a period of years, although the strategy for realizing them was not defined.

Another positive result of this planning approach is that it acquainted developers and architects with artists in the area and gave both groups a taste of the collaborative process of integrating public art into the design process. However, in most cases the proposals were not effectively synchronized with the development cycle of particular private sector projects. Ironically, Nancy Holt's piece, Dark Star Park, which inspired this competition cost so much more than was originally budgeted that this may discourage subsequent public art commissions, since the county is obligated to match funds for the proposals generated by the plan, and is concerned about escalating costs.

Phoenix, Arizona's 1984 art plan illustrates a different type of action-oriented approach. Like the Arlington County plan, it relates the commissioning process to site-inspired art, but the city of Phoenix also coordinates art proposals with ongoing urban design projects. The plan (actually a draft report) integrates public art into a streetscape improvement scheme planned by the city for a downtown redevelopment area. The city commissioned environmental artist Mark Lere to recommend guidelines for integrating public art into this target area. After analyzing what type of art ideas might best serve the sites, Lere proposed street furniture, fountains, trellises and entranceways to be created by artists that will complement other urban design improvements, such as planting and street widening. Although only some of his ideas and illustrations were included in the final streetscape plan, his analysis of the requirements for the public art and his consequent emphasis on art that serves a functional purpose represents a new trend in art planning. Another element of the Phoenix plan is an explicit awareness of the role that public art has played historically in the United States prior to the recent era of 'parachute' Minimalist sculptures. The Phoenix plan acknowledges the earlier integration of sculptural or architectural elements in other cities and other times to enhance street life—and proposes decorative facades to stimulate eye level vistas of passersby, benches and other street furniture, and artist-designed bus shelters and arcades to shield pedestrians from the intense Phoenix sun.

Perhaps the most advanced example of "the state of the art" plan is "Artwork Network—A Planning Study for Seattle—Art in the Civic Context," published in 1984.[25] It is not surprising that this offspring of the most innovative and prolific public art organization in the states—the Seattle Arts Commission—cuts the leading edge. Seattle was one of the first cities to initiate a one-percent-for-the-arts ordinance in 1973 and the first to promote collaborative public art projects with city funding. In 1976 Seattle's plan, appropriately labeled a "study," because it is theoretical as well as action-oriented, develops an analytic framework, devised to evaluate potential art sites.

This plan begins by analyzing public art from the macro view of the entire cityscape and works its way down to a micro examination of various districts in downtown Seattle. By reviewing the past twenty years of public art in Seattle, the study analyzes the different ways in which public art appeals to its audience—"aesthetic, didactic, functional, symbolic"—and to its site.[26] These include "artworks whose artistic intention is not related to the specifics of a particular site, artwork designed for a particular site whose artistic intent could be transposed to other sites, under similar conditions; and artwork whose artistic intent is inseparable from the particulars of a unique site."[27] Although the function of some public art is too complex to be so simply categorized, this typology is still a useful tool for making decisions about commissioning public art. It offers a framework in which a community can appraise its own public art needs.

The plan then uses Seattle as a case study in which to evaluate potential public art sites. To give credence to their strategy of matching site selection and performance guidelines for downtown sites, the authors refer to two urban design studies written by well-known planners. William H. Whyte's *The Social Life of Small Urban Spaces*[28] and Kevin Lynch's *Image of the City*[29] outline ways to analyze urban spaces which the staff of the public art commission in Seattle has been able to apply to public art planning. They acknowledge that their research "revealed that in the many discussions of art in public places, rarely has there been much appreciation for the different types of public places which occur in cities or of their varying roles in civic life. Artists and administrators need to understand public places on

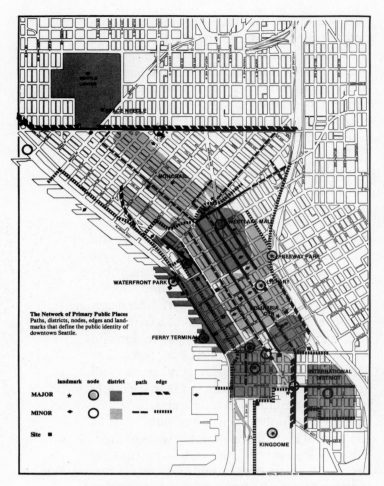

The Network of Primary Public Places
Paths, districts, nodes, edges and landmarks that define the public identity of downtown Seattle.

	landmark	node	district	path	edge
MAJOR	★	◯	■	▬▬	▬▬
MINOR	◆	◯	▨	▬ ▬	▦▦
Site	■				

A graphic display of one of the urban design approaches the Seattle Arts Commission used in their art plan to assess Seattle's potential for public art. This analysis is based on urban planner Kevin Lynch's *Image of the City*.

their own merits prior to evaluating them as prospective locations for art."[30] These sources offer insights into what kinds of city spaces people most like, such as "small spaces marked by a high density of people,"[31] or how people often perceive cities as networks of "paths, districts, nodes, edges, and landmarks."[32] Their choices for the siting of public art are based on these observations about urban design. Clear diagrams and mapping techniques are used to locate, by district, 1) existing public art, 2) existing public places, and 3) proposed development. A rating is then given to each site, labeling it as a priority site, a future site, or a temporary site. This plan is a more complex,

future-thinking and comprehensive approach to public art planning, successfully borrowing substantive and illustrative components of urban design plans.

Seattle's plan together with those described here form an important apparatus for other communities that want to devise a public art strategy. Like other planning processes, a framework for commissioning public art need not be invented over and over again, despite differences in cities' geography, population, history, and spatial organization. These documents on proposed art work record an evolving framework that can be important to other planners, whether or not particular art proposals in these cities are realized. Other communities can adapt these systems into their art planning, and tailor them to their own needs. The art plans reviewed here have evolved over a ten-year span and reflect, in our opinion, a progressive change; as art planning continues to develop, so do the strategies that shape it. Summarized here are what we see as emerging trends, based on discussions with art planners across the nation and reviews of these and other art plans:

1. Public planning is becoming increasingly comprehensive, even if implementation remains incremental. Plans cover larger geographical units and include linking various art projects into networks across districts and even encompassing entire cityscapes.

2. Art plans in the 1970s consisted largely of inventories of potential sites without much guidance on what kind of public art should be chosen, or what kind of analysis might contribute to commissioning decisions. Since that time, art plans have moved beyond inventory to evaluation and analysis, including general research on art planning, specific site constraints, user behavior and historic associations with particular locales.

3. Art plans are becoming prescriptive,

offering performance guidelines for public spaces based on more sophisticated systems of analysis.

4. Art planners are making their plans more accessible to the public through explanatory brochures, newspaper flyers, public hearings, seminars, exhibitions and catalogues of proposed work, and other communication devices.

5. Public art sponsoring often takes the form of public/private partnerships. A few sophisticated planning offices, usually with an urban design staff, are using incentive zoning to achieve public art plans for new development, in which the developer and city agency work together toward integrating public art and amenities into the design (see Bethesda, p. 198). City arts councils have begun to take a more active role in fundraising for and shaping public art proposals for their constituencies rather than leaving those tasks to the private sector, even when the sites are privately owned.

6. More cities are finding ways to involve a community response that goes beyond the tokenism of an advisory role where the public has sometimes felt hoodwinked. For example, in Palo Alto, one Art-in-Public-Places project sponsored an exhibition of sculpture in a city park for an entire summer. Then the public was encouraged to complete a ballot, voting for their three favorite pieces. The three favorite works were purchased by the city and installed in three different public locations. This procedure may not guarantee the highest quality art, or even the site specific art we are encouraging, but it demonstrates an increased concern about popular review of content as well as the process of obtaining public consent.

7. Public art is more often including the creation of amenities—benches, railings, kiosks, pavings—which combine practical and artistic purposes. Artists are once again crafting these street furnishings with the

View of the "Lone Pine" Square adjacent to the theatres that are the heart of the proposed Richmond arts district.

The Townscape Institute devised this art plan for Richmond's proposed arts district. The drawing conceptualizes the spatial/visual relationships linking these diverse proposed art elements—wall murals, painted crosswalks, sculptures, benches, illuminated facades and artifacts, like the milk bottles commemorating a nearby dairy, and a theatrical backdrop. The ensemble of works fulfills urban design objectives of street animation, thematic connection between different art elements, cultural interpretation of the neighborhood and a history of Richmond's artistic achievement, and encourages a sense of physical movement through the district as each art element pulls the eye toward the next.

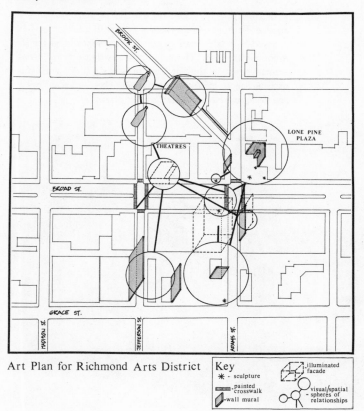

Art Plan for Richmond Arts District

Key
* - sculpture
▦ - painted crosswalk
▱ - wall mural
▨ - illuminated facade
◯ - visual/spatial - spheres of relationships

same care and attention given to sculpture and murals.

8. There is more evidence of a collaborative effort—with teams of artists and between artists, developers and architects. This presages a closer connection of art to both architecture and the site planning of new developments, though at present there is still limited cooperation in most projects, and very few examples of successful collaboration involving very significant changes in building textures or forms.[33]

9. An increasing number of public art pieces are being sited in untraditional locations such as roadside rest areas, shopping malls, electric power substations, and subway stops where they have an impact on a much broader audience—stimulating both public interest and expectations.

These bronze mustangs run wild as they did on the Texan plains, symbolizing the region's heritage at Las Colinas, a new commercial center near the Dallas/Fort Worth Airport. Located on the 300' × 300' Williams Square Plaza, they represent a renewed interest expressed by the private sector in representational art at a monumental scale. The plaza is left wide open to intentionally simulate the flat barren Texan prairie, once the natural habitat of the mustangs. Benches and plantings are kept on the periphery of the plaza.

Bethesda "Zones"—An Art Strategy

The Chairman of the Community Arts Council of Arlington, Kathleen Freshey, was not aware of either the Houston and Phoenix art plans or those of other American cities when she initiated the arts plan for Arlington County. She was inspired by an article in the *Washington Post* entitled "Bethesda's Beauty Pageant."[34] There she discovered that in adjacent Montgomery County the county planning agency was using a special zoning overlay district in Bethesda, a prosperous Washington suburb, to encourage developers to make increased commitments to public art. Although Arlington intended to encourage the commissioning of artworks for existing as well as new developments and, though they had no zoning laws that offered such incentives to developers, the Community Arts Council found that some aspects of the Bethesda plan could be adapted for their own quite different use. In Arlington, the emphasis was on larger open spaces adjacent to commercial development or defined by large highways.

In Bethesda the urban design staff of the county planning agency, the Maryland National Capital Park and Planning Commission, utilizes a zoning bonus to encourage developers to list their proposed art commissions at the time when the site plans are reviewed. In exchange for such public benefits as public art as well as open space, open space management, and residential housing in their proposed projects, developers are granted greater density for buildings. This form of "optional" zoning is based on an absolute calculation of the total building density allowed within the overlay district which extends about three blocks from the new metro stop at the center of the commercial area. The planners made a calculation of the number of automobiles that could be comfortably accommodated on Bethesda streets during the peak rush hours, and then this quantity of vehicular traffic was related to the square footage of building

This cast-iron and glass bus shelter in the historic Lowertown section of St. Paul, Minnesota, shows how customizing the standard street furniture elements, which usually come out of a catalogue, can enhance the particular character of a neighborhood or district. It is the successful realization of a similar idea proposed at about the same time for the Richmond Arts District. The Richmond bus stop's concept also included the idea of utilizing historic photographs of each block along the bus route as part of the shelter design.

density (by type) that would generate that amount of vehicular traffic by subtracting the existing square footage of development. The county planning office then had a framework for defining the acceptable level of measured growth—at a time when there was enormous demand. Through this down zoning approach which was accomplished by amending the master plan in 1976, the county created a climate for productive negotiation with the private sector. By pushing down the zoning envelope and then allowing the increased density only where certain additional amenities are provided, the county created a device for upgrading

the quality of development and ensuring at the same time a superior level of project plan review missing in earlier development.

However, this art planning approach, which remains ad hoc, depends not only on having a viable zoning incentive in the face of market demand, but also on the skill and commitment of an urban design staff and their consultants. While the county planning staff has neither specific authority to coordinate the configuration of different building projects so that they might create some larger urban design nor even the power to alter the interior skin of the buildings, they have used a close project review and a streetscape plan to tie many disparate elements together.

By December of 1982 ten development teams (several working under the aegis of the same developer) had chosen to accept the zoning bonus of increased FAR (floor area ratio) and had submitted applications for projects which were to include public art. At this point, the urban design staff led by John Westbrook called on Ronald Lee Fleming of The Townscape Institute to consult with each development team on an equal time basis in review of their preliminary application and again before their project plans were completed. Mr. Westbrook made the central decision that the art planning should not be frozen at the time the developers turned in their project plans. He said: "I felt that the creative process should not stop at that point and that the artists who don't work under a set time should be allowed to continue to enrich their art proposals."

As a result of earlier and less productive experiences, the urban design staff determined that the art proposals had to be thoroughly developed in the year between project plan submission and site plan approval and that they would be treated as part of the construction budget so that funds would have to be expended for the art *before* the developer received an occupancy permit.

This was a propitious time for the urban design staff and The Townscape Institute to

The brickwork pavement pattern by the artist Jerry Clapsaddle for Gateway Center, a new commercial development in Bethesda, Maryland, demonstrates how simple animation elements can enrich a walkway. The brick design creates a sense of movement that guides visitors from the building's frontage on Wisconsin Avenue around the corner to an adjacent public park on the side street. The sidewalk was part of developer David Burka's response to a county zoning incentive that encouraged public art and managed open space in exchange for the bonus of larger floor area ratio (FAR) for office construction.

encourage the developers to enrich their art plans because many site decisions were still in a state of flux. The result was a considerable reworking of some site plans which not incidentally expanded the proposed role of the artists. There was even a rethinking of some building footprints to create more viable public spaces. The design staff and the consultants sought to relate the public art to the urban design objectives espoused in the first chapter of this book:

• to connect the circulation systems of the different buildings by means of small encounters with works of public art,

• to encourage art elements to support the animation of major spaces,

• to foster works of art that would relate certain activities and industries to Bethesda's nineteenth century history as a transportation center and trolley line terminus,

• to employ art to direct visitors toward the metro station tunnels, and

• to add some larger urban design elements that would give motorists passing through the district some sense of entry into a special district.

To achieve this last objective, the developers were encouraged to construct pavillions on the Wisconsin Avenue edge of their properties. The resulting row of pavillions proposed on the southern edge of the optional zoning district were planned to serve as gateposts to the area; at night they might eventually appear as lanterns glowing at intervals down the street.

The most remarkable features of this art strategy—which has produced individual site-specific proposals and depends on the market place to stimulate developer response—are the high proportion of the submissions that have been approved (9 of the 10 proposed developments) and the fact that art works have been commissioned from more than a score of different artists. Several of the artists proposed doing a series of works that would be integrated throughout the development and would relate to its various parts. In Bethesda Place, Ned Smythe has utilized the Biblical story of the "waters of Bethesda" to thematically link a series of fresco and mosaic works that appear along a water course and terminate in a pool, that encourages pedestrian movement through a mixed commercial and residential development. Raymond Kaskey, who is both sculptor and architect and is known for his interest in naturalistic and classical forms, has proposed nautical designs in a colonnade that separates the park near the Salisbury Building from the street. For example, the capitals of the colonnade are capped with nautilus shell-like forms in cast concrete. In addition, an enormous clam shell will provide a transition from upper to lower gardens, and Tom Supensky, in collaboration with Kaskey, has designed a ceramic wave that will emerge from the reflecting pool. In Chevy Chase Plaza, Martin Puryear, working closely with the landscape architect James van Sweden, is using a garden theme to develop a fountain, outdoor seating, and entrance features, along with garden arbors, walls, trellises, interpretive stones which engrave the history of Bethesda, and a bridge over a pool.

In another unusual collaboration, artist Patsy Norvell, known for naturalistic plants and flowers etched on glass, will work with the architects of Keyes, Condon, Florance "to shape and illuminate the entire pedestrian and retail area" in the glass arcades and pavillions of the 4600 East–West Highway Building.

While some of the placemaking emphasis in the original proposals was eroded after the architects hired their own arts consultants and commissioned the artists, enough remains, particularly in these more comprehensive approaches, to affirm a particular feeling of place identity in those projects.

The site plans that the developers presented to the planning board required ex-

plicit commitments to art that would be legally enforceable. The developers and their lawyers were required to submit written answers to such questions as "Please show the relationship between the different elements in your art plan for this development project. If a child was lost in this building, are there any narrative elements to your art plan that could lead him out? Will any of the art elements have surfaces of a kind that people would enjoy touching?" These questions,

Drawing of Bethesda's Art Plan, generated by incentive zoning and the site specific determination of the county's urban design staff, illustrates how public art will be integrated into building and amenity design. Ten new or proposed projects within a three-block radius near the metro are scheduled to commission more contemporary public art than now exists in Maryland outside of Baltimore.

BETHESDA ARTISTS

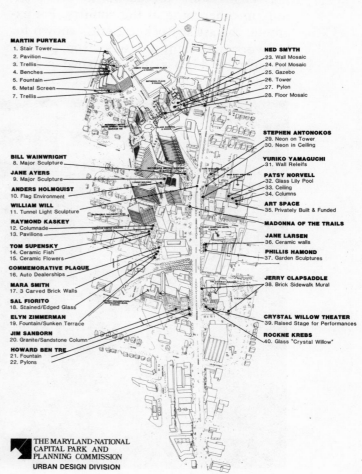

MARTIN PURYEAR
1. Stair Tower
2. Pavilion
3. Trellis
4. Benches
5. Fountain
6. Metal Screen
7. Trellis

BILL WAINWRIGHT
8. Major Sculpture

JANE AYERS
9. Major Sculpture

ANDERS HOLMQUIST
10. Flag Environment

WILLIAM WILL
11. Tunnel Light Sculpture

RAYMOND KASKEY
12. Columnade
13. Pavilions

TOM SUPENSKY
14. Ceramic Fish
15. Ceramic Flowers

COMMEMORATIVE PLAQUE
16. Auto Dealerships

MARA SMITH
17. 3 Carved Brick Walls

SAL FIORITO
18. Stained/Edged Glass

ELYN ZIMMERMAN
19. Fountain/Sunken Terrace

JIM SANBORN
20. Granite/Sandstone Column

HOWARD BEN TRE
21. Fountain
22. Pylons

NED SMYTH
23. Wall Mosaic
24. Pool Mosaic
25. Gazebo
26. Tower
27. Pylon
28. Floor Mosaic

STEPHEN ANTONOKOS
29. Neon on Tower
30. Neon in Ceiling

YURIKO YAMAGUCHI
31. Wall Releifs

PATSY NORVELL
32. Glass Lily Pool
33. Ceiling
34. Columns

ART SPACE
35. Privately Built & Funded

MADONNA OF THE TRAILS

JANE LARSEN
36. Ceramic walls

PHILLIS HAMOND
37. Garden Sculptures

JERRY CLAPSADDLE
38. Brick Sidewalk Mural

CRYSTAL WILLOW THEATER
39. Raised Stage for Performances

ROCKNE KREBS
40. Glass "Crystal Willow"

THE MARYLAND-NATIONAL CAPITAL PARK AND PLANNING COMMISSION
URBAN DESIGN DIVISION

part of the process of the Environmental Profile (see Appendix), were developed with the staff and The Townscape Institute to reinforce the seriousness of the planning process and to encourage a holistic approach.

Despite the number of artists involved in the planning, the instances of actual collaboration between architect and artist were comparatively few. However, there were more collaborations between artists and landscape architects. Martin's Puryear's collaboration with James van Sweden and Ned Smythe's collaboration with Land Design Research, on projects across from one another on Old Georgetown Road, appear to be the most innovative and comprehensive in plan. However, individual artist-designed elements have found their way into some of the architecture, and these breakthroughs may create some precedents for arts planning in other parts of the country. For example, the artist Rockne Krebs, known for his work with light in lasers, neon, prisms, plexiglas and glass, has designed a freestanding sculpture pavillion that serves as

a potential bus shelter along Wisconsin Avenue. Composed of glass panels that cascade down its sides and are laminated with prisms that cast bands of spectral light in all directions, this pavillion will stand at the intersection of Wisconsin and Willow Lane, continuing the line of trees on Willow Lane—hence its name "The Crystal Willow"—while serving also as a visual landmark identity on the edge of the district. Across the street the three cut glass and copper columns of Howard Ben Tré serve as counterpoint to this pavillion and form the other "gatepost" as entry to the commercial district.

In another piece of artist-designer interaction, Jim Sanborn, a sculptor of sliced rock forms, will be creating a 23-foot three-sided

Kiosks on plazas in the new Bethesda projects are urban design elements that the county encouraged developers to provide with the optimal zone method. Pictured here is artist Rockne Kreb's proposed "Crystal Willow." This gazebo is composed of 100 rectangular panels of pre-cut tempered glass. Attached to these panels are some 400 glass prisms that are designed to shimmer in the light like the leaves of a willow.

structural column for the Artery Headquarters building under the arboretum and on axis with the Crystal Willow pavillion and Howard Ben Tré's cut glass and copper fountain. By contrasting both color and materials, the design will draw the viewer in from the street. Each face of the column will have a different motif. Classical elements include red Grecian columns in relief on grey sandstone combined with symbols in brass celebrating extra-terrestrial forces. A brass shooting star and thunderbolt image literally "bolt" this column dramatically to the Artery building.

Other artists are creating works for additional building projects, which will include ceramic murals, bronze garden pieces, carved brick (by Mara Smith whose work is discussed on page 41), glass entry screens and a wall mural of bronze elements. The entire prow of 7475 Wisconsin Avenue will be specially lit as a sculpture, with a tower form at its juncture outlined in neon, designed by the lighting artist Stephen Antonokos, and Ellen Zimmerman is creating a cascading waterfall of carved granite forms in the plaza of another building.

The internal cohesion that some of the art elements achieve should mark one of the most successful recent examples of the integration of art and architecture. Perhaps not since Rockefeller Center in the 1930s has so much public art been integrated with architecture within an area of a few square blocks in this country. While the planning agency has been the catalyst for this effort, with some staff support provided by the Maryland Arts Council, the developers and their arts consultants have worked out different techniques for the selection of the artists. Bethesda has no minimal percentage of development costs specified for public art, and neither the local arts council nor the planning agency has yet produced an overall strategy for public art in the area or required a specific dollar amount of art commissions. Yet, despite the absence of defined objectives in a written plan, the zoning incentive and the close attention of the urban design staff in the county planning department has made the difference. As John Westbrook— the committed chief of Urban Design who nourished this process—said, "We have the most innovative zoning tools to weigh and balance the different resources. We look collectively, not at isolated cases. That is what is unique; that is what has never been done before."

Art Planning for Content

Once we have accepted this thesis that there are urban design objectives that can and should be used to evaluate public art proposals, these criteria can be deployed to determine the comparative merits of different proposals in terms of their capacity to make a compact with public places. Public art clearly served some of these urban design functions in an earlier age. Beaux Arts planning schema and the City Beautiful movement in this country used sculpture to define and articulate vistas and *ronds points*. The planned environment provided physical direction through space and some suggestion of cultural domination if not interpretation. Today's deft notion of using public art to animate space was probably not a necessary part of late nineteenth-century planning schemes in an age when society appears to have needed no special encouragement to promenade regularly in public spaces,[35] although there were certainly constraints on the kinds of animation permitted in most public spaces.

The use of a broad set of urban-design-related objectives to evaluate public art proposals requires that both the commissioning body and the artist consider multiple purposes for a given proposal. Armed with a set of criteria that includes purpose, we may avoid some of the worst excesses of what is becoming widely known as "plop" art. Only a few years ago, any shaft of steel pivoted into a public place was honored in progressive art circles as a civic virtue. Now, quite suddenly, great numbers of people are voicing their skepticism about such arti-facts or at least about their siting in public spaces. But even adding urban design cri-teria to the evaluating of a proposal may not result in a level of accessible meaning—the content the general public may expect if, in fact, public monies are being allocated for a project. To the extent that the public wants art of recognizable content, they should have available the procedures that are most likely to secure it.

This is not to propose that all works of art need to have a content that is accessible to the general public, but it is fair to suggest that the mystique of inaccessible art be-comes an object of worship for only a small elite.[36] If we are to build any real confidence in a tradition of public art that can be in-tegrated into our national culture—art that "speaks" to users in neighborhood centers and town squares across the country in con-trast to the mute monuments of recent vin-tage in corporate and governmental plazas or the turf around the art museum—then we had best empower local communities with the planning tools that can give them some confidence in the result.

Conducting a process that pays more at-tention to community content than the art-ist's personal agenda does not necessarily produce a banal or boring result—the kind the critics dismiss with code words such as "mundane or predictable." Nor does respect for community context lead ineluctably to work that is didactic—a view propagated by some artists and critics who have been steeped in artistic prerogatives that equate the "avant-garde" with a certain alienation, and hence a disregard for societal con-straints. Permanent installation of public art pieces in public places require the acknowl-edgement of societal restraints; this is part of the compact that allows them to be in public space. The whole spectre of "socialist realism," the fear in some art circles that if art funding supports representation, public spaces will be overrun with mannequins performing quasi-heroic acts, seems to us a red herring. What we are proposing is that commissioning boards do their *homework* and demand that the artists respect, even celebrate, the identity and interests of a community or site. To some extent then, those who judge art proposals should them-selves have some sense of commitment to the place, and the will to find the resources for this kind of process. The job of com-missioning art is commonly given to a panel of "experts," in a society that may well ca-tegorize people into such boxes because it lacks confidence in its own judgment—and thus through the compartmentalization of expertise perpetuates in still another form the aridity of single use zoning that has made our cityscapes so boring. The assignment of such panels should require more than just comparing folios of slides of work by artists competing for a commission, and then, with hardly a backward glance at the site, se-lecting one of them the winner, and retreat-ing back to academia or the gallery place.

First, there needs to be a much more *thoughtful and documented evaluation of place.* This is the element in the planning process that is the most neglected in public art competitions. In our judgment, it is still not adequately defined in either the NEA Art-in-Public-Places grant applications or the procedures for GSA's Art-in-Architecture grants.

Duncan Plaza: A Cautionary Tale—A Precedent for Environmental Profile but without Effect

An interesting but aborted effort to build this information-gathering process into a public art competition took place in New Orleans in 1980.[37] The American Institute of Architects' design charette for Duncan Plaza assembled some useful information about this park site adjacent to City Hall and the Public Library on the edge of the commercial district. Supported by an NEA Design Arts grant, the AIA's R/UDAT (Regional Urban Design Assistance Team), a multidisciplinary group of architects from around the country, assisted by local architectural students, spent four full days in January 1980, developing some general recommendations for increasing the utility and improving the comfort of this rather banal 1950s style park of concrete benches, paths and grass.

After an informal community hearing, a sort of "inventory of desires" was recorded and the R/UDAT team then drafted a statement about the context, including a brief history of the site, the social milieu, the appropriate scale for future improvements, the impact of seasonal change on the potential use of the space, some proposed public choreography, and rather generic recommendations for social uses and physical improvements. The report was published in the expectation that it would serve as useful background information for a subsequent arts competititon to enhance the site.

This competition was based on the notion of an integration of the work of both environmental artists and landscape architects. The principal innovation suggested by the NEA design advisers was to have selected environmental artists, choose the landscape architectural teams with which they wished to collaborate, and to serve as team leaders in order to encourage the artists to take an aggressive role in shaping the competition proposals.

Unfortunately, the teams that were selected for the competition made scant use of the research that came out of the earlier design charette by the R/UDAT team, including the information on community priorities. The jury, with a majority not connected to the city, selected as the winning proposal a design for an enormous aviary with tropical lagoons and plantings that completely covered the site. So impressed were they by its grandeur and eccentricity that the jury failed to heed the well-documented local desire for a place in which people could gather comfortably. The two other proposals, both more modest in scope and realistic in budget, also made only limited reference to the R/UDAT recommendations, though Martin Puryear's included an inventive interpretation of the cast iron work so characteristic of New Orleans architecture. Sadly enough, the expenditure of almost $100,000 by the NEA and privately matched New Orleans funds did not produce a practical result. A public survey organized by the mayor, who had initially supported the idea of the competition, showed such opposition to the winning proposals as well as to its price tag of more than triple the city's budget—that the restoration of Duncan Plaza appears to have been dropped. A progressive mayor who wanted to nurture the arts felt embarrassed because both the artists' teams and jury of arts experts had

Chicago artist Martin Puryear, a finalist for the ill fated Duncan Plaza design competition, included a radial plan with traditional elements—grill fencing of cast iron, brick paving, and plantings of palm trees located concentrically around a one-hundred-foot circle containing a pool and sunken amphitheatre. He designed the space to encourage office workers located nearby to use it for lunch, as well as for musical and theatrical performances. Another more grandiose proposal covering the space in a vast aviary and ignoring the cost constraints won the competition review dominated by jurors not accountable to the city. It was rejected after popular protest embarrassed the city government, which had initially welcomed the idea of a competition.

paid little attention to the city's priorities expressed in the documentation. Consequently, the local constraints such as budget, consumer desires, place characteristics, were ignored.

The cautionary tale of the New Orleans' R/UDAT and its aftermath is but one of a number of competitions that, in spite of their high cost, have not always resulted in usable projects. The selection process would no doubt have benefited from more pertinent information gathering and, a more conscientious use of that material and of the priority objectives when the arts proposals were being solicited and evaluated. It may be that a checklist of certain generic pieces of information should be established for communities, one that can easily be adapted to a variety of different arts projects; we make bold to suggest one approach in the Appendix.

To celebrate the 50th anniversary of the sit-down strike that affirmed the bargaining power of the United Auto Workers to represent workers in the General Motors plants in Flint, Michigan, the union and the city commissioned The Townscape Institute to create a commemorative art work. In collaboration with Johann Sellenraad, a New York artist, Townscape developed the concept of a memorial wall on the river front across from the downtown area that would provide a sequential narration of events both inside and outside the factories at the time of the forty-four day strike in the winter of 1936–37.

The focal point of the ensemble is a wall divided into two sections with columns, resemblling those in the factory, at its apex and sides. Both sides of the wall will be tiled with scenes painted by Johann Sellenraad which recall the memorable photographs of the struggle as it occurred inside and out of the factory. On the wall facing downtown, visitors will see the inside of the factory with the unifying element of the assembly line behind workers sitting on automobile seats and Fisher Body One strikers marking the strike calendar.

On the outside, facing Auto World, a new amusement park celebrates the automotive history; the wall will depict scenes of farmers supporting the strikers by passing food through the windows, the protest marches of the Women's Auxillary Brigade, picketing children, and scenes of reconciliation when labor and management sign the historic agreements acknowledging the union as the bargaining agent, and the triumphant victory march of the workers. The role of the Reuther brothers and John L. Lewis, and the effect of the governor's decision to send in the National Guard will also be part of this narrative series of panels.

On the river side of the wall piece, large ceramic benches inspired by the car seats where the workers sat during the strike will allow visitors actually to place themselves in the shoes and seats of the strikers. Behind the benches and the tiled wall is a concrete aqueduct, a feature existing in this park in the 1970s; it is supported by simple columns similar to those in the automobile factories. By collaging some tiles to the concrete structure, this backdrop can be transformed into a piece of the assembly line.

The memorial seeks to realize urban design objectives as an entry marker to Auto World, a major economic investment designed to attract visitors to this depressed blue collar city with high unemployment. The memorial also serves as an animator of a somewhat forlorn landscaped area that people now have little reason to visit, and, of course, as a major focal point of cultural orientation that wittily co-opts an aqueduct to develop more fully the theme of inside and out. The project is being accomplished through the leadership of Mayor James Sharp and City Administrator Robert Collier, and with the support of eight local chapters of the United Auto Workers Union.

Appendix: The Environmental Profile

DEFINING THE TASK

We have alluded frequently to the collection of site information and the process of generating metaphors from it as a significant determinant in encouraging art that makes some compact with the public. This process of defining the Environmental Profile was described first in an article in *Landscape Architecture* (Jan. 1981)[38] and later in *Public Interest*'s issue on public art (Jan. 1982).[39] Since that time we have had the occasion to further refine this approach at public art workshops for the Historic Staunton Foundation in Staunton, Virginia, for the Flint Department of Community Development and the Carriagetown Historic District in Flint, Michigan, for the Federated Arts Council in the proposed arts district in Richmond, Virginia, and in the commissioning of the Rindge Field Brickworker and Ballplayer sculpture (see page 128) by the

One-Percent-for-Public-Art Commission in Cambridge, and in eight NEA funded public art competitions for Boston neighborhoods and adjacent communities.

The goal of the Environmental Profile is first to produce a clear and concise statement about site information, contextual constraints and opportunities, and a behavioral analysis of the use to be expected of the site. This material, called the "Brief," then becomes the bedrock for mining themes and metaphors that can generate some community validation and can become a catalyst for both stimulating artistic creation and providing a framework for evaluating the content of artists' proposals. The metaphors and themes may be first identified, or later confirmed, in community meetings or workshops.

This Environmental Profile process in fact

becomes a means of community empowerment, because it puts the community in touch with the sources of its own identity and encourages the artists to create within a context that respects this identity or *potential* identity. In an age when many artists take umbrage at being asked to move beyond their own private language or vision, one can understand, perhaps even sympathize, with those artists who are unprepared to shed their own cultural baggage and respond to a problem that has been partly defined for them by the community . . . and yet the failure to do this often reveals an ignorance too profound to be remedied by individual artistic intuition.

Ultimately an Environmental Profile should not inhibit artistic creativity, but rather challenge it. There is a long tradition of art that acknowledges defined constraints at the outset and it appears masterly. Al-

though El Greco painted commissions for religious clients who told him what biblical tale, theme, or subject he was to put on canvas, this mandate appears not to have inhibited his creativity or the strong sense of personal identity that is characteristic of his brushwork. Pope Julius II made some rather site-specific decisions for Michelangelo, his artist-in-residence for some decades—providing both setting and theme, but the results from Michelangelo's hand are far

In the Boston area, the covers and pages of these neighborhood-based telephone directories became an innovative way of reaching a larger audience to discuss public art issues and publicize upcoming public art competitions for community sites. The design competition staff carefully researched each locale so that design opportunities and constraints, site associations, and behavorial analysis helped to define some themes and metaphors. The resulting "environmental profiles" served as community sanctioned grounding and contextual frame for artistic inspiration.

Public Service Advertisement • THE CAMBRIDGE PHONEBOOK 1983

Why is Ben Franklin Wearing a Fire Helmet and Sneakers in Inman Square?

Because Benjamin Franklin, a Boston native, started America's first fire insurance company. So he fits in with the portraits of the firemen of the Engine company #5 on the wall of their Inman Square Headquarters. The artist, Ellary Eddy, equipped Ben with sneakers possibly to give him a running start at a new age. George Washington is also in the picture because he served as a volunteer fireman. Having their moniker on the side of the handsome old fire station encouraged the firemen to support the renovation of this Inman Square landmark; it also helped Cambridge gain national recognition for public art that affirms neighborhood identity. Since 1975 some fifty six public art works ranging from carved tree trunks and tiled play yards to wind sculptures and painted newspaper kiosks have appeared along Cambridge streets, on walls, and in playgrounds under the aegis of the Cambridge Arts Council. Another twenty works were commissioned in 1982 and will appear soon. They are the result of the MBTA's commitment o the "Arts on the Line" as a part of the Red Line subway construction projects and Cambridge's new one per cent for public art ordinance which allocates money from public construction projects. Soon the Lechmere Canal development, subway stations, renovations, and housing projects will include sculptures of neighborhood residents, tiles of enamel and brass depicting local flora, fauna, and neighborhood history, bollards will be carved with the textile patterns of the different groups who have lived around Porter Square from Penobscot Indians to French Canadians... all these are projects which reveal, reinforce, or enrich a sense of place.

How Can Public Art Affect Cambridge?

The Inman Square Firemen were partners in a public art process which both affirmed their identity and supported the neighborhood. There can be many more partners for such projects in Cambridge. The universities, burgeoning industries, and private developers as well as community organizations and neighborhood groups can play a more effective role in defining what they wish to affirm not only through public art on walls, in lobbies and courtyards, or in the pavement but also in the character of such basic amenities as benches, bus shelters, and trash baskets. At a time of change, when the skyline is being transformed by new construction and when a third of the Cambridge population moves every five years, the need to connect people to places is stronger than ever before. Here are some ideas which can encourage more place responsive art:

Work with the character of the site: not just the scale and building materials of the context, but the history, geography, past and current uses, and special events and personalities associated with it. Collecting this information can encourage artists' proposals which are inspired by the "mental landscape" of the site. Consider how artisans as well as artists might be involved in creating surfaces that people want to touch. Examine how the art can involve the participation of the people it will affect, and how events can be organized around its production, installation, and integration into the community. Question whether the art belongs in a gallery or is designed for a particular site and to what extent it can strengthen the urban design of an environment. How can it be related to other works of art or urban design. Ask whether such functional objects as benches, gates, fences, and pavements can be made by artisans and artists. And then ask what art you can propose or what information you can provide that will enable Cambridge to more fully realize in its new art the diverse heritage of its neighborhoods, the crowded history of its citizens' achievements, and the vision of its future.

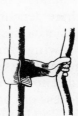

Part of the proposed "Glove Cycle" by Mags Harries for the Porter Square Subway Station.

If you would like to share information or ideas about place responsive public art or would like to be informed about opportunities for commissioning public art, including competitions, please write (do not telephone): **The Townscape Institute, 2 Hubbard Park, Cambridge, MA 02138**

This information about the public art process is provided through the courtesy of The Townscape Institute, a not-for-profit public interest planning organization in Cambridge. The principals, Ronald Lee Fleming and Renata von Tscharner recently wrote the book, *Place Makers: Public Art That Tells You Where You Are* (New York: Hastings House) which describes art and urban design projects across the country affirming a sense of place.

Firemen's Mural, Ellary Eddy

Boxing in Central Square, Lisa Carter and Michael Stanton

Tree Sculpture, Fred Faller

photos courtesy of The Townscape Institute
Cover design by Holly

from slavish as revealed in the ceiling of the Sistine Chapel.

If the goal of the Environmental Profile is to produce a clear and concise statement for both the creator and the commissioning body, then the objective is to do this in a way that acknowledges economies of time and resources so that the process can meet the budget of the commissioning body with modest funds—which is usually the case. Indeed one of the hurdles under the NEA's Art-In-Public-Places program is the cost of the preliminary planning which the local agency must assume, including the travel expenses and honoraria of panelists often from outside the locale. The process outlined here depends chiefly on coordinating an interactive assemblage of local resources and allowing time for public feedback, so that many diverse interests are at least considered, if not always accommodated, during the process of commissioning public art.

Accordingly, we conclude *Place Makers* with a brief outline of a prototype for this Environmental Profile Process. We believe it is flexible enough to fit local conditions, but that the questions included with each informational component suggest some of the possibilities which may be considered and which we hope will expand its potential application.

An Annotated Outline

1. ASSEMBLING THE TEAM

An organization that wishes to commission public art—a local arts council, planning commission or staff, civic beautification group, art museum—begins by assembling a multidisciplinary team. The team might include:

- a local historian

- the designer of the space (if it is a new space and if, alas, the commission has been given before the profile is assembled)

- community chroniclers in the form of several people with long memories, though often without any formal training

- a community leader with proprietary interest in the turf to be considered (someone whose cohorts could stop the project if they chose to, but who might also take the role of defender over the long run)

- several artists and artisans who understand that they are there to generate arts ideas, not to seek a particular commission

- a folklorist who can paint a portrait of the community cultures connected with the area around the space

- the head of the maintenance staff that will oversee the space

- at least one member of the sponsoring agency with an arts background

- a behavioralist—someone who can analyze user patterns in a space.

Where possible, members of the assembled group should be paid small honoraria for their time unless their presence on the panel is seen by them as a matter of civic virtue or municipal duty. The honoraria can dignify the role of the artists and help them to step out of the self-interested posture of promoting their own work, which is, of course, a very understandable instinct. In a small community, it may be difficult to avoid conflicts of interest if the artists who are asked to be on the panel would also like to make a proposal. (This problem may also occur on design review boards when the most talented architect in town often cannot participate on the review board because his or her work is the subject of it.) As noted above, in the best of all possible worlds, this group would develop the profile before a particular architect or landscape architect had been chosen to design the space or building.

2. SETTING THE STAGE: PRELIMINARY STAFF WORK AND MEETING

Once a panel is assembled and provided with clear guidance for its role as evaluators of information and generators of ideas, the members meet on or near the site. They should plan to meet more than once so that there will be time for reflection and for ideas to percolate through the material presented formally. If the space under consideration has a diurnal cycle of use, the panel should try to meet at different times of day.

At the first meeting the sponsoring organization will usually communicate, both visually and in written form, whatever information is by then assembled. The purpose of this initial staff work is not to enable the sponsoring organization to dominate the discussion and impose its agenda, though that is sometimes a tempting option. Rather, it usually takes a professional staff to round up the needed materials—early design proposals for this section of the community (where they exist), other art projects and the community's experience with them, examples of local crafts and building materials that survive in the architecture of the area, photographs that show how the area has evolved and that document the kinds of people and uses that characterize the area. Time-lapse photography can be an effective way to indicate how people now use a space, as behavioral analysis is an important and surprisingly neglected component of public art planning.

3. PREPARING THE AGENDA OF INQUIRY FOR THE ENVIRONMENTAL PROFILE

After the initial briefing, the panel members add their own observations and experience to it and, by utilizing a checklist to ensure comprehensiveness when the complexity of the issues requires it, seek to identify the information they will need to understand the space and its potential for the commissioning of public art. This material can be organized in the following categories. Many sites are not complicated enough to require answers to all these questions, but they may serve as an outline for review.

3.1 Physical Setting

3.1.1. What is the significance of the site in terms of larger urban design issues or relationships? Can it provide a connection to other key nodes in the cityscape? Is there a possibility to include a long vista or to organize series of relations with objects already part of the site configuration? For example, can a group of thematic ideas be translated into objects which move across the site and connect it to a visible landmark in the background or foreground?

3.1.2. What particular constraints and opportunities does the site afford? Should the panel consider a neighboring historic district (or an area that ought to be a district) as a cue to design limits on materials, scale, style, or color palette?

3.1.3. How has this physical setting evolved over time? Have changes been documented that an artist might wish to recall in the new work? Are there outlines or silhouettes from the past that could give the new design some resonance? For instance, in New Haven's Ninth Square, a proposal for a neighborhood park includes new arches that recall a building that stood on the site for seventy years.

3.1.4. What are the larger dynamics of change in the entire cityscape or the quarter where the site is located? Might a proposal including such evidence of the larger cityscape have more significance than one based exclusively on the physical context of the immediate site? A corporate plaza in the warehouse district in Chicago might inspire a garden of fragments that evokes the rebirth of a city from the ruins of the Chicago fire of 1873.

3.1.5. What aspects of the natural history—the geology of the area or the flora and fauna—can be recovered in the design of an arts project?

The proposed mini-park at the dog-leg of Orange Street in New Haven's Ninth Square includes a brace of tall iron arches recalling an earlier sense of place: when the vista was closed by the arched facade of the Gas Company Building, circa 1890. This long time visual association disappeared when the Gas Company was demolished for parking space in 1975. The New Haven Downtown Council commissioned the Townscape Institute to make this NEA funded plan as part of a streetscape design supporting the revitalization efforts of a private development company, Ninth Square Associates.

View of the Old Gas Company Building, New Haven, circa 1890.

3.1.6. What effects will climate have on the use of the site and on the deterioration of art objects? Will snowplows be used on sidewalks that might chip delicate or vulnerable inlays in the pavement? Will a sculpture withstand an 80-mile an hour wind? (This is the design ceiling for the wind tolerance of a new sculpture of figures pulling on a sail for the plaza of James Center, an office building in Richmond, Virginia.)

3.1.7. What is the pattern of artificial lighting in the area, and will the lighting inhibit or encourage night-time use of the site? Can lighting articulate surrounding architectural features that will strengthen the night-time significance of a particular art work? Or does existing lighting in the site bleach out a proposed art piece or environment?

3.1.8. Could a design be planned in which the parts were to be assembled incrementally over a number of years, utilizing the skills and contributions of local people? This concept of leaving some things incomplete so that others can make an imprint is certainly not a part of most designers' formal training, but in case studies we have observed, allowing people to leave a mark on "place" can create a significant act of community empowerment. Out of these personal marks can come a sense of proprietorship that may have measurable benefits in terms of safeguarding the space and protecting the art work. Such events as part of

Nancy Webb's bronze tile inserts recall the flora and fauna on the swampy site of the new Alewife Brook Subway Station (1985). Place-oriented art is a part of the Arts-on-the-Line program sponsored by the Cambridge Arts Council and the MBTA for subway stations in Cambridge and Somerville.

An assessment of this wind responsive sculpture, a forest of rods that clang in the breeze, influenced the James Center art strategy. Located only two blocks away outside the Federal Reserve Bank tower, the sculpture created noise, but not any positive lasting identification.

the building process create uncertainty, which modern contracting methods and regionalized construction crews without individual linkage to a given community are disinclined to contemplate, unless and until there is an advocacy group concerned about them that specifically defines such opportunities in the work agreement.

3.2 Historical, Sociological, Folkloric Content

3.2.1. Can objects in this space serve some larger strategy of cultural interpretation by making connection with other similar efforts in nearby locations? Are there other groups, such as arts councils or preservation organizations with which the panel could jointly support a particular theme? Curiously these organizations often have almost no communication at either local or national levels. (For example, the National Trust for Historic Preservation and the

Developer Henry Faison did not start by worrying about wind pressure. He wanted monumental bronze figures that would extend and reinterpret Richmond's proud tradition of representational sculpture which distinguishes the capitol grounds and configures the rond points along Monument Avenue, the city's great 19th-century boulevard. Faison commissioned sculptures for his new downtown office center along the James River which recall the story of river transport on a site where the Kanawha Canal and turning basin once joined and where sixteen canal boat hulks were excavated for the foundations of a gleaming highrise development that houses CSX Corporation, the largest transportation company in the world. Lloyd Lillie sculpted the eight-to-eleven foot hoisters of sail and Alexandra Kasuba designed the granite "deck" which emerges out of the steps at the entrance to the first building in the new complex. Completed in 1987, this large sculpture is a significant element in a public arts strategy which seeks to assemble a "mental landscape" of associations about the sites, connecting the pedestrian to them. This strategy seeks to humanize the ground plane if not the scale of the structures.

American Council for the Arts seem unaware of each other even though the integration of their interests would strengthen their appeal at the grass-roots level.) A local preservation commission can provide the historical background material inspiring an art council commission (see Brickworker and Ballplayer story, page 128).

3.2.2. What historical events—citywide or regional—took place in the vicinity that strike parallels with our own time?

3.2.3. Does the proximity of neighborhoods give neighborhood history a special importance? In Providence's Federal Hill in the 1980s the fruit stands of early Italian immigrants have been noted on bronze plaques in the market square. Yet their potential as public art is not yet realized.[40]

3.2.4. Are there ethnic traditions in the surrounding area that might be focused on a particular site? Could a folk dance group regularly meeting in the neighborhood be celebrated by a pattern in the pavement?

3.2.5. Is there evidence of an arts and crafts tradition in the built environment of the surrounding area that could be continued or embellished in this particular site? Can salvaged elements be integrated into a new design?

3.2.6. Are there legends, characters, or myths particular to the site or surrounding area that might be in some way commemorated in the space?

As a result of community advocacy, fragments of the old entrance to Cambridge Rindge and Latin High School were salvaged to form this playground gate when the new school was constructed.

3.2.7. Are there unrecorded triumphs or traumas that might become the focus of public art? The East Boston community, proposed that the "mothers of Maverick Street" who in 1976 barricaded their street against airport construction trucks, should be commemorated in new public art projects at the airport nearby.

3.2.8. What human resources in the area could be employed to create public art at the site? Are there people with special crafts whose work is respected in the community and thus might have more meaning than that of an outside artist? The notion of using artisans to work in stone, iron, tile, mosaic, and carved wood work as it relates to many of the surfaces of a site should not necessarily cancel out the monumentality of a single large piece. But artisans' work can greatly increase the claim that the space makes to the general public because it slakes the thirst for intricacy and craft—for the evidence of care and love—that is missing from much of a prefabricated and industrialized building program and the contemporary art monuments which are made in the image and likeness of these materials.

3.2.9. Is there a way in which local school children can be involved in the art process—for instance, making tiles or terra-cotta plaques that might be thematically connected to a space and be added to it over time? Children's contribution will benefit from the fine orchestration of an artist's hand, and the work will usually be more interesting if it is related to some larger theme, which the children can then interpret.

3.2.10. Can an event that the community finds significant be *translated* into a work of public art so that a sense of resonance over time is evoked? For example, in Cambridge a woman's oral history group created a quilt as part of the Bicentennial activity, with each woman telling her story to the others and then sewing a square on that quilt, thus endowed it with enormous meaning for a defined constituency. It might now be translated into a more durable form, becoming an element of architecture such as a carpet of tiles located at the entrance to a community building.

3.3 Behavioral Analysis

3.3.1. What program of activities is contemplated for the space? How do people use the site now, and how do they want to use it? These two questions may require a user survey to establish preferences for the activities to occur in a given space as was done for the Duncan Plaza charette in New Orleans (p. 204).

3.3.2. How do the patterns of sun and shade affect the use of the site and hence enjoyment of the public art in it? William H. Whyte did some pioneering stop motion photography in Manhattan corporate plazas, showing how changing light affected seating behavior, but the effect of light on public art has been given little attention. More recently William Reimann has analyzed the impact of sunlight on the design of the embroidered bollards in Porter Square (see p. 165).

3.3.3. What animation objectives can the public art realize or strengthen? (In Boston's Pemberton Square the podium carved from a salvaged capital enables television news crews to report court news—an unanticipated but welcome use which animates the square.)

3.3.4. What is the choreography of pedestrian movement and how does this affect use of the site?[41] In the competition for the redesign of Boston's Copley Square in 1984 some of the most elegant proposals neglected this fundamental behavioral principle and interrupted the most logical traversing of paths across the site, with such barriers as panels of grass. The majority of the jury decided against giving the first prize to one of these schemes, over the belligerent objections of other members of the jury whose concern for strong design statements overrode their respect for behavioral patterns.

3.3.5. How is the art related to the area where people will predictably congregate in the space? Is the art designed as an inter-

The Women's Bicentennial quilt in Cambridge in which many women each designed a square. As a tiled bench, floor pattern, or wall on a public site, it might exert a stronger emotional pull than works created by single artists.

The Judge's Bench and the trucks of the TV news teams who now use it, thus animating Pemberton Square in downtown Boston.

lude, a respite from more active use of the space, or is it the center of attraction like a Tinguely sculpture with its whimsically coordinated motions or the animated time piece in Louisville on page 50.

3.3.6. Does the art take into consideration the handicapped? Is it meant to be touched or heard? If it is meant to be heard, will it soon become annoying or boring? (The clanging beryllium rods of the untitled sculpture in front of the Federal Reserve Bank in Richmond by Harry Bertoia, for example, is continuous on windy days (made more

Clement Meadmore's iron squiggle installed in Cincinnati in 1984 confronts pedestrians emerging from a new corporate tower, the Cincinnati Commerce Center, which recently replaced the landmark Plaza Theatre. Renovated in 1978, this theatre was demolished soon afterwards when an absence of zoning protection allowed escalating land prices to overwhelm it. Now the installation of a makeshift guard rail prevents the sharp point of the sculpture from ramming people. Seeing it wrapped in plastic, one passerby wryly suggested this was to protect it from graffiti. In fact, it is wrapped to prevent damage by a cleaning solution used on the building. The sculpture appears arbitrary on a site across from Fountain Square that holds theatrical memories for Cincinnati citizens.

George Sugerman's sculpture creates an arcade in front of the Wills Eye Hospital in Philadelphia for those who can see it, but for those who cannot (the blind, a major constituency in this hospital, who are encouraged to follow the large handrail which guides them along the side of the buiding towards the sculpture) there is a sharply felt disaster ahead.

Isaac Witkin's Cor-Ten sculpture "Everglades" installed in 1976 on Springfield's Pynchon Plaza, has been the target of graffiti in a "beautified" and now derelict space of compounded design failures. This non-working fountain and the dangerously steep ascent should have been "Spanish Steps" connecting the Cultural Center above to the downtown.

frequent by the Venturi effect of the high tower) and drives people away from the space.)

3.3.7. Does the art have a special appeal to children? Is there anything to interest a child? Does the art have an intricacy that would intrigue a child? Of course, this may be an important question if the space is predominantly used by children and their guardians or if it is a part of a facility that has a large children's constituency like a zoo, aquarium, park or library.

3.3.8. Could a child become disoriented in the place or could a series of art works create a trail leading them through it? Answering this question was a submission requirement for developers' art plans in the Bethesda optional zoning district (see p. 198).

3.3.9. If tourists are frequent visitors to this space or this area, do the art works provide them with physical or cultural orientation?

4. INTERACTION WITH THE ENVIRONMENTAL INFORMATION—"THE BRIEF"

This long checklist of questions and the assembled answers form what we call the

Environmental Brief. To assemble this material, it is important to have the advice and help of some staff from the sponsoring organization or from some other community agency such as an historical commission or planning office. If the space is part of an on-going architectural project, some behavioral analysis may already have been carried out by the architect. A required environmental impact statement may already have documented this information.

If the discussion takes place at a table, passing some of the exhibits around may elicit comments that would otherwise fail to register if presented in a lecture format. A tape recorder on the table can ensure that a record is kept. People usually forget about it. A luncheon after a tightly packed session may give the participants an opportunity to reflect and expand on particular insights about the character of a space or a neighborhood.

5. CRAFTING THE METAPHOR

The next stop is to translate the assembled brief into metaphors, story lines, themes, symbols. This may take place in a workshop at which the brief from the prior meeting is

The cube and the headhouse present different design sensibilities in Manhattan's Astor Place. On a site embraced by 19th-century architecture including the Victorian façade of the Cooper Union nearby, the iron cube, entitled "Alamo" takes a stand. Installed by sculptor Tony Rosenthal in 1966, it asserts itself, the ultimate inanimate object, defining a self referential focus for the space. In contrast, the addition of a cast iron replica of the original 1904 subway headhouse, part of a $2.5 million station restoration and refurbishment in 1985, represents an integrative, contextual approach. The headhouse picks up the intricacy of Victorian details in the surrounding architecture and seeks to affirm the integrity of the larger space. The Municipal Art Society, one of America's earliest watchdogs of urban design currently uses small models of "Alamo" for its annual awards to civic leaders. It will be interesting to see if the society changes to headhouse models in future years.

Also a similar cube at Univ of Michigan Ann Arbor

summarized. More artists may be invited to join this workshop. But the province of the metaphor cannot be claimed by artists alone; it is astonishing and even moving to see how poetic laymen can sometimes be about their place, and it is a condition generally overlooked by professionals. And even people who cannot find inspiration in the ordinary examination of their milieu may manifest an uncanny capacity to realize when they are being patronized if they are the ones who are ritualistically consulted. The problem of working through metaphors in any depth in a public meeting may take some skill, but usually more than enough content is developed in these sessions to keep designers quite busy responding creatively to the issues raised. It is important to record the themes and metaphors, and the relevant trail of information that inspired them, so that they can be summarized and distributed to other people who were not present.

The statement of metaphors and themes, *combined with* the environmental brief— (a) the physical design constraints and opportunities, (b) the historical and sociological context, and (c) the behavioral analysis—constitute the Environmental Profile. This is the basic document for both informing the artists and evaluating the arts proposals. The Environmental Profile then goes through a period of incubation. It should be widely disseminated to encourage public comment and feedback—even in the certain knowledge that many public questions arouse a constituency for obstruction. The Profile should be accompanied by *realistic* information on the budget.

6. ASSEMBLING THE CAST

The Environmental Profile is now ready to be used to identify and assemble artists and artisans for the proposed project. This, of course, is a delicate task. Since some artists may have already been involved in the assembling of the Environmental Brief and the crafting of metaphors, what is their role

and that of the other community people now that artists are about to be selected to propose projects? There are advantages to keeping this group, which has developed a familiarity and identification with both the place and the proposal, in touch with the project, whether or not they are qualified to evaluate the merit of art works. Often there is a need for some art professionals on the jury that ultimately selects proposals, but their approach should be balanced with community interests and with the documentation and analysis of the place that is contained in the Environmental Profile process.

But for the selection of a modest work of art, a jury of art professionals may not be necessary, though one person trained in art might be added to an existing committee. However, a major commission would benefit from the presence on the committee of a curator or gallery director who is accustomed to making artistic assessments. Since such outside experts may have limited time in which to become really familiar with the community and its concerns, there is added virtue in putting the Environmental Profile into writing and in having on the jury some committee members who were involved in assembling it to make sure that the experts give consideration to its content.

Unless the artists are impressed with the seriousness of the community's concerns, they may simply bring their own preconceived agenda to a community space. The presence of community people on an advisory board along with art professionals may be salutary even if, in the end, only professionals vote to select the artist or proposal. A committee that has carried through an Environmental Profile usually calls for the submission of specific proposals rather than just the solicitation of resumes and slides of artists' work. By doing the extra work of site analysis, the committee prepares itself to undertake a more demanding selection process that should elicit some site-specific proposals. The committee should consider compensating the artists for their preliminary work on proposals if there is a limited request for proposals as opposed to the more general competition, which is often too expensive.

In the selection process there is no substitute for the two-pronged approach of a careful site analysis followed by an exchange of views with each artist under consideration. In spite of the cliché about the camel's resemblance to a horse designed by a committee, a well-instructed group can in fact influence a design by creating the moral authority of the context and encouraging the artist to respect that context.

7. THE ARTIST'S PROPOSAL

Whether artists apply for a project directly, or are commissioned to make a specific proposal, or proposals are solicited through a competition process, the Environmental Profile provides an avenue for background information that should be salutary, even if not sacrosanct. In fact, the Environmental Profile may generate ideas completely different from those anticipated by the sponsoring agency. That is a function of imagination that may separate the artist from the planner. The Profile can serve as a base from which to make the spirit manifest . . . a guide to inspiration. For the jury, however, it serves the added function of providing a fallback position. If a proposal substitutes artistic flights of fantasy (or self-indulgence) for the solution of some basic problems identified in the Environmental Profile, the jury is more easily justified in denying a commission on the grounds that the criteria of the Profile have been ignored.

The Environmental Profile can also help the commissioning body *negotiate* with an artist. The provisions of the Environmental Profile can be invoked to underscore the need for a more comprehensive or more thoughtful presentation. In an age in which much contemporary art deprives laymen of any capacity to evaluate it, the Environmental Profile can reaffirm criteria of public value that will restore their confidence. The jury

should have a clear mandate to deny a commission if an artist's proposal does not adequately serve the public interest. Denial is made easier if those interests are documented, and that is what the Environmental Profile is designed to do.

In conclusion, the process of compiling the Environmental Profile not only encourages interaction among the different constituencies involved in an arts project; it also generates a body of useful information for the artist as well as for the sponsor and the users that neither group alone could as easily acquire. The Profile should not be viewed as a constraint on the artist's creativity, but rather as challenging that creativity to respond to the context of a given environment and to express more fully what that context connotes—*the mental landscape of associations as well as the physical realities*. It should help the artist tap into the energy that is often already invested in place meaning, as well as document for the sponsoring agency the sentiments of the surrounding community. The modest expense of such an effort may avoid the more exorbitant cost of stalemate, outright failure, or lingering community resentment that have characterized a number of public arts projects.

Postlude: The Evaluation

Finally after the implementation of the art project, there needs to be some evaluation. What has been the response to the work? Has it been subjected to graffiti or other forms of abuse? Is it being adequately maintained? Has it served as a reference for the commissioning of other works? Have activities been organized that support or reaffirm its purpose?

This is not to suggest that good planning will necessarily be rewarded with universal public acclaim, but neither does an initial outburst of public fury presage future artistic greatness. The sponsoring agency should keep a clipping file on public response and a record of maintenance problems. Certainly the contract with the artist should give the agency the right to remove, though not to destroy, the work if a public hearing reveals that its design, its execution, or the durability of its materials precludes its serving or continuing to serve the public's larger purpose in enjoying a public space.

The "improved" reconstruction of the 1904 headhouse in Astor Place, New York City, reflects changing sensibilities. It was completed in 1986 by Prentice & Chan, Olhausen, architects.

Notes

Introduction

1. Several other Scots towns now have artists-in-residence who work on projects which affect the everyday life of their occupants. Harding and his associates executed some eighty projects in Glenrothes over a ten-year period. Local residents were often involved in the design and execution of the works.

2. The children who attended the bake sale designed the sign now marking it, which a local woodcarver finished for them.

3. The total cost of the repair and maintenance of the CITGO sign for three years, was $300,000.

4. On this particular sunny February noon hour the glare in the space was so strong that only two people were observed sitting in the 1.6 acre plaza.

5. The panels were graffitied after three years, but only after the first tentative markings on the margin between text and panel photo were allowed to remain for several weeks—demonstrating official negligence and hence inviting disrespect. Anti-graffiti products and sealers should ideally be applied to artwork when it is new as preventative measures against vandalism and exposure to moisture and pollutants.

There are many good products on the market today that remove paint, magic marker, ink, gum and other adhesives. The Central Park Conservancy in New York City and Boston's Park and Recreation Department are having considerable success in removing graffiti from their public sculpture and architectural elements.

Kathy Shea, associate director of the Sculpture Conservation Lab, affiliated with Washington University Technical Association in St. Louis, explains that graffiti not only defaces art but damages the patina, or surface quality. Removing graffiti can cause additional problems, leaving the "cleared" area open to corrosion.

Therefore it is best to do some research to find the anti-graffiti or sealer product that best suits the particular artwork and nature of the problem. There are no rules to follow—every artwork needs special consideration. Products should be used properly and tested before applying, as they can cause damage to the people using them, the artwork, building materials and the environment. For assistance, contact paint manufacturers, your local museum or university with a conservation department, or a fine art conservator. Some local public art councils which have commissioned wall murals might also offer advice.

The following is a selection of organizations that might be of further use.

The American Institute for Conservation for

Historic and Artistic Works can offer information about fine arts conservation. They are located at The Klingle Mansion, 3545 Williamsburg Lane, N.W., Washington, D.C. 20008.

The Conservation Group has a Sculptural Conservation Lab. Their address is: Washington University Technology Associates, 8200 Brentwood Industrial Drive, St. Louis, Missouri 63144.

New York Landmarks Conservancy has a Technical Preservation Services Center. They also have co-published *The Preservation Directory: A Listing of Craftsmen, Craftswomen, Contractors, and Professionals* with the Municipal Art Society. Second Edition, January 1985.

The National Park Service offers technical assistance: The Preservation Assistance Division (424), National Park Service, P.O. Box 37127, Washington, D.C., 20013–7127.

6. Marcel Proust, *Swann's Way*. New York: Vintage Books, 1970.
7. There are 2200 city and county-level arts councils as of May, 1985, according to the National Assembly of Local Arts Agencies, who defines "local arts councils" as any city or county-level agency employing paid or volunteer staffs, whose primary function is to provide money and services to arts organizations, individual artists or the community as a whole. Not included in this figure are the sixty-four state, territory, and regional arts councils operating as of May 1985, according to the National Assembly of State Arts' Agencies, Washington, D.C.
8. Juan Carlo Bonta, *Architecture and Its Interpretation*. New York: Rizzoli, 1979.
9. Leopold Aldo, *Sand County Almanac*. New York: A Sierra Club / Ballantine Book, 1974, p. 251.

Profiles

Miners' Monument

1. Jorn K. Bragmann, *Cumberland Evening Times*, 7 October, 1982, p. 17.
2. Tony Urbas in John Beardsley, *Earthwork and Beyond*. New York: Abbeville Press, 1984, p. 118.
3. Dr. Nelson P. Guild in *Ibid.*, p. 118.
4. Andrew Leicester, *Cumberland Sunday Times*, 3 October, 1982, p. B1.

Grants Tomb

1. *New York Times*, 13 October, 1984, p. 27.

Horse Race Clock

1. Wyatt Wilson cited in Terence Holland, "Baubles, Bangles and Bright's 'Shining Thing,' " *Louisville Today*, December, 1976, p. 47.
2. Holland, *Ibid.*, p. 48.
3. Henry Heuser, *Ibid.*, p. 48.
4. *Louisville Times*, 2 October, 1977, p. B8.

Burke Building

1. *New York Times*, 10 August, 1889 cited by Polly Lane in *Seattle Times* 7 February, 1971.

Judge's Bench

1. Robert Campbell, *Boston Globe*, 1 November, 1983, p. 48.
2. *Ibid.*

Crossroads Mural

1. Mack Wineka, *Salisbury Evening Post*, 3 September, 1981, p. 7.

Krewe of Poydras

1. Roger Green, "Artistic Endeavors on Poydras Street," *Times Picayune/The States Item* 22 January, 1983, p. 12.
2. Theodore Wolff, *Christian Science Monitor*, 1 February 1983, p. 19.
3. Dana Standish, "Pydras Gets a Krewe," *GAMBIT*, 15 January, 1983, p. 37.
4. Mimi Read, "Ida Kohlmeyer" in *Dixie Magazine*, *The Times-Picayune*, 3 April, 1983, p. 10.

Sonja Henie

1. Carl Nesjar, *You Are Here*, M.I.T. catalogue (Cambridge, MA: Center for Advanced Visual Studied, M.I.T., 1976), p. 69.
2. Carl Nesjar, *Olympic Newsletter* (National Fine Arts), 1980.
3. Barbara Fred, *Daily Camera*, 1 May, 1974 (Boulder, CO).
4. Nesjar cited in Mary Reinman, *Lake Placid News*, 2 August, 1979, p. 6.

Asaroton

1. Pamela Allara, "Arts on the Line Unveiled/Porter Square," *Art New England*, February, 1985, pp. 13, 18.

Steelmakers

1. *New York Times*, August 28, 1980.

Pioneer Murals

1. Mayor Graham F. Bruce cited by Cheryl Coull in "The town that is painting itself out of the red and onto the map," *Beautiful British Columbia* Winter, 1983, p. 31.
2. *Urban Innovation Abroad*, VIII, no. 12 December, 1984, p. 5.
3. Christy Lapi, *Ladysmith-Chemainus Chronicle*, 30 January, 1985, p. 8.

Riverwalk

1. Mud Island Press Information, 7 January, 1983.

Cat and Dog Fountain

1. Gerard Chapman, *Berkshire Eagle*, 5 September, 1978, p. 25.
2. *Ibid.*, p. 25.

Harvard Square Theatre Mural

1. Keim-Mineros Industries, based in New York City, manufactures Keim, a color coating based on liquid silicate technology and earth pigments which provide a long-lasting medium for muralists working on masonry surfaces—brick, concrete, stucco and stone. The concept originated 110 years ago in Bavaria, developed for creating a fresco-appearance with the ease of paint technique. Keim, created in the 1970s, was updated to accommodate contemporary building surfaces and has been available in the U.S. since 1980. Keim is also light-fast and resistant to ultra-violet rays. The company guarantees that colors will not fade for at least ten years.
2. The artists used a two-part epoxy anti-graffiti glaze that also waterproofs the mural. Available from major paint companies, they range from matte to glossy finishes. Another option for sealing the mural is to use a polyurethane or vinyl sealer, available in hardware or paint stores.

Community Murals

1. Plastic Shield, made by Danacolors of San Francisco, is a sealer that protects the murals from exposure and graffiti. It is a plastic varnish with an ultra-violet screening agent to reduce fading.
2. *San Francisco Examiner*, 6 April 1981.

Creature Pond

1. *Landscape*, November, 1982, p. 79.
2. Robert Campbell, "Learn from the Past or Fail in the Future, The Livable City" (special issue) *The Boston Globe*, 11 November, 1984, pp. 36–37.

Flower Stand

1. *Times Star*, 23 August, 1932.

Viewlands/Hoffman—Creston/ Nelson Substations

1. Matthew Kangas, "Electrifying Substations," *Seattle Voice*, June, 1982, p. 32.
2. Richard Hobbs cited in Nancy Joseph, "Artists on Design Teams," (Special Issue), *Seattle Arts Commission Newsletter*, November, 1983, p. 1.
3. Nancy Joseph, *Ibid.*, p. 4.
4. Buster Simpson, *Ibid.*, p. 3.
5. Buster Simpson, *Ibid.*, p. 3.
6. Rae Tufts, *The Seattle Times*, 26 August, 1984, p. D–5.
7. *Ibid.*, p. D–5.
8. Regina Hackett, *Seattle Post-Intelligence*, 29 June, 1982, p. D–1.
9. Rae Tufts, *Seattle Times*, 26 August, 1981, p. D–5.
10. Matthew Kangas, *Ibid.*, p. 32.

PUBLIC ART PLANNING

1. When Jimenez presented his design at a series of community meetings—a prerequisite for obtaining the matching funds from the Community Development Block Grant program—some community members requested a more traditional piece, like a bust of a Chicano hero. After several meetings, both the area residents and the City Council accepted the sculpture.
2. A recent study group convened by the Art in Public Places program in 1984 concluded that there needed to be a higher quality art coming out of the commissioning process, and that as a result of their grant giving, the program was particularly well suited to perform a clearinghouse

function, informing arts administrators about what was going on in public art throughout the country. This could be particularly useful if public art "disasters" were tallied and evaluated.

3. Professor Sam Hunter in Donald Thalacker's *Art in the World of Architecture* (New York: Chelsea House Publishers, 1980), p. ix.

4. *Ibid.*, p. ix.

5. Information concerning the erstwhile maze project near the Cambridge Rindge and Latin High School was collected in conversations with William Insley, artist, New York; Nancy Rosen, panelist, New York; Pamela Worden, arts administrator, Cambridge, Massachusetts; Chris Connaire, executive director of Cambridge Arts Council, Cambridge, Massachusetts; and Graham Gund, panelist, Cambridge, Massachusetts.

6. Tom Wolfe, "The Worship of Art," *Harpers* October, 1984, p. 61–68.

7. Richard Serra, cited by Wolfe, *Ibid.*, p. 67.

8. The interviews were conducted by Ronald Lee Fleming in a cultural planning charette organized by the Greater Hartford Arts Council and Partners for Livable Places (Washington, D.C.) on June 23–6, 1984. Mr. Fleming was one of a panel of six experts called in to assess cultural planning and design opportunities for downtown Hartford.

9. Douglas Stalker and Clark Glymour, "The Malignant Object: Thoughts on Public Sculpture," *Public Interest*, 66 (Winter, 1982), p. 17.

10. Ronald Lee Fleming, "Public Art Planning," *Public Interest* 66 (Winter, 1982), p. 28.

11. Janet Kardon, "Street Wise/Street Foolish," *Urban Encounters—Art. Architecture. Audience* (Institute of Contemporary Art and University of Pennsylvania, 1980), p. 8.

12. *Ibid.*, p. 8, 10.

13. *Ibid.*, p. 10.

14. Conceptual artist Robert Barry from New York City wrote these words to accompany the eighty contemporary works of art on loan from the Count Panza Collection exhibited at the Museum of Contemporary Art, Los Angeles, California, February 13–September 29, 1985.

15. Calvin Tompkins in *The New Yorker* 20 May, 1985, p. 95.

16. Roberta P. Degnore, "Statement: GSA-Serra Hearings", New York, 7 March, 1985.

17. Donald Gray, "The Rape of Federal Plaza" (Statement for Serra hearing, New York, 7 March, 1985).

18. Rilke spoke of the

. . . swift vanishing of so much that is visible, whose place will not be supplied. Even for our grandparents a "house," a "well," a familiar tower, their very dress, their cloak was infinitely more, infinitely more intimate; almost everything was a vessel in which they found and stored humanity. Now, there comes crowding over from America empty, indifferent things, pseudo-things, Dummy-Life. A house in the American understanding, an American apple or vine, has nothing in common with the house, the fruit, the grape, into which the hope and meditation of our forefathers had entered . . . The animated, experienced things that share our lives are coming to an end and cannot be replaced. We are perhaps the last to have still known such things.

From a letter written by Rainer Maria Rilke, November 13, 1924, to his Polish translator, Witold von Hulewicz. In Rainer Maria Rilke's *Duino Elegies* translated by J. B. Leishman and Stephen Spender. (New York: W. W. Norton Co., Inc. 1939).

19. *Public Art in Public Spaces.* (Houston: Houston City Planning Department, 1976).

20. *Ibid.*, p. 1.

21. *Artplan 1982–1983.* Cambridge, MA.: Cambridge Arts Council, 1982).

22. *Sited Toward the Future–Proposals for Public Art Sculpture in Arlington County.* (Arlington, Virginia: Arlington Arts Center, 1984).

23. Mark Lere, *Final Report for Artworks Program for the City of Phoenix* (draft) 1984.

24. Lynda Roscoe Hartigan, "Proposed—in the Present/Sighted—Toward the Future" in *Sited Toward the Future*, p. 10.

25. *Artwork Network. A Planning Study for Seattle: Art in the Civic Context.* (Seattle: Seattle Arts Commission, 1984).

26. *Ibid.*, p. 18.

27. *Ibid.*, pp. 21, 22.

28. William H. Whyte, *The Social Life of Small Urban Spaces.* (Washington, D.C.: The Conservation Foundation, 1980).

29. Kevin Lynch, *Image of the City* (Cambridge, MA: MIT Press, 1960).

30. *Artwork Network. A Planning Study for Seattle: Art in the Civic Context* (Seattle: Seattle Arts Commission, 1984), p. 13.

31. William H. Whyte cited in *Artwork Network. A Planning Study for Seattle: Art in the Civic Context* (Seattle: Seattle Arts Commission, 1984), p. 10.

32. Kevin Lynch's System of Visual Cues cited in *Ibid.*, p. 11.

33. Ben Carpenter, the entrepreneur who is the

driving force of the Los Colinas Corporation, envisioned the plaza concept for Williams Square outside Dallas and personally chose Robert Glen's "Galloping Mustangs" as a centerpiece to attract people and give identity to the 300' x 300' plaza. The landscape architects from SWA Group, Dallas worked closely with developer, artist, and architects from SOM, San Francisco. A schematic design review of the three adjacent buildings sought to make them compatible with the mustangs—the focal-point and only work of art in the plaza.

34. "Bethesda's 'Beauty Pageant' " in *The Washington Post*, 19 February, 1983, F1, F13.

35. Richard Sennett. *The Fall of Public Man.* (New York: Alfred A. Knopf, 1976).

36. Tom Wolfe, *Harpers*, October, 1984.

37. The following sources supplied information concerning Duncan Plaza:

The Public's Place in Art for Public Place—The Duncan Plaza Experience (New Orleans: City of New Orleans, 1982), *Regional Urban Design Assistance Team, Duncan Plaza* (City of New Orleans and the American Institute of Architects, 1980), and interviews with city officials—Matthew Kuluz, city planner and John Pecoul, special assistant to the mayor, New Orleans, Louisiana.

38. Ronald Lee Fleming, "A Modest Proposal: More Lovable Objects As A Part Of Urban Design Rather Than As A Reaction To It," *Landscape Architecture* (January 1981), pp. 27–31.

39. Ronald Lee Fleming, "The Meaning of Place," *Public Interest* (January 1982).

40. This project had good intentions but was unimaginative. Why not celebrate the early vendors with a huge pile of ceramic fruit? A version of this idea was actually proposed by Mark Mandell in the Chelsea, Massachusetts Streetscape Revitalization Project, 1977 (see p. 134) to commission a sculpture in granite of an early morning marketing truck with racks of ceramic fruit, but unfortunately the truck was sited to take up a parking space, and the politicians would not push it through.

41. Funded with the support of NEA's Art in Public Places Program, Isaac Witkin's sculpture has not been a catalyst for building public proprietorship in this space. Stair access has been officially barricaded because of the dangerous angle of descent (the governor fell down a few steps at the dedication), and the fountain in the park below remains empty most of the time. New proposals include wall panels on the stairway which would interpret "the cultural quadrangle" of museums on the hill above as well as commemorative successive layers of community history which could be related to the levels of ascent.

In Gratis

The process of discovering and researching the projects included in this book involved much correspondence, astonishing telephone bills, and at least a few encounters as whimsical as some of the projects uncovered during the quest for *Place Makers*. We are grateful for all of the work that was done by an army of artists, arts administrators, public interest groups, architects, friends and colleagues which made the project first conceivable, and then possible. We have attempted to list them all, and of course, have failed. We apologize, and hope that subsequent editions which add new *Place Makers*, will enable us to recognize any of our helpmates who may have been overlooked.

Ellen Abar, Reference Librarian, Frostburg State College, Frostburg, Maryland

Rita Abraham, Pennsylvania Avenue Development Corporation, Washington, D.C.

Flavia Alaya, The Passaic County Historical Society, Paterson, New Jersey

Malcolm Alexander, Sculptor, Santa Barbara, California

Robert Allen, Director, Olympic Center, Lake Placid, New York

James Allerton, GSA Real Properties Contracts Division-Region 10, Auburn, Washington

Dean Amhaus, Legislative Assistant, American Council for the Arts, Washington, D.C.

Gail Anderson, Marketing Assistant, Cambridge Seven Associates, Cambridge, Massachusetts

Richard Andrews, Director, Art-in-Public-Places Program, NEA, Washington, D.C.

A. Eric Arctander, Artist, New York, New York

Richard Armstrong, Management Assistant, Cultural Center, City of Palo Alto, California

Cynvia Arthur, Artist, Salisbury, North Carolina

Ruth Asawa, Artist, San Francisco, California

John Ashworth, Planner, City Planning Department, New York, New York

Robert Ballou, Director of Urban Design, Community Development Department, Highland Park, Illinois

Linda Bank, Architect, Boston, Massachusetts

Fred Bassetti, Architect, Seattle, Washington

David Beard, Office of Citizen Participation, Creedmoore Hospital, Queens, New York

Susanne Beck, Associate Director, Springfield Central Inc., Springfield, Massachusetts

Robert Behrens, Artist, San Francisco

Bertram Berenson, Professor of Architecture, University of Cincinnati, Ohio

David Bermant, Developer and Co-owner of Hamden Plaza Shopping Center, Hamden, Connecticut.

Donald Beyer, Jr., Owner of Volvo Dealership, Falls Church, Virginia

Richard S. Beyer, Sculptor, and Margaret Beyer, Seattle, Washington

Robert Bivens, President, Louisville Central Area, Inc., (LCA) Louisville, Kentucky

William G. E. Blaire, Architect, Seattle, Washington

J. Blaine Bonham, Jr., Director of Philadelphia Green, The Pennsylvania Horticultural Society, Philadelphia, Pennsylvania

Boston Parks and Recreation Department, Boston, Massachusetts

David B. Boyce, Sidney Janis Gallery, New York, New York

James Branch, Federated Arts Council of Richmond, Richmond, Virginia

Mara Brazer, Parkfriends, New Haven, Connecticut

Joseph Bresnan, Director, Historic Parks, City of New York, Department of Parks and Recreation, New York, New York

Barney Bright, Artist, Louisville, Kentucky

Judy Brody, American Institute for Conservation of Historic and Artistic Works, Washington, D.C.

Tom Brophy, Photographer, Brookline, Massachusetts

David Brown, Executive Director, Historic Staunton Foundation, Staunton, Virginia

Greg Brown, Artist, Palo Alto, California

Kate Burke, Artist, Hyde Park, Massachusetts

William Cadogan, Electrical Engineer, Townsend, Massachusetts

Avé Cadwallader, former Director Rowan Art Guild, Salisbury, North Carolina

Lisa Carter, Muralist, Cambridge, Massachusetts

Judy Chalker, Ohio Arts Council, Columbus, Ohio

Sarah S. Chamberlin, The Saint Louis Art Museum, St. Louis, Missouri

John Chandler, former Administrator one percent commission, Cambridge Arts Council, Cambridge, Massachusetts

Laurie Moon Chauvin, National Trust for Historic Preservation, Boston, Massachusetts

Peter Chermayoff, Principal, Cambridge Seven Associates, Cambridge, Massachusetts

Cityarts Workshop Inc., New York, New York

City Walls, New York, New York

Jerry Clapsaddle, Artist, Alexandria, Virginia

Diana H. Cohen, Assistant, Cambridge, Massachusetts

Gerald Cohen, Retailer, Waban, Massachusetts

Robert Collier, City Administrator, Flint, Michigan

Clair Colquitt, Artist, Seattle, Washington

Michael G. Contompasis, Headmaster Boston Latin, Roxbury, Massachusetts

Dale Conway, Editor, Cambridge, Massachusetts

Daniel Coolidge, Architect, Shepley, Bulfinch, Boston, Massachusetts

James Corson, Chief of Interpretation, National Park Service, New York, New York

Jessica Cusick, Project Director, Public Art Fund, New York, New York

Barbara Davis-Probert, Youngstown Arts Council, Youngstown, Ohio

Brian Day, former Executive Director FEAT, (Flint Environmental Action Team) Flint, Michigan

Diane Dayson, Site Supervisor, National Park Service, New York, New York

Dennis deWitt, Architect, Boston Architectural Center, Boston, Massachusetts

Roberta Degnore, Environmental Psychologist, New York, New York

Joseph Disponzio, Planner, City of New York Parks and Recreation Department, New York, New York

Jenny Dixon, Director, Public Art Fund, New York, New York

Al Dobbins, Engineer, Richmond Renaissance, Richmond, Virginia

Jennifer Dowley, former Director, Arts-on-the-Line Project, Cambridge Arts Council, Cambridge, Massachusetts

Timothy Duffield, Sculptor, Edgemont, Pennsylvania

Kathrine Dwyer, Program Officer, Eugene and Agnes E. Meyer Foundation, Washington, D.C.

Annette Eddlund, Martin Selig Real Estate, Seattle, Washington

Ellary Eddy, Artist, Greenwich, Connecticut

Jared Edwards, Partner, Smith Edwards Architects, Hartford, Connecticut

Peter Epstein, Planner and Writer, Alexandria, Virginia

Donald K. Erickson, Planner, Department of Community Development, Seattle, Washington

Elliot Erwitt, Photographer, New York, New York

Jeffrey Figly, Sidney Janis Gallery, New York, New York

Beth Fisher, Public Information Officer, Ohio Arts Council, Columbus, Ohio

Karen Fonkunis, Department of Slavic Language, Harvard University, Cambridge, Massachusetts

Gay Foster, Public Relations, Anatole Hotels, Dallas, Texas

Rick Friedman, Photographer, Cambridge, Massachusetts

Pat Fuller, former director, Art-in-Public-Places Program, National Endowment for the Arts, Washington, D.C.

Daniel Galvez, Artist, Oakland, California

Flora Maria Garcia, Arts Administrator, Houston Arts Council, Houston, Texas

Chris Garett, Public Relations, Hotel Waverly, Altanta, Georgia

Howard Garnitz, Sculptor, Washington, D.C.

Dineo Coleman Gary, Arts on the Line, Cambridge Arts Council, Cambridge, Massachusetts

Alexander Gerard, Architect, Hamburg, Germany

Dimitri Gerakaris, Sculptor, New Canaan, New Hampshire

Herbert Gleason, Esq., former Corporation Counsel, City of Boston, Boston, Massachusetts

Marsha Goldberg, National Assembly of Local Arts Agencies, Washington, D.C.

Abby Goodman, Intern, Harvard Graduate School of Design, Cambridge, Massachusetts

Al Gowan, Dean of Design, Massachusetts College of Art, Boston, Massachusetts

Steven Graham, Director, Zoological Parks Department, Royal Oak, Michigan

Donald Gray, Artist, New York, New York

Ann Grear, Muralist, Boston, Massachusetts

Roger Green, Writer, *Times-Picayune*, New Orleans, Louisiana

George Greenamyer, Artist, Marshfield, Massachusetts

Jane Greengold, Artist, New York, New York

Chuck Greening, Artist, Seattle, Washington

Kathy Greenough, Neighborhood Development and Employment Agency, Boston, Massachusetts

Anne Grimmer, National Park Service, Washington, D.C.

Jeff Gunderson, Reference Librarian, Indiana Historical Society Library, Indianapolis, Indiana

Cathy Gupta, Cityarts, New York, New York

Richard Haas, Muralist, New York, New York

Lauri Halderman, former Director of Publications, Townscape Institute, Cambridge, Massachusetts

Bunty Hales, Gallery Manager, Federation of Canadian Artists, Vancouver, B.C., Canada

Barbara Hancock, Manager of Special Programs, Louisville Central Area, Inc., Louisville, Kentucky

David Harding, Artist, Dartington Institute, Totnes, South Devon, England

Daryl Y. Harnisch, Sidney Janis Gallery, New York, New York

Denise Harper, Public Relations Manager, Hyatt Hotel, San Francisco, California

Mags Harries, Artist, Cambridge, Massachusetts

Susan Harris, Public Relations Coordinator, Graham Gund Associates, Cambridge, Massachusetts

Roy Harrover, Architect, Harrover and Associates, Memphis, Tennessee

Lynda Roscoe Hartigan, Guest Curator, Arlington Arts Center, Arlington, Virginia

Mary Moon Hemingway, Writer, Kittery Point, Maine

Robert Henry, Associate, Cambridge Seven Associates, Cambridge, Massachusetts

Hera, Artist, New York, New York

Kay Herring, Alyeska Pipeline, Anchorage, Alaska

Henry Heuser, President of the Henry Vogt Foundation, Louisville, Kentucky

Michael Higgs, Artist, Baltimore, Maryland

Richard Hobbs, Partner, Hobbs, Fukui Associates, Seattle, Washington

Barry W. Hodges, Manager of Architecture, Metropolitan Atlanta Rapid Transit Authority, Atlanta, Georgia

Isabel K. Hogan, Mayor, City of Kent, Washington

H.P. Hood, Dairy Products, Boston, Massachusetts

Vipen Hoon, Vice President, Louisville Central Area, Inc., Louisville, Kentucky

Caroline Hopkins, Lake Placid Olympic Organizing Committee, Lake Placid, New York

William Morris Hunt, former theater director, Boston, Massachusetts

Steven Huss, Assistant, Art in Public Places Program, Seattle Arts Commission, Seattle, Washington

Jonathan C. Hyde, Director of Public Relations, Children's Museum, Boston, Massachusetts

Penelope Jencks, Artist, Boston, Massachusetts

J. Seward Johnson, Jr., Artist, Princeton, New Jersey

Ilze Jones, Architect of Jones & Jones, Seattle,

Washington

Stella Jones, Federated Arts Council, Richmond, Virginia

Nancy Joseph, former Assistant, Art in Public Places Program, Seattle Arts Commission, Seattle, Washington

David Judelson, Artist, Arlington, Massachusetts

David Kahn, National Park Service, New York, New York

Leon Kaplan, Director, Arts In Public Places, Palo Alto, California

Lyn Kartiganer, Project Manager, Arts in Public Places, Seattle Arts Commission, Seattle, Washington

Catherine Keene, The Passaic County Historical Society, Paterson, New Jersey

Harry Keiner, Archivist, Corporate Library, The Travelers Companies, Hartford, Connecticut

Cindy Kelly, Director, Visual Resource Center, Maryland Arts Council, Baltimore, Maryland

Caroline King, Intern, Tufts University, Medford, Massachusetts

Richard King, Keim-Mineros Industries, New York, New York

Kirk Kinsell, Vice President, Trammel Crow Hotel Company, Dallas, Texas

Kathleen Kinsella, Executive Director, Lake Placid Chamber of Commerce, Lake Placid, N.Y.

Lou Anne Kirby, Community Relations Coordinator, Seattle Department of Parks and Recreation, Seattle, Washington

Stephen Knapp, Artist, Worcester, Massachusetts

Ann Windus Knight, Artist, Seattle, Washington

Ida Kohlmeyer, Artist, New Orleans, Louisiana

Rockne Krebs, Artist, Washington, D.C.

Bruce Kriviskey, R/UDAT Program Director, The American Institute of Architects, Washington, D.C.

Matthew Kuluz, Planner, City of New Orleans, New Orleans, Louisiana

Jean Kunkel, Director of Development, New York City Landmarks Conservancy, New York, New York

Lynn Lampey, Intergovernment Relations, City of Seattle, Seattle, Washington

Polly Lane, Editor, *Seattle Times*, Seattle, Washington

Debbie Latter, Office of the Mayor, Cincinnati, Ohio

Mary Leen, Bostonian Society, Boston, Massachusetts

Gregg LeFevre, Artist, Waltham, Massachusetts

Andrew Leicester, Artist, Golden Valley, Minnesota

Glen Leiner, National Park Service, Washington, D.C.

Charles A. Lewis, Morton Arboretum, Lisle, Illinois

Barbara Lillie, Artist, Newton, Massachusetts

Lloyd Lillie, Artist, Newton, Massachusetts

Delores Locasho, Department of Parks and Recreation, New York, New York

Melanie Lockman, Intern, Smith College, Northampton, Massachusetts

Lois Loeblein, Director, Waterworks Gallery, Salisbury, North Carolina

Palas Lombardi, Director, Arts on the Line, Cambridge Arts Council, Cambridge, Massachusetts

Weiming Lu, Director, Lowertown Redevelopment Corp., St. Paul, Minnesota

Cindy Mackey, New England Aquarium, Boston, Massachusetts

Jack Mackie, Artist, Seattle, Washington

David Maclagan, Muralist, Chemainus, British Columbia

Lee Major, *Chicago Tribune*, Chicago, Illinois

Gerald Malcolm, Architect, McAdoo, Malcolm and Youel, Seattle, Washington

Dennis Marks, Artist, Santa Cruz, California

Steven Masler, Museum Director, Mud Island Mississippi River Museum, Memphis, Tennessee

Pastor Martelino, Jr., Sculptor, Smyrna, Georgia

Marsha Mateyka, Marasha Mateyka Gallery, Washington, D.C.

Judith McCanna, Community Development, City of Chelsea, Chelsea, Massachusetts

McDuffie Associates, Architects, Atlanta, Georgia

John McGary, Planner, Community Development Department, Flint, Michigan

Jill McGuire, St. Louis Arts and Humanities Council, St. Louis, Missouri

George McLaughlin, Jr., Attorney, Boston, Massachusetts

Edward McMahon, Director, National Institute for Citizen Education in the Law, Washington, D.C.

Robert McNulty, President, Partners for Livable Places, Washington, D.C.

Russel Melies, Designer, Boston, Massachusetts

Proctor Melquist, former Editor, *Sunset Magazine*, Menlo Park, California

Molly Miller, former Assistant Director, Cambridge Arts Council, Cambridge, Massachusetts

Sherrie Miller, Publicity Manager, Mud Island Mississippi River Museum, Memphis, Tennessee

Norman Mintz, Designer, New York, New York

Victoria Mohar, SITE, New York, New York

Christopher Moore, Typist, Cambridge, Massachusetts

James Moore, Department of Public Works, Corning, New York

Shirley Muirhead, Designer, Boston Redevelopment Authority, Boston, Massachusetts

Carl Nesjar, Artist, Oslo, Norway

Fran Nugent, Engineer, Department of Public Works, City of Chelsea, Chelsea, Massachusetts

Becky Nyberg, Lowertown Redevelopment Corporation, St. Paul, Minnesota

Jeff Oberdorfer, Architect and Artist, Santa Cruz, California

Denise Ott, Project Assistant, Duncan Plaza Project, New Orleans, Louisiana

Robin Peach, Neighborhood Development and Employment Agency, Boston, Massachusetts

Duane R. Pearson, Manhattan Director, National Park Service, New York, New York

John Pecoul, Special Assistant to the Mayor, New Orleans, Louisiana

Robert Livingston Pell, formerly with Central Park Task Force, New York, New York

Beverly Pepper, Sculptor, Todi, Italy

Gale Peterson, Director, Cincinnati Historical Society, Cincinnati, Ohio

Patricia C. Philips, SITE, New York, New York

David Phillips, Artist, Somerville, Massachusetts

Pauline Pierce, Curator, Stockbridge Library Association, Stockbridge, Massachusetts

Marianne Pincentini, Director, Houston Arts Council, Houston, Texas

Kate Pouncey, Curator of Education, Mud Island Mississippi River Museum, Memphis, Tennessee

Doris Power, Designer, Pacific Palisades, California

Sherry Proctor, Cambridge Seven, Cambridge, Massachusetts

Martin Puryear, Artist, Chicago, Illinois

Paul Rafferty, Assembly of British Columbia Arts Councils, Vancouver, British Columbia, Canada

James Reeves, Landscape Architect, SWA Group, Dallas, Texas

Maurice A. Reidy, Principal, Maurice A. Reidy Engineers, Boston, Massachusetts

William Reimann, Artist, Cambridge, Massachusetts

Grace C. Rhoads, Johnson Atelier, Technical Institute of Sculpture, Princeton, New Jersey

Vincent Ricci, Sculptor, Boston, Massachusetts

Robert Richardson, Architectural Management Office, Cincinnati, Ohio

Thomas Johnston Robertson, Muralist, Chemainus, British Columbia

Sydney Roberts Rockefeller, Artist, Boston, Massachusetts

William Roe, Ben Thompson Associates, Cambridge, Massachusetts

Lilli Ann Killen Rosenberg, Artist, Newton, Massachusetts

Bonnie Rychlak, Assistant to Isomu Niguchi, Long Island City, New York

Pamela Sams, SITE, New York, New York

Raiza Sánchez de Morales, Assistant, Boston, Massachusetts

Thomas J. Schlereth, Professor of American Studies, University of Notre Dame, Notre Dame, Indiana

Donald Schon, Professor, MIT, Cambridge, Massachusetts

Karl Schutz, Director of the Chemainas Festival of Murals, Chemainus, B.C., Canada

John Sedelak, MARTA Architectual Coordinator, Atlanta, Georgia

George Segal, Sculptor, New York, New York

Martin Selig, Real Estate, Seattle, Washington

Mary Shannon, Executive Secretary of Boston Art Commission, Boston, Massachusetts

Cathy Shea, Associate Director, The Conservation Group, Washington University Technology Associates, St. Louis, Missouri

Paul Shell, President, Cornerstone Development Co., Seattle, Washington

Carol Sherwood, National Building Museum, Washington, D.C.

Dorothea Silverman, Director, AREA (Artists Representing Environmental Art), New York, New York

George Slavak, Architect, Beran and Shelmire, Dallas, Texas

Douglas Smith, Artist, Brookline, Massachusetts

Mara Smith, Sculptor, Denton, Texas

Peter Sollogub, Associate, Cambridge Seven Associates, Cambridge, Massachusetts

Drew Souerwine, Public Relations, Children's Museum, Boston, Massachusetts

Emilio Sousa, SITE, New York, New York

South Street Seaport Museum, New York, New York

G. H. Southworth, Program Director, Corning Glass Foundation, Corning, New York

Valerie Spieth, Savannah Area Convention and Visitors Bureau, Savannah, Georgia

St. Louis Parks Department, St. Louis, Missiouri

Paula Stoeke, Curator, J. Seward Johnson, Sculpture Placement, Washington, D.C.

Charles Sullivan, Director, Cambridge Historical Commission, Cambridge, Massachusetts

Frederika Taylor, Lower Manhattan Culture Council, New York City

Donald Thalacker, Director, Art in Architecture Program, General Services Administration, Washington, D.C.

Marietta Tree, Planner, New York, New York

Mark Ukelson, director, On Broadway Tours, Seattle, Washington

Barbara Urban, Wadsworth Atheneum, Hartford, Connecticut

Robert A. Van Deen, John Graham and Company, Seattle, Washington

Sheryl Voegler, St. Louis Art Museum, St. Louis, Missouri

Bruce Voeller, Mariposa Foundation, Pasadena, California

Wilhelm V. von Molkte, Professor Emeritus of Urban Design, Harvard University, Cambridge, Massachusetts

Marcia Wagoner, former Director, Seattle Arts Commission, Seattle, Washington

Eve Wahrsager, Researcher, New York, New York

Roger Webb, President, Architectural Heritage Foundation, Boston, Massachusetts

Fredrica W. Wechsler, Director, Arts-in-the-Academy, National Academy of Sciences, Washington, D.C.

Polly Welch, Architect, Boston, Masachusetts

Margo Wellington, former Director, Municipal Arts Society, New York, New York

Sandy Wernick, Public Relations, Union Square Hyatt Hotel, San Francisco, California

John Westbrook, former Chief of Urban Design, Maryland National Capital Parks and Planning Commission, Silver Spring, Maryland

Mary Wilkinson, Senior Interpreter, Mud Island Mississippi River Museum, Memphis, Tennessee.

Ann Williams, Executive Director, Historic Salisbury Foundation, Salisbury, North Carolina

Joshua Winer, Artist, Cambridge, Massachusetts

James Wines, SITE, New York, New York

Nancy Wolf, Artist, New York, New York

Glossary

This brief compendium is intended only to elucidate particular terms that are utilized in some of the placemaker studies, and is obviously not a comprehensive inventory of words that can describe artistic and architectural elements, styles, or conditions.

Abstract Art A general term describing all art—especially painting or sculpture—that depicts an object or form in a non-realistic manner, or employs non-realistic use of form. The works of sculptor Beverly Pepper and painter Jackson Pollack exemplify this approach.

Acrylic Artist's colors made by dispersing pigments in a vehicle made from a polymethylmethacrylate solution and mineral spirits used in paints such as acrylic latex exterior paint, which do not yellow and dry quickly.

Allegorical Art A term referring to any art work—visual or written—in which the characters or figures act as symbols representing ideas or principles. A blindfolded woman holding up a scale is an often-used allegorical figure, representing justice.

Analemmatic Sundial A type of sundial, first conceived by the ancient Greeks, in which a person stands in the center of a surface and reads the time from his own shadow.

Architectonic Relating to architecture, or the structural qualities of form; specifically, artworks which echo the qualities of architecture through strong emphasis on structure or function.

Art Deco A term originated about 1860 referring to the style of art and architecture popular between WWI and WWII, characterized by streamlined forms, geometric patterns, boldness, simplicity, and, in sculpture, popular use of aluminum as a medium.

Art Nouveau A term referring to the style of art and architecture popular during the period 1880–1910, characterized by curved, slender, elegant lines, the most frequent motif of which was the lily; the style was especially popular in France.

Arts and Crafts English movement in applied arts and, indirectly, in architecture, during the second half of the 19th century, emphasizing the importance of craftsmanship and high standards of design in everyday objects as a reaction against the Industrial Revolution.

Arts-on-the-Line A term referring to the incorporation of various types of art pieces into the design of the Red Line subway extension in Cambridge, Massachusetts. Among the artworks are sculpture, street furniture, pavement and wall tiles, and light, sound and kinetic pieces.

Baroque A style of art and architecture first developed during the Renaissance in reaction to the severity of Classical forms; and as the design strategy of the counter reformation, it is characterized by use of curves, elaborate scrolls, and carved ornamentation.

Bas Relief A sculpture, carving or frieze with little depth, or only slight projection from the background.

Beaux-Arts French for "Fine Arts"; a movement in architecture and art which originated at the Ecole des Beaux-Arts in Paris, and lasted from 1870–1930, characterized by emphasis on ornamentation, embellishment, and grandeur with use of classical form; includes wide use of ornate public statuary.

Bollard Upright post, usually stone or metal, originally used as a hitching-post; employed in present times to protect pedestrian and restricted areas from automobile traffic.

Bronze An alloy of copper and tin, frequently including other elements, often used for cast sculpture, public monuments, and other durable metal works.

Brutalist A school of architecture popular since 1950, characterized by predominant use of concrete, use of massive, geometric shapes, articulation of functional elements such as heat ducts, and no ornamentation. The style is exemplified by Alison and Peter Smithson's 1965 Economist Building in London.

Bust A sculpture representing the head and neck, and often the shoulders and chest, of a human figure; also known as a portrait bust.

City Beautiful A movement launched at the 1893 Chicago Exposition, popular for several decades, whose aim was the beautification of cities through humanistic design elements, such as parks, gardens and public art in a classical style.

Classical A style of architecture or art following the traditions of ancient Greece or Rome, characterized by frequent use of columns, simple, heavy symmetry, and triangular pediments over entrance ways.

Coffered A surface, usually a ceiling, vault or dome, formed by recessed panels which create a continuous pattern.

Cornice The projecting horizontal section of a building, used to frame the top of a structure, or its windows, often carved as embellishment in classical or neoclassical architecture.

Doric The oldest and simplest of the three ancient Greek orders of architecture, characterized by fluted columns with plain rounded capitals.

Diorama A miniature landscape showing trees, houses, people, etc., often displayed in museums to present a panoramic overview of an area at a certain time.

Eclecticism A term referring to that approach in art and architecture which attempts to draw the best elements from various, unrelated styles.

Environmental Art A term usually describing three-dimensional art located both indoors and outdoors. Most environmental art pieces attempt to change the observer's perception by manipulating such elements as light, color, power, shape and sound. Many environmental art pieces encourage the public to participate by entering into the piece or by affecting certain changes. The "Spiral Jetty" by Robert Smithson at the Great Salt Lake in Utah is among the best known environmental art pieces of the 1970s.

Epoxy A group of synthetic thermo-setting resins used in carpentry and for repairing masonry and sculpture.

Facade The ornamented or plain exterior front surface or surfaces of a building, usually facing a street.

Federal A style of architecture popular in the United States in the late 18th and early 19th centuries, which is more restrained than the earlier Georgian style and is characterized by a low pitched roof, smooth façade, and often an elliptical fanlight over doorways with slender flanking sidelights.

Frieze A horizontal band of sculpture in bas-relief used as ornament along the outside of a building, often placed along a building's roofline.

Gargoyle A grotesque sculptural projection, usually of a bizarre creature, used frequently in Gothic architecture; often fitted with a lead pipe to drain water from the roof.

Gazebo A free-standing roofed structure, usually opened on the sides, often used as a summerhouse, a viewing spot (as on a belvedere), a sales stand or information booth.

Gothic A style of architecture popular in the 13th, 14th and 15th centuries in Europe, usually associated with stone cathedrals; characterized by emphasis on verticality, and use of pointed arches and stone tracery, often supported by elaborate flying buttresses. The Cathedral at Chartres is among the most famous examples.

Gnomon The shaft positioned in the center of a sundial, which indicates time through the position of its shadow.

Grotesque A carved sculptural projection, similar to a gargoyle, usually depicting a caricatured animal or human figure, associated with Gothic architecture, originally designed to direct rainwater.

GSA Art Program The General Services Administration of the United States federal government, which owns and manages federal office buildings, sponsors an art-in-architecture program. The agency has been responsible for numerous artworks, amounting to approximately one half of one percent of the construction cost.

In situ A term describing an object in its natural or original position, often used in reference to relief panels carved onto the walls of a building after the stone has already been set in place.

Ionic One of the three orders of ancient Greek architecture, in which the capitals of the columns are carved with a pair of scroll-like devices.

Italianate A style of architecture popular during the late 19th century, which revived elements from Italian architecture, ranging from the Renaissance to the Baroque, characterized by a wide, protruding roof and asymmetrical towers. The Morse-Libby Mansion in Portland, Maine, built 1859–1863, is a well-known example.

Keystone The center stone in the crown of an arch, usually larger than the others and regarded as binding of the whole.

Kinetic Pertaining to motion; often used in art to describe abstract modern sculpture which is designed to move through space.

Landmark An object or structure, such as a stone, tree or building that is of unusual historic or aesthetic significance, or that is conspicuous against a landscape and can be used as a point of orientation.

Lost Wax Process A technique for casting bronze sculpture, which consists of forming a wax-surfaced model, molding it, then melting the wax so the vacant mold can be refilled with molten bronze.

Mausoleum A stone building above the ground used to store the dead; a large tomb or sepulchre.

Miniature A small figure or object which replicates a large original sculpture, monument, building or other structure.

Minimalism A style of art prevalent in the 1960's and 70's which sought to reduce sculpture to its most direct properties as object in space. Richard Serra's large Cor-Ten steel sculptures exemplify this style.

Mission Style A style of architecture used in churches and monasteries of the Spanish religious orders in Mexico and California, mainly during the 18th century, characterized by red tile roofs, stucco exteriors, and small windows. This style was revived in the southwestern United States in the early twentieth century.

Modern Movement A style of architecture popular from the 1930s to the present, exemplifying the philosophy "form follows function," characterized by such building technologies as high-rise, pre-cast concrete, extreme cantilevers, reflective glass façades, curtain walls, flat roofs, and the lack of decoration. It is also called the international style because it avoids any particular national, historical, or regional design references.

Montage An arrangement of photographs, or other artistic elements, used as a means of pictorial expression, to present a visual essay.

Monument A building, statue or other structure erected to commemorate a person, group of persons, or event, usually in recognition of some type of outstanding public service.

Mosaic An inlaid surface of small pieces of colored glass, tile, or stone which form a design or pattern, especially popular during the Byzantine and Art Nouveau periods.

Mural A wall painting, usually created to enhance a large empty exterior or interior surface; may be painted directly onto wall, or onto another surface which is then attached to the wall.

NEA The National Endowment for the Arts of the United States federal government; agencies include the Art in Public Places program, which provides matching funds for public art, and the Design Arts program, which supports projects involving art and design.

Neoclassical Pertaining to the revival of the styles of ancient Greek and Roman art and architecture, a movement especially popular in the United States from 1810–1850 and 1890–1930.

Objet Trouve French phrase meaning "found object." A term used in art for everyday items which by their treatment gain artistic value. French artist Marcel Duchamp was among the first who introduced this technique of viewing ordinary things as art.

One Percent for the Arts   An ordinance or policy adopted by cities, states, planning commissions, architects or developers, which sets aside one percent of construction costs of a building or development for public art.

Participatory Art   A term referring to artwork that encourages or requires interaction with a viewer or viewers; in some cases the audience helps produce the artwork.

Patina   A film, usually green, formed on metal sculptures and surfaces by long-term exposure to a moist atmosphere; also can be a surface discoloration artificially formed by treatment with acids.

Pedestal   The supporting base for a column or sculpture, usually of stone or bronze, which raises the object above street or ground level.

Pergola   A structure, usually of timber or metal, used to shelter pedestrians in public places; also used in gardens to cover paths, or to support climbing plants.

Pilaster   A rectangular wall-projection, in the shape of a pillar, usually spanning floor to ceiling, and consisting of a base, shaft and capital.

Pop Art   A term derived from "popular art" describing that style of art which originated in the 1960's, often characterized by bright colors and references to commercial images, and objects of the "vernacular culture" not ordinarily thought of as art. Andy Warhol's Campbell's Soup Cans are among the best known Pop images.

Post-Modernism   An architectural style which followed the Modern Movement, or International Style; it started in the mid 1970's, and emphasized the sculptural quality of buildings, using an eclecticism of past stylistic elements, usually less severe and formally ordered than in the Modern Movement style, sometimes whimsical.

Representational Art   A general term referring to art in which elements are composed or arranged to resemble a person, structure, object, scene, or other artifact; it can be stylized or naturalistic.

Revivalism   An architectural style which employs elements of earlier periods, particularly popular during the 19th century.

Romanesque   A style of architecture popular during the 11th, 12th, and 13th centuries in Europe particularly in France, Spain, and Germany, based on the Roman principles of architecture; it was characterized by use of round arches, barrel vaults and cross vaults. Henry Hobson Richardson's Trinity Church in Boston (1875) is considered among the most influential Romanesque Revivalist buildings.

Rond-point   A rotary; a place where several roads meet.

Roundel   A small circular panel or window; specifically, a circular niche deeply recessed, often decorated with a bust in high relief, or in late neoclassic design filled by a free-standing bust.

Site-Specific Art   A term referring to artworks in which either form or content relate to surrounding landscape, community or physical environment, which are designed for a specific location and reinforce association with place. Mags Harries' *Asaroton 1976* in Haymarket, Boston is one example of such an approach.

Social Realism   A movement in art, especially painting, merging realistic style with social or political commentary, usually focusing sympathetically on the workers, or members of the proletariat; most closely associated with Soviet and Chinese art and propaganda, exemplified in American painting in the period between WWI and WWII, in WPA-sponsored public art.

Strip Architecture   A term referring to the type of buildings predominant along highways, including gas stations, fast food places, motels and shops; characterized by large, colorful, sometimes flashing signs, gimmicky design, and use of cheap materials such as plastic, with emphasis on attracting auto-borne customers.

Superrealism   A movement in art of the 1970's, in which naturalistic detail is rendered with acute fidelity, in an extreme reaction to abstraction; epitomized in painting by Richard Estes' urban landscapes, and in sculpture by Duane Hanson's polyester-fiberglass sculptures of fully-clothed middle-class Americans.

Tableau   A three-dimensional sculptural grouping or a painted scene, focusing on the interaction between an ensemble of people, or between people and objects.

Terra-cotta   A molded and fired clayware used extensively for low-relief sculptural panels on buildings during the period 1870–1920.

Trompe l'oeil   A term referring to murals, usually painted on walls and ceilings, often as part of an architectural treatment, which attempt to disguise themselves through careful perspective and naturalistic use of color and form as actual sculptures, scenes, or architectural extensions; the device was particularly popular during the Renaissance, and is exemplified by the dome and vault painted by Pozzo in the St. Ignatius church in Rome.

Selected Bibliography

Alloway, Lawrence. "The Public Sculpture Problem." *Studio International*, 1971.

———. "Public Sculpture for the Post-Heroic Age." *Art in America*, October 1979.

American Council for the Arts. *The Arts and City Planning*. New York, 1980.

Armstrong, Tom, et al. *200 Years of American Sculpture*. New York: Whitney Library of Design, 1976.

Artwork Network. A Planning Study for Seattle: Art in the Civic Context. Seattle: Seattle Arts Commission, City of Seattle, 1984.

Balken, Debra Bricker. *Aspects of New Narrative Art*. Catalogue for Exhibition at The Berkshire Museum, 4 August–23 September, 1984. Pittsfield, Massachusetts.

Barnard, Julian. *The Decorative Tradition*. Princeton: The Pyne Press, 1973.

Barthes, Roland. *The Eiffel Tower and Other Mythologies*. New York: Hill and Wang, 1979.

Beardsley, John. *Art in Public Places*. Washington, D.C.: Partners for Livable Places, 1981.

———. "Personal Sensibilities in Public Places." *Artforum*, 19 (1981).

———. *Earthworks and Beyond*. New York: Abbeville Press, 1984.

Berger, Joseph. " 'Tilted Arc' To Be Moved From Plaza at Foley Sq." *The New York Times*, 1 June, 1985, pp. 25, 28.

Blake, Peter. *Form Follows Fiasco: Why Modern Architecture Hasn't Worked*. Boston: Atlantic, 1977.

Bonta, Juan Pablo. *Architecture and its Interpretation*. New York: Rizzoli, 1979.

Bongartz, Roy. "Where the Monumental Sculptors Go." *ARTnews*, February 1976.

Brenson, Michael. "The Case in Favor of a Controversial Sculpture." *The New York Times* (Arts & Leisure Section) 19 May, 1985, pp. 1, 35.

Brolin, Brent C. *The Failure of Modern Architecture*. New York: Van Nostrand Reinhold, 1976.

Brolin, Brent C. and Richards, Jean. *Sourcebook of Architectural Ornament*. New York: Van Nostrand Reinhold, 1982.

Cambridge Arts Council. *1% for Public Art Ordinance*. 1979.

———. *Arts on the Line*. Catalogue for exhibition at Hayden Gallery, MIT, February–March 1980.

———. *Administrative Structure, Policy, and Operating Guidelines for 1% for Art for the City of Cambridge*, 1980.

———. *Artplan 1982–83*. 1982.

Canaday, John. *What is Art: An Introduction to Painting, Sculpture, and Architecture*. New York: Alfred A. Knopf, 1980.

Carpenter, Edward K. "Urban Art." *Design and Environment*, Summer, 1974.

Castle, Ted. "Art in its Place." *Geo 4*, September 1982.

Clay, Grady. "Earthworks Move Upstage." *Landscape Architecture 70* (1980).

Cockcroft, Eva, et al. *Toward A People's Art: The Contemporary Mural Movement*. New York: E. P. Dutton, 1977.

Cooper, Graham and Sargent, Dough. *Painting the Town*. Edinburgh: Phaidon, 1979.

Crimp, Douglas. "Richard Serra's Urban Sculpture." *Arts Magazine*, November 1980.

Davis, Barbara A., et al. *The Effects of Environmental Amenities on Patterns of Economic Development*. Washington, D.C.: The Urban Institute, 1980.

Davis, Douglas. "Public Art: The Taming of the Vision." *Art in America*, May–June 1974.

d'Harnoncourt, Anne. *Celebration, Buildings, Art and People*. Washington, D.C.: U.S. General Services Administration, 1976.

Dean, Andrea, ed. "Art in the Environment" (special issue on the impact, problems, and promise). *AIA Journal*, October 1976.

Diamonstein, Barbaralee, ed. *Collaboration: Artists and Architects*. New York: Watson-Guptil Publications, Whitney Library of Design, 1981.

Dixon, Jenny. "Resolving the Polarities in Public Art." *PLACE* 3 (January 1983.)

Doezema, M. and Hargrove, J. *The Public Monument and Its Audience*. Bloomington, Indiana: Indiana University Press, 1977.

Dupont, Robert L. and Arnett, Stuart. *The Public's Place in Art for Public Places—The Duncan Plaza Experience*. New Orleans: City of New Orleans, 1982.

Fachard, Sabine. *L'Art et la Ville: Interventions des Artistes dans les Villes Nouvelles*. Paris: Secretariat des Villes Nouvelles, 1976.

Filler, Martin. "Art Without Museums." *Urban Open Spaces*. New York: Cooper–Hewett Museum, 1979.

Fleming, Ronald Lee. "Neighborhood Value—Reinvestment by Design." *Public Management*, August 1977.

———. "Images of a Town." *Historic Preservation*, October 1978.

———. "Local Government and the Arts: The Cambridge Arts Council," *Management Information Service*, International City Management Association, December 1978.

———. "Strategies for a Lovable Environment." *Environmental Comment*, Urban Land Institute, May 1979.

———. "Aesthetic Policy and Community Identity" and "Cultural Tithing in Cambridge." *Local Government and the Arts* by Louise Kreisberg, American Council for the Arts, October 1979.

———. "Seeds for the Soul: Beyond Landscape: Strategies for Lovable Places." *The 1980 Longwood Program Seminars* (12). Newark, Delaware: University of Delaware, 1980.

———. "Gritty Cities: Appealing to the Landscape of the Mind." *Landscape*, January 1981.

———. "Lovable Objects Challenge the Modern Movement." *Landscape Architecture*, January 1981.

———. "Interpreting and Enhancing Townscape: Appealing to the Landscape of the Mind." *Small Town Design Resource Book for Small Communities*, November–December 1981.

———. "The Meaning of Place." *Public Interest*, January 1982.

———. "Public Art and Place Meaning: Some Comparative Impressions of Europe and the United States." *Livability*, Spring, 1982.

———. *Facade Stories: Changing Faces of Main Street Storefronts and How to Care for Them*. New York: Hastings House, 1982.

———. "Place Makers—The City as Public Art." *Design for Arts in Education*, 83 (1983).

———. "The New Senate Building." *Wall Street Journal*, 4 February, 1983.

———. "Art On a Neighborhood Scale." *Art New England*, 5 (June 1984).

Foote, Nancy. "Monument—Sculpture—Earthwork." *Artforum*. October 1979.

Forgey, Benjamin. "A New Vision: Public Places with Sculpture." *Smithsonian*. October 1975.

———. "It Takes More than an Outdoor Site to Make Sculpture Public." *Artnews*, September, 1980.

———. "The Perils of Street Sculpture." *The Washington Post*, 13 February, 1985.

Franz, Gina. "How Public Is Public Sculpture?" *The New Art Examiner*, February 1980.

Freedman, Doris. "Public Sculpture." *Design and Environment*, Summer, 1974.

Fried, Frederick and Gillon, Edmond V. *New York Civic Sculpture*. New York: Dover Publications, 1976.

Friedman, Mildred, ed. "Site: The Meaning of

Place in Art and Architecture." *Design Quartlery* 122 (1983).

Fundaburk, Emma Lilia and Davenport, Thomas G. *Art in Public Places in the United States.* Bowling Green, Ohio: Bowling Green University, Popular Press, 1975.

Gingold, Dianne J. *Business and the Arts: How They Meet the Challenge.* Washington, D.C.: National Endowment for the Arts, 1984.

Glueck, Grace. "New Sculpture under the Sun, from Staten Island to the Bronx. *The New York Times.* 3 August, 1979.

———. "Art in Public Places Stirs Widening Debate." *New York Times,* 23 May, 1982.

———. "Serving the Environment." *New York Times,* 27 June, 1982.

———. "What Part Should the Public Play in Choosing Public Art?" *The New York Times,* 3 February, 1985, pp. 27, 28.

Goldin, Amy. "The Esthetic Ghetto: Some Thoughts About Public Art." *Art in America,* May–June 1974.

Goldwater, Robert. *What is Modern Sculpture?* New York: The Museum of Modern Art, 1969.

Goode, James M. *The Outdoor Sculpture of Washington, D.C.* Washington, D.C.: Smithsonian Institution Press, 1980.

Gortazar, Fernando Gonzalez. "Sculptures as 'Vitalizing Elements' in Superficial Urban Settings." *Landscape Architecture,* November 1976.

Gowan, Al. *Nuts and Bolts: Case Studies in Public Design.* Cambridge: Public Design Press, 1980.

Green, Dennis. *$ for Art, New Legislation Can Integrate Art and Architecture.* New York: ACA Publications, 1976.

Green, Kevin, ed. *The City as a Stage: Strategies for the Arts in Urban Economics.* Washington, D.C.: Partners for Livable Places, 1983.

Greenberg, David, Smith, Kathryn and Teacher, Stuart. *Big Art: Megamurals and Supergraphics.* Philadelphia: Running Press, 1977.

Haas, Richard. *An Architecture of Illusion.* New York: Rizzoli International Publications, 1981.

Harney, Andy Leon. "The Proliferating One Percent Programs for the Use of Art in Public Buildings." *AIA Journal,* October 1976.

Harris, Stacy Paleologos, ed. *Insights/On Sites— Perspectives on Art in Public Places.* Washington, D.C.: Partners for Livable Places, 1984.

Henry, Diane. "Some Residents of Hartford Are Throwing Stones at Sculptor's Extended 'Se-renity of the Graveyard.' " *The New York Times.* 5 Sept. 1977.

Higgins, Richard. "The Gospel According to Tom." *Boston Globe.* 9 December 1984.

Hoelterhoff, Manuela. "Tilting Over the Arc: Art of Abomination?" *Wall Street Journal,* 14 March 1985.

Houston City Planning Department. *Public Art in Public Spaces.* Houston: City of Houston, 1976.

Huxtable, Ada Louise. "Public Sculpture—A City's Most Pervasive Art." *The New York Times,* 15 September 1974.

Kardon, Janet, ed. *Urban Encounters—Art Architecture Audience.* Catalogue. Philadelphia: Institute of Contemporary Art, University of Pennsylvania, 1980.

Kramer, Hilton. "Sculpture is Having a Coming-Out." *The New York Times,* 19 February, 1978.

———. "Sculpture on the Streets." *The New York Times,* 15 July 1979.

Kreisberg, Louise. *Local Government and the Arts.* New York: American Council for the Arts, 1979.

Krier, Rob. *Urban Space.* New York: Rizzoli International Publications, 1979.

Larson, Kay. "The Expulsion from the Garden: Environmental Sculpture at the Winter Olympics." *Artforum.* April 1980.

Lere, Mark. *Artworks Program for the City of Phoenix.* (final draft) 1984.

Linker, Kate. "Public Sculpture: The Pursuit of the Pleasurable and Profitable Paradise." *Artforum.* March 1981.

Lynch, Kevin. *Image of the City.* Cambridge, Massachusetts: M.I.T. Press, 1960.

———. *What Time is this Place?* Cambridge, Mass: M.I.T. Press, 1972.

Maldonado, Tomas. *Design, Nature, and Revolution: Toward a Critical Ecology.* New York: Harper and Row, 1972.

McNulty, Robert H., Jacobson, Dorothy R. and Penne, R. Leo. *From the Economics of Amenity: A Policy Guide to Urban Economic Development.* Washington, D.C.: Partners for Livable Places, 1985.

McGill, Douglas. " 'Tilted Arc' Removal Draws Mixed Reaction." *The New York Times,* 6 June, 1985, p. C21.

Miles, Don C., Cook, Robert and Roberts, Cameron B. *Plazas For People.* New York: New York City Department of City Planning, 1978.

New Orleans, City of, and the American Institute of Architects. *Duncan Plaza*, Regional Urban Design Assistance Team, 1980.

Nochlin, Linda. "The Realist Criminal and the Abstract Law." *Art in America*. May–June 1974.

O'Doherty, Brian. "Public Art and the Government: A Progress Report." *Art in America*. May–June 1974.

Oldenberg, Claes and Coosj, V. *Large Scale Projects 1977–1980*. New York: Rizzoli, 1980.

Page, Clint and Cuff, Penelope, ed. *Negotiating for Amenities: Zoning and Management Tools That Built Livable Cities*. 2 vols. Washington, D.C.: Partners for Livable Places, 1982.

Partners for Livable Places. *Tools for Leadership: Building Cultural Partnerships*. Washington, D.C.: Partners for Livable Places, 1982.

———. "Cultural Planning Charrette, Hartford, Connecticut, June 3–6, 1984". (unpublished) Washington, D.C., June 30 1984.

Percival, Arthur. *Understanding Our Surroundings: A Manual of Urban Interpretation*. London: Civic Trust, 1979.

Perlman, Bennard B. *1% Art in Civic Architecture*. Baltimore: Maryland Arts Council, 1979.

Proust, Marcel. *Swann's Way*. New York: Vintage Books, 1970.

Redstone, Louis G. *Art in Architecture*. New York: McGraw-Hill Book Co., 1968.

Relph, E. *Place and Placelessness*. London: Pion Limited, 1976.

———. *Public Art—New Dimensions*. New York: McGraw-Hill, 1980.

"Richard Serra." (Special section) *Arts Magazine* 55 (1980).

Roberston, Jacquelin. "The Current Crisis of Disorder" in *Education for Urban Design*. New York: The Institute for Urban Design, 1982.

Robinette, Margaret A. *Outdoor Sculpture: Object and Environment*. New York: Whitney Library of Design, 1976.

Rosen, Nancy. *Ten Years of Public Art: 1972–1982*. New York Public Art Fund, Inc. 1982.

Schon, Donald A. "Problems, Frames and Perspectives on Designing." *Design Studies* 5 (1984).

Scott, Nancy. "Politics on a Pedestal. *Art Journal*, Spring 1979.

Schjeldahl, Peter. "Artistic Control." *Village Voice*, 14–20 October 1981, p. 100.

Senie, Harriet. "Urban Sculpture: Cultural Tokens or Ornaments to Life?" *Artnews*, September 1979.

Sinclair, Stephen. "When Art Meets the Community." *Cultural Post*, March–April, 1980.

Slavin, Maeve. "Art and Architecture: Can They Ever Meet Again?" *Interiors*. March 1980.

Sommer, Robert. *Street Art*. New York: Links Books, 1975.

Sonfist, Alan. "Natural Phenomena as Public Monuments." *Tracks*, Spring, 1977.

Stearn-Phillips, Daydre. *Western's Outdoor Museum*. Bellingham, Wash.: Western Washington University, 1979.

Stendhal (Marie Henri Beyle). *On Love*. Translated by Philip Sidney Woolf and Cecil N. Sidney. New York: Peter Pauper Press, n.d.

Stevens, Mark, Hager, Mark and Malone, Maggie. "Sculpture Out in the Open," *Newsweek* 18 August 1980.

Tarzan, Dolores. "Art, The Public, and Public Art." *Seattle Times*, 21 September 1980.

Thalacker, Donald W. *The Place of Art in the World of Architecture*. New York: Chelsea House, 1980.

Tomkins, Calvin. "The Urban Capacity." *The New Yorker*, 5 April 1982.

———. "The Art World: Like Water in a Glass." *The New Yorker* 21 March 1983.

———. "Perceptions at All Levels," *The New Yorker*, 3 December 1984.

———. "Tilted Arc." *The New Yorker*, 20 May, 1985.

U.S. Department Of Transportation. *Design, Art and Architecture in Transportation*. Washington, D.C.: U.S. Government Printing Office, 1977–1978.

———. *Aesthetics in Transportation*. 1980.

Von Eckhardt, Wolfgang. "Toward More Livable Cities." *Time Magazine*, November 1981.

Von Tscharner, Renata and Fleming, Ronald Lee. *New Providence, A Changing Cityscape*. San Diego: Harcourt Brace Jovanovich, 1987.

Von Tscharner, Renata. *City Identity Software*. Cambridge: City Identity System Associates, 1987.

Venturi, Robert. *Complexity and Contradiction in Architecture*. New York: The Museum of Modern Art Papers on Architecture, 1966.

Warren, Geoffrey. *Vanishing Street Furniture*. North Pomfret, VT.: David & Charles, 1978.

Whyte, William H. *The Social Life of Small Urban Spaces*. Washington, D.C.: The Conservation Foundation, 1980.

Willard, L. F. "Would You Pay $87,000 for These 36 Rocks?" *Yankee Magazine*, February, 1978.

Wolfe, Tom. "The Worship of Art." *Harpers*, October, 1984, pp. 61–68.

Photo Credits

PHOTO CREDITS NOT LISTED IN PROFILE SUMMARIES

Index